MOONTIME DIARY® 2023

In Tune With The Moon
Northern Hemisphere

If you find this diary please arrange for its return to:

Name   ....

Phone   ....

Address   ....

Email   ....

Thank you

© Moontime Diary® 2023 Northern Hemisphere
ISBN 978-0-6454361-0-5
Edition 3 © 2020, 2021, 2023.
Published by Moontime Diary®
PO Box 1200
Mullumbimby
NSW 2482
Australia
moontimeoffice@gmail.com
www.moontimediary.com.au

To Leon

PLEASE NOTE

The Moontime Diary® for the Northern Hemisphere works with

Greenwich Mean Time GMT and the Tropical Zodiac.

Name	Description	Relative to GMT
GMT	Greenwich Mean Time	GMT 0:00 hour
UTC	Universal Coordinated Time	GMT 0:00 hour
ECT	European Central Time	GMT + 1:00 hour
EET	Eastern European Time	GMT + 2:00 hours
CNT	Canada Newfoundland Time	GMT - 3:30 hours
IET	Indiana Eastern Standard Time	GMT - 5:00 hours
EST	Eastern Standard Time	GMT - 5:00 hours
CST	Central Standard Time	GMT - 6:00 hours
MST	Mountain Standard Time	GMT - 7:00 hours
PNT	Phoenix Standard Time	GMT - 7:00 hours
PST	Pacific Standard Time	GMT - 8:00 hours
AST	Alaska Standard Time	GMT - 9:00 hours
HST	Hawaii Standard Time	GMT - 10:00 hours
MIT	Midway Islands Time	GMT - 11:00 hours

Please consider Daylight Saving Times in your time zone.

Every effort has been made to provide accurate information. If you find any mistakes, please inform us and accept Moontime Diary's apologies. Views expressed by contributing authors are not necessarily those of the publisher.

The Moontime Diary® gives no medical advice. Please take your dis-ease seriously, seek professional advice and make informed choices.

For more info and to subscribe to our newsletter, visit our website:

www.moontimediary.com.au

CONTENTS

Thank you for purchasing our
NORTHERN HEMISPHERE
MOONTIME DIARY®

This annual almanac combines a diary and moon calendar with planetary data and traditional knowledge regarding seasons and cycles in the Northern Hemisphere.

The information is relevant for people interested in health and wellbeing, home, gardening, Astrology, Pagan traditions and night sky watching.

The Moontime Diary features well-known artists and experienced astrologers who are passionate about our natural environment.

The Moontime Diary promotes reducing our ecological footprint by aligning activities to nature's seasons and cycles. Like a sailor, who takes the tide out, instead of struggling against it, you too can time your activities and achieve better outcomes.

The Moontime Diary keeps beginners and professionals
informed and inspired throughout the year.

Iris Detenhoff ~ Author and Publisher of the Moontime Diary

I started working as a general nurse in Munich, Germany, before migrating to Australia in 1987. Since 1990 I have lived in the NSW Northern Rivers Area, where I developed a deep interest and commenced studies in natural health, astrology, sustainable building and Anthroposophy.

All of the above, combined with the urge to live a healthy, more sustainable life with my son, led me to explore the lunar phases. To integrate the Moon, I needed daily reminders, and this is how I conceived the Moontime Diary in 2006. *www.moontimediary.com.au; email: moontimeoffice @gmail.com*

Katarzyna Bruniewska-Gierczak ~ Zodiac Illustrations

Licensed under Dreamstime

Katarzyna is a graduate of the Faculty of Humanities of the Bydgoszcz Academy of Casimir the Great, in the field of Protection of Cultural Heritage. Katarzyna was born in Poland on April 12, 1979. She discovered her passion for painting in her early childhood and started using oil paints at the age of 16. Later, oil paint was replaced by watercolour, which resulted in the creation of numerous illustrations, many of them decorate the covers of books and magazines around the world. From the very beginning, the central place in her paintings has been occupied by a woman, her emotions and sensitivity.

To view more of or purchase Katarzyna's artwork, *visit: http://bruniewska.com/*

Brian Clark ~ Power to the People

Brian Clark has been a consulting astrologer and educator for most of his adult life. He is the creator of the Astro*Synthesis distance learning program, which has been shaped from his experience as an astrological educator and author.

His books and articles have been translated into numerous languages. Brian's most recent publications are The Family Legacy, Vocation, and From the Moment We Met: The Astrology of Adult Relationships, all available through Amazon or Astro*Synthesis.

www.astrosynthesis.com.au

Marilyn Hillier ~ Facebook Posting

Marilyn has been studying Astrology for the past 25 years and is very involved within the astrological world. She teaches at the Gold Coast, is the President of the Gold Coast Astrological Society, a member of the QFA (Queensland Federation of Astrologers), and a member of the FAA (Federation of Australian Astrologers).

Having her natal Moon in the watery sign of Pisces, Marilyn is very much in touch with the lunar aspects. She thoroughly enjoys sharing her and Moontime Diary's astrological knowledge about the Moon by writing Moontime Diary's Facebook posts.

Email: marilyn_astro@hotmail.com

My Heartfelt Thanks and Acknowledgements to

- Solarfire: www.esotech.com.au
- Time and Date: www.timeanddate.com
- Sea & Sky: www.seasky.org

And many others, INCLUDING YOU, without whom this work would not be possible.

I wish you all the best for 2023,
With Love and Moonlight,

Iris and Monty

Sun ~ Moon & Earth Cycle

The ever-changing Moon orbits around the Earth and, together with the Sun and our tilted Earth, causes the seasons and cycles as we know them.

When these three planets line up exactly, they present us with fascinating events such as Full Moons, some Super ~ Blood or Blue Moons, Eclipses, Solstices and Equinoxes.

Dark Moon

The day before a new Moon, when the Moon is not visible, is called Dark Moon.

New Moon

The Moon is between the Earth and the Sun; therefore, it is invisible from Earth.

Full Moon

At full Moon, the Moon and Sun are opposite each other, with the Earth in between. From Earth, we see the fully illuminated Moon.

Super Moon

A Super Moon occurs at either a full or new Moon, which coincides with the Moon's closest approach to the Earth (perigee).

Therefore Super full Moons appear bigger and brighter than usual and cause higher tides, called Perigean spring tides.

Blue Moon

A Blue Moon occurs when two full Moons rise in the same zodiac sign or calendar month.

Folklore also says that if a season has four full Moons, the third full Moon is called a Blue Moon.

This happens approximately every 33 months and two Blue Moons in one year occur roughly once every 19 years. Blue Moons never occur in February because it takes 27.3 days for the Moon to complete one orbit.

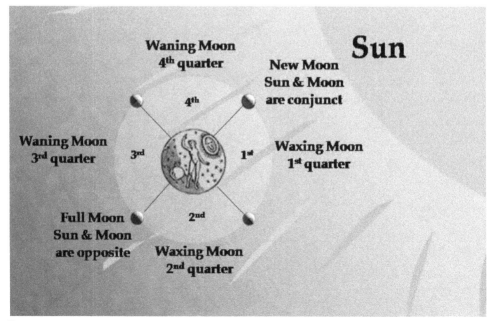

Eclipses

Eclipses are natural phenomena and only happen at those new and full Moons when the Sun, Moon, and Earth line up exactly, which usually occurs four times a year and always in pairs 14 days apart.

LUNAR ECLIPSE

A lunar eclipse happens only at full Moon when the Sun and Moon are opposite. The Earth passes between the Sun and the Moon and partially or fully blocks (occults) the Sun's rays, causing the darkening of the Moon.

You can safely observe a lunar eclipse without eye protection.

SOLAR ECLIPSE

A solar eclipse happens on the new Moon when the Moon passes between the Earth and Sun. It partially or fully blocks (occults) the Sun's rays and causes the sky's darkening.

It is crucial to never watch a solar eclipse without protective eyeglasses or shields.

BLOOD MOON

A full Moon fully eclipsed often turns red and is called a Blood Moon. This is due to a phenomenon named 'Rayleigh Scattering', a scattering of light that also causes spectacular sunrises and sunsets.

EQUINOX

Twice a year, when the Sun crosses the celestial equator, day and night are of equal length.

The March equinox, known as Ostara, marks the beginning of spring.

The September equinox, known as Mabon, marks the beginning of autumn in the northern hemisphere.

SOLSTICE

Summer solstice, Litha, marks the longest day of the year. The Sun reaches its highest point in the sky at noon and is most intense.

Winter solstice, known as Yule, marks the shortest day of the year when the Sun is at its lowest point in the sky at noon and least intense.

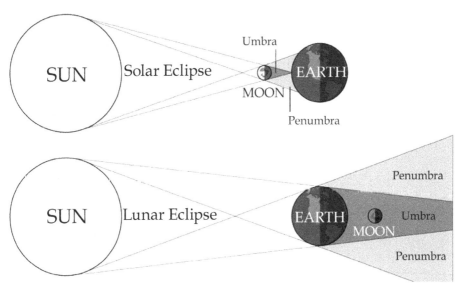

For specific times and visibility, visit *www.timeanddate.com.au* and *www.seasky.org*

Moon Phases for Health and Wellbeing

The Moon's gravitational pull not only affects ocean tides; it also influences humans, animals and plants.

Human beings consist of approximately 65%, fish about 80% and plants between 80-90% of water, as in blood, lymph, cerebral fluids and sap. Therefore, the Moon's gravitational pull affects our physical and emotional wellbeing and the growth and decay cycle of plants.

Once you realise how you can take advantage of the lunar cycle, it will make sense to plan health and beauty treatments for those days when they are most effective. Knowing the days which are counter-productive can also be an advantage. Either way helps you improve your health and daily routine.

Tradition says it is particularly beneficial to support and strengthen the organ and body part related to the zodiac sign (see Affinity Table page 190) the Moon moves through. E.g. drinking Stinging Nettle tea while the Moon moves through Libra supports and conditions your kidneys.

Anything that puts stress on this organ/body part is more detrimental at this time; therefore, operations (considered stressful to the organ) are, if possible, avoided.

E.g. a knee operation often is elective surgery and allows you to plan:

Capricorn rules the knee (see Affinity Table page 190). It is best to avoid the 2.5 days each month when the Moon moves through Capricorn. Most importantly, avoid the Capricorn full Moon in June or July.

NOTE: Do not postpone Emergency operations!

New Moon

New Moon is the best time to rest, fast, contemplate or kick a bad habit. Meditative self-inquiry helps you to set goals and work out steps to achieve them. If you want to be more specific, look at the Affinity Table (page 190). You find that every zodiac sign relates to a particular body part.

Waxing Moon

While the Moon waxes, the two weeks are divided into the first and second quarters.

During this growth and expansion phase, cells absorb and retain moisture, information, stimulants and toxins. This can result in fluid retention, weight gain, and heightened sensitivity at full Moon.

Being aware of this can help you plan and manage mood swings, children, allergies, hangovers and migraines.

Make the most of the waxing phase by enjoying nourishing, regenerative, strengthening and refreshing treatments during these two weeks.

Full Moon

When the Moon and Sun occupy opposite signs, the full Moon rises approximately at the time as the Sun is setting. You see the Moon as a whole disc, reflecting the Sun's light brightly.

The day towards the full Moon can be very intense. We tend to have interrupted sleep and often feel more impulsive and emotional than usual.

We find this particularly true when the full Moon aspects a personal planet in our birth chart, illuminating areas in

Timing Table for Health and Wellbeing

Activities	Best Phase	Best Sign for the Moon
DEEP CLEANSE TREATMENTS	WANING MOON	SEE AFFINITY TABLE PAGE 190
DENTIST TREATMENT	WANING MOON	VIRGO, SCORPIO, AVOID ARIES AND TAURUS
DENTAL HYGIENE, CLEANING	WANING MOON	CAPRICORN, AQUARIUS, VIRGO
FASTING AND DETOX	WANING/NEW MOON	SCORPIO, VIRGO
FOOT REFLEX MASSAGE	WAX/WANING	PISCES
HAIR COLOUR & STREAKS	WAXING MOON	LEO, VIRGO, SAGITTARIUS, ARIES
HAIRCUT STRONG REGROWTH	WAXING MOON	LEO
HAIR REMOVAL	WANING MOON	AQUARIUS, CAPRICORN
HAIR WASHING	WANING MOON	AVOID WATER SIGNS (PROMOTES DANDRUFF)
LYMPHATIC DRAINAGE	WANING MOON	WATER SIGNS
MANICURE AND PEDICURE	WAXING MOON	CAPRICORN, AQUARIUS, ARIES, AVOID PISCES
MASSAGE	WAX/WANING	SEE AFFINITY TABLE PAGE 190
MOISTURISING TREATMENTS	WAXING MOON	TAURUS, VIRGO, LIBRA, CAPRICORN
OPERATIONS	AVOID FULL MOON	PREFER WANING MOON, SEE PAGES 10, 190
START WEANING BABIES	WAXING MOON	AQUARIUS, STOP AT FULL MOON
REMOVE SUN SPOTS ETC.	WANING MOON	AVOID WAXING AND FULL MOON
VACCINATION	AVOID FULL MOON	AVOID TAURUS, VIRGO, CAPRICORN

our life which might need attention. Try to avoid operations close to or on the full Moon because there is a higher chance of complications.

◖ Waning Moon

The two weeks, while the Moon is waning, are divided into the third and fourth quarters. As the Moon gets smaller, cells release moisture, pent-up energy can flow out and the pressure reduces.

During these two weeks, cleansing facials, lymphatic drainage and detox mud wraps are more effective because they support the body's tendency to release and eliminate.

The waning Moon phase is the favourable time for operations and removing sunspots, moles, warts and plaque. Generally, there are fewer complications, less scar formation, and less pain sensitivity.

For example, schedule a lymphatic drainage massage for a day when the Moon is waning and in a water sign.

Sign	Health Zodiac
Aries	A fire sign, relates to the head, eyes, brain and outer layer of the skin. People who get headaches and migraines are more likely to have one while the Moon is in Aries, particularly when it is waxing and/or full. A hangover at full Moon in Aries is usually worse than at other times.
Taurus	A very fertile earth sign, relates to the ears, throat, voice box, jaw, teeth, neck and tonsils. A good time for gentle singing exercises and neck/shoulder massages. Try to avoid major dental work while the Moon is in Taurus, especially while waxing and closer to the full Moon.
Gemini	An air sign, relates to the breath, lungs, shoulders, arms, hands and nervous system. Working with paints, chemicals and solvents affect the lungs more while the Moon is waxing or full in Gemini. Stretches and exercise for shoulders, arms and hands have a beneficial effect.
Cancer	A very fertile water sign, relates to our emotions, the lymphatic system, breasts, stomach, liver and kidneys. While the Moon is waxing and full in a water sign, we tend to retain fluids and are more emotional. Lymphatic drainage massages are more beneficial in the waning phase.
Leo	A fire sign, relates to the back, heart, blood circulation and diaphragm. While the Moon is waxing enjoy an invigorating back massage and while the Moon is waning a more relaxing one. At full Moon, try to avoid operations and anything stressful to the heart and back.
Virgo	An earth sign, relates to the lips, hands, digestive system, spleen, nerves and pancreas. Pure water and clean, natural, nutritional food are essential to keep the digestive and nervous systems going strong.
Libra	An air sign, relates to the lower back, hips, kidneys and bladder. Prevent stones, infections and urination problems by drinking Stinging Nettle tea. In the waxing phase, this tea delivers nutrients, while in the waning period, it is an effective diuretic, flushing kidneys and bladder.
Scorpio	A fertile water sign, relates to emotions, sexual organs, liver, urethra and lymphatic fluids. While the Moon is waxing and full, we tend to retain fluids and are more emotional. Improve the digestive system by eating bitter-tasting herbs, e.g. Rocket or taking 'Swedish Bitters'
Sagittarius	A fire sign, relates to the hips, thighs, venous system and liver. To stimulate your circulation, dry brush your legs while the Moon is waxing in Sagittarius. To remove old skin cells, dry brush your skin while the Moon is waning in Sagittarius.
Capricorn	An earth sign, relates to skin, hair, nails, teeth, bones, joints, particularly the knees. Try to avoid bone, knee, joint operations and major dental work while the Moon is in Capricorn, especially at Capricorn full Moon.
Aquarius	An air sign relates to the mind, shins, ankles, the venous and nervous system. Extra magnesium, staying hydrated and active conditions both the venous and nervous systems. Too much table salt contributes to the hardening of the arteries and skin complaints
Pisces	A fertile water sign relates to emotions, lymphatic fluids, feet and toes. While the Moon is waxing and full, we tend to be more emotional and retain fluids. This affects the feet, making them more sensitive. If you buy shoes which are comfortable then, they will stay comfortable later.

PAGAN WHEEL OF THE YEAR

We visit the four seasons physically, emotionally and spiritually many times during a day and countless times during our life. Each time we do, we have new experiences and hone our skills. We find a greater understanding of the significance of life cycles, the four directions, the four seasons and the elements, all of which govern much of our life.

Every morning the Sun rises in the east, the direction of the most significant light, wisdom and consciousness. The air is crisp, and the energies are synonymous with spring, the season of new growth and fertility.

At high noon, the Sun is at its peak strength and sits directly overhead to the south. The air is hot, and the energy is synonymous with summer, the season of fruition and fulfilment.

As the Sun moves across the sky, we witness it sinking in the west. The air is cooling down, and the energy is synonymous with autumn, harvest, the season for introspection and meditation.

And finally, at midnight, the Sun has retired and darkness rules. Symbolically we are now in the north, experiencing winter. The coldest season relates to old age, wisdom and knowledge.

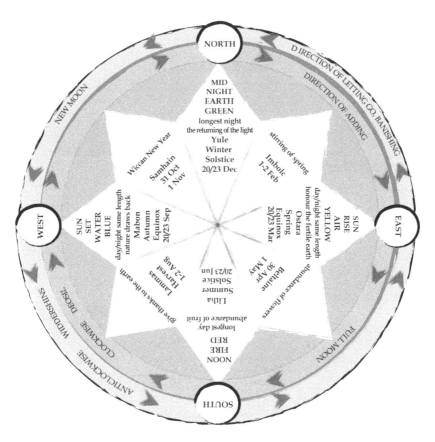

Moon Phases for Home and Work

With awareness of the Moon phases, you can create and maintain a healthy, pleasant atmosphere in your home and work.

The waxing phase lends itself to gardening activities such as planting, watering and fertilising (see page 16).

Housekeeping and maintenance jobs such as cleaning windows, tiles and floors, laundry, sorting out cupboards, and repairs have better results when done while the Moon is waning.

New Moon

The new Moon is the first visible crescent after the Sun and Moon were conjunct.

The first two days after the exact new Moon gives you the best opportunity to plan for the next cycle. Take some quiet time for a personalised ritual to plan, set goals and work out steps to achieve them.

Timing Table for Home and Maintenance

Activities	Best Phase	Best Sign for the Moon
CHARGING CRYSTALS	WAXING/FULL MOON	AQUARIUS, VIRGO, CAPRICORN, TAURUS
DIVINING FOR WATER	WAXING/FULL MOON	CANCER, SCORPIO, PISCES
DRILLING FOR WATER BORES	WAXING/FULL MOON	CANCER, SCORPIO, PISCES
AIRING BEDDING	WANING MOON	AIR AND FIRE SIGNS
CAR WASH	WANING MOON	VIRGO, LIBRA, CAPRICORN, AQUARIUS, GEMINI
CLEANSING CRYSTALS	WANING/NEW MOON	TAURUS, VIRGO, CAPRICORN, AQUARIUS
CLEANING WINDOWS	WANING MOON	FIRE AND AIR SIGNS
CONCRETING, EXCAVATIONS	WANING MOON	TAURUS, VIRGO, CAPRICORN
LAUNDRY	WANING MOON	CANCER, SCORPIO, PISCES
LAYING WOODEN FLOORS	WANING MOON	TAURUS, VIRGO, CAPRICORN
MAINTENANCE	WANING MOON	TAURUS, VIRGO, CAPRICORN
MAJOR CLEAN-UP	WANING MOON	ARIES, VIRGO, SCORPIO
MOPPING FLOORS	WANING MOON	FIRE AND AIR SIGNS
PAINTING AND GLUE JOBS	WANING MOON	ARIES, LEO, LIBRA, AQUARIUS
PAINTING AND GLUE JOBS	WANING MOON	AVOID FULL MOON AND MOON IN GEMINI
REMOVING MOULD	WANING MOON	LIBRA, AQUARIUS, GEMINI
SET FENCE/HOUSE POSTS	WANING/NEW MOON	TAURUS, VIRGO, CAPRICORN

☽ Waxing Moon

In the two weeks between the new and full Moon, the Moon waxes and gets bigger. Projects started on the new Moon are gathering momentum, growing and expanding.

Use this time to research, add, adjust, stock and place your orders.

Be aware that materials such as timber absorb moisture from the atmosphere and expand while the Moon is waxing.

○ Full Moon

This is a short but very intensive time with high cellular pressure. Avoid installing wooden floors and fence posts because, after the full Moon, wood will release moisture, shrink and leave gaps in the floor.

☾ Waning Moon

While the waning Moon is getting smaller, it is best to put things together, consolidate projects, release surplus and remove waste. This time favours general work, maintenance, repairs and cleaning.

Materials like wood are now releasing moisture and shrinking a little. Therefore, the third quarter Moon days are ideal for installing timber floors, fences and house posts.

At dark Moon (the day just before a new Moon), we cannot see the Moon at all. This is a time for rest and contemplation. Meditative self-inquiry helps you clarify issues you would like to resolve before the next cycle starts.

Timing Table for Planning and Work

Activities	Best Phase	Best Sign for the Moon
PLAN, START CAMPAIGN	NEW AND WAXING MOON	GEMINI, VIRGO, CAPRICORN
START NEW JOB	NEW AND WAXING MOON	LEO, CAPRICORN, VIRGO, TAURUS
START NEW PROJECT	NEW AND WAXING MOON	RELATE TO ZODIAC SIGN PAGES 21–43
TRAVEL PLANNING	NEW AND WAXING MOON	VIRGO, SAGITTARIUS, CAPRICORN
FINANCIAL PLANNING	NEW AND WAXING MOON	TAURUS, CANCER, VIRGO, SCORPIO
FINANCING, INVESTING	WAXING MOON	TAURUS, VIRGO, SCORPIO, CAPRICORN
CONFERENCES, NETWORKING	WAXING OR WANING MOON	AQUARIUS, CAPRICORN, GEMINI
WEDDING	WAXING MOON	LIBRA, CANCER, TAURUS
WEDDING	AVOID 3 RD QUARTER UNTIL NEW MOON	
JOB INTERVIEWS	JUST AFTER FULL MOON	LEO, GEMINI, AQUARIUS
BOOKKEEPING, TAX	WANING MOON	TAURUS, VIRGO, SCORPIO
GIVING NOTICE	WANING MOON	JUST BEFORE NEW MOON
MOVING HOUSE	WANING/NEW MOON	TAURUS, CANCER, LIBRA
PLAN AND SET GOALS	JUST AFTER NEW MOON	RELATE TO ZODIAC SIGN PAGES 21–43

Moon Phases in the Garden

Many gardeners and farmers successfully prepare the soil, plant, water, fertilise, harvest and preserve food by the Moon phases. They grow healthy and nutrient-rich food without chemical fertilisers, toxic herbicides and insecticides.

New Moon

The Moon and Sun are conjunct in the same sign at the new Moon. We cannot see the Moon from Earth because it is so close to the bright Sun.

This is considered a resting period in the garden, and the soil is getting ready to exhale

Waxing Moon

The two weeks while the Moon waxes are divided into the first and second quarters.

As the Moon becomes fuller, plants transport their sap (which contains nutrients and medicinal constituents) up the stem into the leaves, flowers and fruits.

Simultaneously, the Earth exhales, releasing moisture and nutrients for plants to absorb and metabolise.

Therefore the second quarter is the most favourable time to plant, water, fertilise and harvest above-ground vegetables.

Seeds planted in the second quarter absorb more water, germinate better and grow well.

During droughts, try to plant seeds close to the full Moon.

Eating organically grown, above-ground food straight from the garden in a waxing phase towards the full Moon delivers the most nutrients and medicinal properties.

Full Moon

On the full Moon, the Moon and the Sun occupy opposite signs. The full Moon rises on the eastern horizon simultaneously as the Sun sets in the west. It is a very intense time with high internal pressure.

Herbs, fruits and flowers harvested at full Moon are very juicy, flavourful, high in nutrients and medicinal properties.

Waning Moon

The two weeks while the Moon wanes are divided into the third and fourth quarters.

As the Moon becomes smaller, the Earth inhales, absorbing water, nutrients, and anything else disolved (e.g., fertilisers or chemicals).

Simultaneously, plants exhale, releasing moisture, dropping leaves, flowers and fruit.

The third quarter is the most effective time to vitalise the soil with fertiliser and manure, planting and tending to below-ground vegetables, like Potatoes and Ginger.

Drying, preserving and storing herbs, flowers and fruit in the waning phase prevents mould growth.

To make teas and tinctures, harvest and dry roots in the fourth quarter and dark Moon. This way, you ensure the medicinal properties are in the roots of the plant.

Healthy soil is vital to growing healthy plants that are more resilient to disease and fungal infections and more nutritious.

Therefore, improving and keeping your soil in top condition is essential and relatively easy. By adding animal and plant manure to your soil, you provide an excellent feed to the tiny microbes. Give them some time, and they convert manure to nutrients your plants thrive on.

1. Animal Manure

Cow, horse and sheep manure comes from grazing animals. It is generally lower in nutrients but is excellent to build up organic matter in the soil.

Chicken manure is high in nitrogen and phosphate, making it an ideal soil conditioner and fertiliser for vegetables and herbs.

Worm castings are a highly concentrated mixture of microorganisms, bacteria, enzymes, remnants of plant matter and manure. They are a super boost for the whole garden, and vegetable growers love worm castings.

2. Plant Manure

Lucerne hay, alfalfa and comfrey leaves supply potassium, nitrogen, calcium and other trace elements. Worked into the soil, they break down easily and enhance the soil's drainage capacity.

Fertilising teas are rich in nutrients and a quick way to fertilise plants when they need a boost, e.g. after transplanting when flowering or setting fruit.

For Fertilising Teas, you can use:

• Lucerne/alfalfa hay or meal, fresh grass clippings, kelp and wood ashes are high in nitrogen and potassium.

• Comfrey is rich in calcium, phosphorus, potassium, magnesium, vitamins A, B & C and trace minerals.

• Stinging Nettle tea is high in iron, nitrogen, phosphorus, potassium, calcium, zinc and magnesium.

Please note: Stinging Nettle tea promotes leafy growth but can stunt fruiting and flowering!

Promote Healthy Root Development

After the harvest, prepare the soil with animal and plant manure. Allow the microbes to do their magic as they enrich the soil. This way, you provide excellent conditions for the new seedlings to establish a healthy root system.

Fertilise with phosphorus and nitrogen the week after the full Moon (waning) when the Moon moves through an earth sign.

Enhance Strong Leaf Growth

To enhance above-ground growth, fertilise with nitrogen and potassium-rich fertiliser the week before the full Moon when the Moon waxes in a water sign.

Enhance Flowering

Supply extra phosphorus and potassium the week before the full Moon while the Moon waxes and is in an air sign.

Support Fruit Formation

Supply nitrogen and potassium the week before the full Moon when the Moon moves through a fire sign.

Timing Table for Gardening

Activities	Best Phase	Best Sign for the Moon
CUTTINGS	JUST BEFORE FULL MOON	DEPENDS ON FLOWER, FRUIT, LEAF, ROOT
FERTILISE TO BOOST FRUIT GROWTH	WAXING/FULL MOON	ARIES, SAGITTARIUS, AVOID FULL MOON IN LEO
GRAFT TREES	WAXING NEAR TO FULL MOON	ARIES, LEO, SAGITTARIUS, CAPRICORN
MOW TO STRENGTHEN LAWN	WAXING MOON	PISCES, SCORPIO, CANCER
PRUNE FRUIT TREES FOR BETTER GROWTH	NEW AND EARLY WAXING MOON	SAGITTARIUS, LEO, ARIES
REPOT AND TRANSPLANT	2ND AND 3RD QUARTER	VIRGO
SOW LAWN AND LAY TURF	WAXING MOON	TAURUS, VIRGO, CAPRICORN
SOW, PLANT AND HARVEST FRUIT PLANTS	WAXING MOON	ARIES, LEO, SAGITTARIUS
SOW, PLANT AND HARVEST ABOVE-GROUND VEGETABLES	WAXING MOON	TAURUS, CANCER, SCORPIO, CAPRICORN, PISCES
SOW, PLANT AND HARVEST FLOWERS AND HERBS	WAXING MOON	TAURUS, GEMINI, CANCER, LIBRA, SCORPIO
TRANSPLANT WATER PLANTS	WAXING MOON	CANCER, VIRGO, SCORPIO, PISCES
WATER AND FERTILISE TO BOOST ABOVE-GROUND GROWTH	WAXING/FULL MOON	CANCER, SCORPIO, PISCES
TEND TO YOUR COMPOST	WANING MOON	TAURUS, VIRGO, CAPRICORN
DRY FRUIT AND HERBS	WANING MOON	AVOID WATER SIGNS
FERTILISE TO BOOST ROOT GROWTH	WANING MOON	TAURUS, VIRGO, CAPRICORN
MAINTENANCE	WANING MOON	VIRGO, CAPRICORN, ARIES, AQUARIUS
MOW TO RETARD LAWN GROWTH	WANING MOON	AQUARIUS
MULCH	WANING/NEW MOON	TAURUS, VIRGO, CAPRICORN
PRUNE TO RETARD GROWTH	FULL/WANING MOON	AQUARIUS
SOW AND HARVEST ROOT CROPS	WANING MOON	TAURUS, VIRGO, CAPRICORN
WEED AND PEST MANAGEMENT	WANING MOON	AQUARIUS, VIRGO, GEMINI, LIBRA
WATER AND FERTILISE POT PLANTS	WAXING/WANING	CANCER, SCORPIO, PISCES, VIRGO
PRUNE SICK PLANTS AND TREES	NEW MOON	AVOID AQUARIUS

SIGN	GARDEN ZODIAC
Aries	A fire sign, relates to the fruit of the plant. It is a favourable time to plant and tend to fruiting plants, especially fast-growing ones. Graft fruit trees when the Moon is waxing or close to full. Waning Moon is also is a good time for weed and pest management.
Taurus	An earth sign, relates to the root of the plant. It is a favourable time to plant and tend to root vegetables. Leafy vegetables do well too because Taurus is a very fertile sign. Good time to water and fertilise.
Gemini	An air sign, it relates to the flowers of the plant, to vines and creepers. This is a favourable time to plant and tend to beautiful fragrant flowers and vines. Harvest medicinal flowers/herbs when the Moon is full.
Cancer	A very fertile water sign relates to the leafy parts of the plant. The best time for planting (especially green, leafy vegetables), transplanting, grafting, watering and fertilising is while the Moon is waxing. Mow your lawn now if you want vigorous re-growth.
Leo	A fire sign relates to the fruit of the plant. It is a favourable time to plant and look after fruiting plants and vegetables. Graft fruit trees when the Moon is waxing or close to full. Avoid watering and fertilising when the Moon is full in Leo. The soil is not absorbing very well, and fertilisers tend to burn plants or dissipate.
Virgo	An earth sign relates to the root system of plants. This is a favourable time to plant (third quarter) and care for your root vegetables, general garden maintenance, watering and fertilising, mulching, starting a compost, sawing and laying turf, re-potting and transplanting.
Libra	An air sign it relates to the flowers of the plant, to vines and creepers. This is a favourable time to plant and tend to beautiful fragrant flowers and vines. Harvest medicinal flowers/herbs in the second quarter or even better when the Moon is full.
Scorpio	A water sign relates to the leafy parts of the plant. It is a very fertile sign - the best time for planting (especially green, leafy vegetables), transplanting, grafting, watering and fertilising. The full Moon in Scorpio is also an excellent time to harvest medicinal plants.
Sagittarius	A fire sign relates to the fruit of the plant. It is a favourable time to plant onions and tend to fruiting plants. Graft fruit trees when the Moon is waxing. Avoid weeding plants that spread via the root system because it encourages healthy regrowth.
Capricorn	An earth sign relates to the root system. This is a favourable time to plant (third quarter) and care for root vegetables, general garden maintenance, watering, fertilising and mulching. Harvest roots when the Moon is new in an earth sign when nutrients and medicinal properties are in the root.
Aquarius	An air sign it relates to flowers, vines and creepers. This is a favourable time to plant and tend to beautiful and fragrant flowers and vines. It is best to harvest medicinal flowers and herbs when the Moon is waxing, or even better when it is full in an air sign.
Pisces	A very fertile water sign relates to the leafy parts of the plant. The best time for planting (especially green, leafy vegetables), transplanting, grafting, watering and fertilising is while the Moon is waxing. Mow your lawn now if you want vigorous regrowth.

CAPRICORN

Capricorn ♑, a cardinal earth sign, is symbolised by the sea goat and ruled by the planet Saturn ♄.

Capricorn relates to 10th House affairs such as ambition, career, status, government, one's public standing.

POSITIVE TRAITS: practical, responsible, patient, constructive, ambitious, cautious, determined.

NEGATIVE TRAITS: despondent, heartless, dogmatic, selfish, calculating, conventional, miserly.

KEYWORDS: ambition, authority, prudence, structure, business.

When the Sun or Moon moves through the constellation of Capricorn, we tend to be more ambitious, practical and disciplined. Use this opportunity and positively focus on your work, career and business goals.

Harmonious aspects to the Sun or Moon in Capricorn help you advance everything related to Capricorn. Stressful aspects can trigger fears of losing your reputation. You might be pessimistic, insensitive, even cruel to yourself and others.

FORECAST FOR 2023 *by Narelle*

This year, reflection is the key to your success, as 2023 starts with Mercury retrograding through your sign until 18 January. What are your strengths and weaknesses? Where do you feel most self-empowered? Figure out how to play to your strengths to truly transform your world and capitalise on what 2023 has on offer, particularly Capricorns born 18-20 January.

If you do not like your current situation, be the change rather than waiting for the change to happen to you. This can be particularly true for Capricorns born 5-14 January, who may experience more restlessness than usual this year.

The need to spread your wings and try something new could see you reinventing yourself. Thinking outside the box comes easy, allowing you to come up with alternative options that others may not readily see.

Many Capricorns can draw on their creativity to birth great things in 2023 that bring them great pleasure to both themselves and those they love.

Original Artwork © Katarzyna Bruniewska-Gierczak, liscensed under Dreamstime

AQUARIUS

AQUARIUS ♒, a fixed air sign is symbolised by the water bearer and ruled by its traditional ruler Saturn ♄ and its modern ruler Uranus ♅. Aquarius relates to 11th House affairs such as hopes and wishes, friends, acquaintances, groups and societies.

POSITIVE TRAITS: inventive, humanitarian, freedom-loving, friendly, idealistic.

NEGATIVE TRAITS: eccentric, rebellious, erratic, unpredictable, irritable, straining to be unconventional.

KEYWORDS: original, innovative, independent, humanitarian.

When the Sun or Moon moves through Aquarius, we are more aware of social issues, friendly and yet detached. We tend to be motivated by intellect rather than emotion and want to be heard.

Harmonious aspects to the Sun or Moon in Aquarius help you advance in your endeavours. Stressful aspects can trigger fear of losing your freedom or individuality; you might be eccentric or tactless.

FORECAST FOR 2023 by Narelle

Consider 2023 a year that will bring you many opportunities to clean out your closet of things that are no longer useful and have been taking up valuable space in your life. You can start this while Mars is retrograding through Gemini from 1-12 January. Take a look at your inventory and consider selling, giving to charity, or reinventing anything that has passed its use-by-date. With the newly cleared space you have created, there can be an abundant flow of novel ideas on how to best use your environment.

It can be a good idea to run these ingenious plans by others just to check-in and get an objective point of view. It could be all too easy to over-compensate and take on too much during the second half of the year, particularly for Aquarians born 21 January - 5 February.

Venus retrograding through your opposite sign during 23 July – 4 September can see allies and opponents giving you pause to reconsider your position on things. Take heed when your ideas or objectives are seemingly blocked and consider taking a detour.

PISCES

PISCES ♓, a mutable water sign, is symbolised by two fish bound together by a cord. Its traditional ruler is Jupiter ♃, and its modern ruler is Neptune ♆.

Pisces relates to 12th House affairs such as solitude, institutions such as hospitals, universities and prisons.

POSITIVE TRAITS: sensitive, kind, compassionate, receptive, intuitive, imaginative, romantic, artistic, creative.

NEGATIVE TRAITS: vague, impractical, indecisive, escapist, confused, impressionable.

KEYWORDS: sensitive, sympathetic, romantic, the urge to merge.

When the Sun or Moon moves through Pisces, we tend to be more sensitive, gentle and kind. Avoid becoming a martyr or victim; instead, use your compassion and imagination creatively.

Harmonious aspects to the Sun or Moon in Pisces help you advance everything related to Pisces. Stressful aspects tend to be confusing; you might feel separate, indecisive, and forgetful.

FORECAST FOR 2023 *by Narelle*

This year can be a period of taking life seriously and getting your 'ducks lined up in a row'. Think bigger, life milestones like making important relationship commitments, setting down roots, and building your career. From March, time-keeper planet Saturn makes his once in a 28-year visit to your sign, helping you lay down the foundations of important long-term goals.

Pisces born 19-26 February may find themselves in positions where making decisions in 2023 can profoundly impact their future. Seek wise counsel if the burden of such decision-making is weighing heavily on you and use Mercury retrograding through your opposite sign during 23 August – 15 September to refine your plans.

Think long-term investments, the objective is to put in the hard work now so that you can reap the profit of your labour in the future. Use your Pisces dreamer quality to conjure up your most ideal situation and then take baby steps to bring it into reality.

Original Artwork © Katarzyna Bruniewska-Gierczak, liscensed under Dreamstime

ARIES

ARIES the ram ♈, a cardinal fire sign is symbolised by its horns and ruled by the planet Mars ♂.

Aries relates to 1st House affairs such as physical appearance, personal traits, general outlook, first impressions.

POSITIVE TRAITS: pioneering, bold, independent, direct, decisive, takes the initiative, courageous.

NEGATIVE TRAITS: selfish, impulsive, aggressive, impatient, wants everything now, foolhardy.

KEYWORDS: initiating action, assertiveness, adventurous, forceful, me, myself and I.

When the Sun or Moon moves through the constellation of Aries, we tend to feel more energetic, self-centred and impatient. This increases the risk of headaches, migraines and (head) injuries.

Harmonious aspects to the Sun or Moon in Aries help you advance everything related to Aries. Stressful aspects can trigger fear of personal attack and loss of identity.

FORECAST FOR 2023 *by Narelle*

The self-discovery and growth that began in mid-2022 continue to broaden your horizons for the first five months of 2023. Big ideas may flow, and a boost in confidence can jolt you into action. But before you go 'gung-ho' with saddles blazing, there is an opportunity to reflect and refine your plans during the first couple of weeks of January whilst your ruler Mars is retrograde. If you start things prematurely, you could find mistakes costly.

Taking time to reflect on your inner and outer world during this time could help you channel the abundant raw energy at your disposal into productive and rewarding outcomes when you are clear on the end goal. This can be particularly true for Aries, born 1-10 or 18-20 April, who can find this year deeply transformational.

A solar eclipse in your sign on 20 April could signal the starting point for new beginnings. Take the lead and consider this your time to set the tone of your environment. Call on your inner warrior, be bold, and manifest your dreams into reality.

Original Artwork © Katarzyna Bruniewska-Gierczak, liscensed under Dreamstime

TAURUS

TAURUS the bull ♉ is a fixed earth sign. It is symbolised by the crescent above the circle and ruled by Venus ♀.

Taurus relates to 2nd House affairs such as matter, personal resources, cultivation, growth, values.

POSITIVE TRAITS: practical, patient, reliable, enduring, strong-willed, affectionate, good business sense.

NEGATIVE TRAITS: lazy, possessive, rigid, stubborn, resentful, dependent, opinionated.

KEYWORDS: stable, reliable, permanent, pleasure, possessions, comfort, security.

When the Sun or Moon moves through the constellation of Taurus, we tend to be more practical and patient, appreciate earthly beauty, love to indulge our senses in good food and wine.

Harmonious aspects to the Sun or Moon in Taurus help you advance anything related to Taurus. Stressful aspects can trigger fear of poverty or personal loss and leave you resentful and stubborn.

FORECAST FOR 2023 *by Narelle*

2023 is a growth year for many Taureans, particularly those born 21 April – 6 May. The generous planet Jupiter enters your sign in May to ignite your curiosity for seeking truth and knowledge through exploring outside your comfort zone. This could see you indulging in a spiritual and physical make-over, signing up for a course, taking on a novel hobby, or hitting the road for an exciting adventure.

Change is on the horizon, particularly for Taureans born 5-15 May. Think bigger picture, outside the box concepts that will take you on a new path of self-discovery. Inspiration may come through listening to wise souls who help you make solid plans and commit to materialising long-term goals.

Mercury retrogrades through your sign during 22 April – 15 May, alerting you to any glitches in your plans. Miscommunication or schedule disruptions arising can heighten your senses to things that require your focused attention. Make the necessary adjustments to re-set your compass for smooth sailing. Use the 29 October lunar eclipse in your sign to fertilise and nourish your plans into existence.

Original Artwork © Katarzyna Bruniewska-Gierczak, liscensed under Dreamstime

GEMINI

GEMINI ♊, a mutable air sign, is symbolised by two columns and ruled by the planet Mercury ☿.

Gemini relates to 3rd House affairs such as siblings, education, communication, neighbourhood, short-distance travel.

POSITIVE TRAITS: versatile, adaptable, communicative, quick-witted, inquisitive, a flair for writing.

NEGATIVE TRAITS: restless, scattered, superficial, cynical, ambivalent, two-faced.

KEYWORDS: mind, communication, changeable, transportation, curious, commerce.

When the Sun or Moon moves through the constellation of Gemini, we tend to be more talkative, curious and social. Make the most of it and allow yourself to be spontaneous.

Harmonious aspects to the Sun or Moon in Gemini help you advance anything related to Gemini. Stressful aspects can cause restlessness, change of mind, superficiality and gossip.

FORECAST FOR 2023 *by Narelle*

For many Geminis, it can feel like a slow start with your ruling planet Mercury retrograding, in addition to Mars retrograding through your sign, during the first couple of weeks of January. Momentum will build, but it may take until mid-February before you feel you are getting any traction. This could test your patience, and for some Geminis, particularly those born 22-29 May, a theme of ongoing delays and restrictions could seem to plague the year.

The gift of this cycle is to discover what can be achieved through aligning to a slower pace or another person's point of view. What can be learned from this experience that makes you a better and more resilient person? This could be confusing for Geminis born 14-19 June, but there is light at the end of the tunnel.

Clarity can come from chaos. Meditate, put yourself in the other person's shoes, consider a variety of different options, and look for the silver lining to come out the other side of this year a wiser person.

Original Artwork © Katarzyna Bruniewska-Gierczak, liscensed under Dreamstime

CANCER

CANCER ♋, the crab, a cardinal water sign, is symbolised by the two breasts of a nurturing mother and ruled by the Moon ☽.

Cancer relates to 4th House affairs such as home and family, mothers, babies, early childhood environments.

POSITIVE TRAITS: sensitive, kind, strong maternal instinct and family ties, imaginative, cautious, protective.

NEGATIVE TRAITS: changeable, moody, unreliable, untidy, gullible, holds on to a grudge, self-pitying.

KEYWORDS: mother and child, family, fertility, receptive.

When the Sun or Moon moves through Cancer, we are more sensitive, sentimental, nurturing and protective and nourish ourselves and others with food.

Harmonious aspects to the Sun or Moon in Cancer help you advance anything related to Cancer. Stressful aspects can make us moody and bring up fears of not belonging or being emotionally corrupted.

FORECAST FOR 2023 by Narelle

This year, you can leave a lasting impression on others, particularly those Cancerians born 22-29 June. Your strong work ethic comes from previous years of hard work and is evident in your honour code, which garners a formidable reputation. This allows you to capitalise on your character equity, harness the support of others, and build on your ambitions.

Think "big", like going for that promotion, pay rise, home loan, or opening that business. Picking up any extra responsibilities can be shouldered more readily now, and a sense of fulfilment comes from a job well done. Consider this a 'no-frills' year of patience, determination, duty, and achieving stability.

For many Cancerians born 4-23 July, this could also mean being realistic and unapologetic about one's weaknesses and strengths, allowing you to make compensations where necessary.

Unexpected events can help you see the world through a whole new lens, providing you with a refreshing new perspective. Whilst some doors will be closed forever, the light shining through shuttered windows left ajar beckons you to open them.

Original Artwork © Katarzyna Bruniewska-Gierczak, liscensed under Dreamstime

LEO

LEO ♌, a fixed fire sign, is symbolised by the lion's mane and tail and ruled by the Sun ☉.

Leo relates to 5th House affairs such as children, love affairs, creative self-expression, fun and games.

POSITIVE TRAITS: creative, romantic, generous, frank, affectionate, dignified, vital, loves performing.

NEGATIVE TRAITS: extravagant, condescending, overbearing, proud, arrogant, conceited, fixed.

KEYWORDS: self-expressive, dramatic, creativity, power.

When the Sun or Moon moves through the constellation of Leo, we enjoy showing kindness and need more affection and recognition for ourselves. Allow yourself to be fun-loving, courageous and creative at this time.

Harmonious aspects to the Sun or Moon in Leo help you advance anything related to Leo. Stressful aspects can trigger fears of being insignificant; you might act vain and proud, snobbish and pompous.

FORECAST FOR 2023 by Narelle

This year, grand plans for advancement and self-improvement may dominate your waking moments, but it will take a good plan and discipline to bring them to reality. Unrealistic and idealised concepts may lead to disappointment. Heed the advice from trusted allies before over-investing in grandiose notions only you believe in. Growth is possible when ideas are filtered and channelled into a step-by-step plan that has been overseen and approved by group consensus.

Venus retrograding through your sign from 23 July – 4 September can give you pause to identify who and what is important (when it comes to reviewing the workability of your support group). Apply the HALT rule of decision-making by delaying judgement when hungry, angry, lonely, or tired until after Venus moves direct on 5 September.

For Leos born 23 July, this can be confronting when important relationships end with permanent goodbyes as Pluto enters your opposite sign Aquarius and teaches the life cycle lesson of beginnings, endings, and new beginnings.

VIRGO

VIRGO ♍, a mutable earth sign is symbolised by the letter m and ruled by the planet Mercury ☿.

Virgo relates to 6th House affairs such as health, work, daily routine, service, acquired skills, small domestic animals.

POSITIVE TRAITS: modest, tidy, meticulous, discriminating, literary talent, specialised.

NEGATIVE TRAITS: hypercritical, demanding, high expectations, lacking perspective, worrying.

KEYWORDS: critical, analytical, practical, perfectionism, orderly, organised, service orientated.

When the Sun or Moon moves through Virgo, we have an excellent eye for detail and a good sense for numbers; we are more meticulous, analytical and appreciative of routines.

Harmonious aspects to the Sun or Moon in Virgo help you advance anything related to Virgo. Stressful aspects can trigger fears of being criticised or ill and cause you to worry and be hypercritical.

FORECAST FOR 2023 *by Narelle*

2023 signals a year of opportunity and exciting change for Virgos. The world is your oyster in many ways, but can you spot the pearl when its dull and sharp outer shell cloaks it?

Virgos born 7-16 September are uniquely positioned to think outside the box. When Virgos dare to walk unknown and possibly uncertain paths, they can reap the rewards from following their innovative and creative spirit. Meanwhile, Virgos born 24-31 August may find opponents, both friendly and unfriendly, creating the space to rise to any challenge and take responsibility for their actions, including receipt of any profits.

A surge of personal power can awaken Virgos, born 20-23 September, to their ability to mesmerise, ensnare, and influence others to their cause. Intensity, endurance, and passion permeate every cell in your body to be channelled into healthy obsessions. Whilst many advances in personal and professional goals may be realised, use Mercury retrograding through your sign during 23 August – 15 September to review, refine, and readjust your plans, particularly when delays or hiccups arise.

Original Artwork © Katarzyna Bruniewska-Gierczak, liscensed under Dreamstime

LIBRA

LIBRA ♎, a cardinal air sign is symbolised by a pair of scales and ruled by the planet Venus ♀.

Libra relates to 7th House affairs such as relationships, marriage, business partnerships, and agreements.

POSITIVE TRAITS: amiable, appreciative of beauty and harmony, kind and tactful, romantic, refined.

NEGATIVE TRAITS: indecisive, gullible, ambivalent, lazy, easily influenced.

KEYWORDS: relationship, harmony, beauty, balance, sympathy.

When the Sun or Moon moves through Libra, we appreciate peace, beauty and harmony. We tend to feel and communicate more diplomatically.

Harmonious aspects to the Sun or Moon in Libra help you advance anything related to Libra. Stressful aspects can trigger fears of disagreements, disharmony and being alone. You might be gullible, indecisive and changeable.

FORECAST FOR 2023 *by Narelle*

The start of the year could feel a little more testy than usual as disruptions to schedules, delays, and unfulfilled obligations affect yourself and those around you. It can feel like everything is out of whack, compelling you to right the balance, particularly Librans born 2-17 October.

The first half of the year can feel like you are a horse galloping down the racetrack with a jockey on your back and an urgency to cross the finish line. The demands forged by others could take their toll if you do not stand up for yourself and take a steady pace, particularly Librans born 5-13 October.

The solar eclipse in your sign on 15 October can renew your energy and mark the revitalisation of yourself, your place in the world, and the influence you generate in creating harmony around you.

The power is at your fingertips, particularly for Librans born 21-23 October. Do not let it slip through your fingers nor give it away to another. Hold onto it, cherish and use it wisely.

Original Artwork © Katarzyna Bruniewska-Gierczak, liscensed under Dreamstime

SCORPIO

SCORPIO ♏, a fixed water sign is symbolised by the running snake and ruled by passionate Mars ♂ and transformer Pluto ♀.

Scorpio relates to 8th House affairs such as cycles of life and death, sex, money, inheritance, and other peoples resources.

POSITIVE TRAITS: purposeful, determined, persistent, powerful feelings, highly imaginative.

NEGATIVE TRAITS: secretive, jealous, stubborn, brooding, intense, resentful.

KEYWORDS: elimination, transformation, death and rebirth, passion.

When the Sun or Moon moves through the constellation of Scorpio, there is a sense of intensity. We are highly sensitive and imaginative and can be moody. Avoid confrontations and complications.

Harmonious aspects to the Sun or Moon in Scorpio help you advance anything related to Scorpio. Stressful aspects can trigger fears of being involved or out of control. You might be secretive and resentful.

FORECAST FOR 2023 *by Narelle*

Whilst your natural instincts may be to control and take charge, you could find benefit from listening to the wisdom of others and allowing their influence to reflect in your decision-making this year.

Corrective and productive change can come through the innovation of partners and significant others in your life. Adopt a curious mindset and create an environment that allows the space for others to contribute. In fact, major personal and professional growth can occur most when you are relating with another person who shares like-minded values. Use your instincts to connect, forge, and cement alliances that will stand the test of time and yield long-term benefits for you both.

Use Mercury retrograding through your opposite sign 21 April – 15 May to listen to other people's perspectives and iron out any differences of opinion. The lunar eclipse in your sign on 6 May could signal a period of three to six months of reaping results from past actions and the ending and beginning of a new 18-year cycle, particularly for Scorpios born 7 November.

Original Artwork © Katarzyna Bruniewska-Gierczak, liscensed under Dreamstime

SAGITTARIUS

SAGITTARIUS ♐ is a mutable fire sign. It is symbolised by the arrow pointing to the future and ruled by Jupiter ♃.

Sagittarius relates to 9th House affairs such as foreign countries, travel, culture, religion, law, higher education.

POSITIVE TRAITS: expansive, optimistic, generous, compassionate, loving justice and equity, dependable.

NEGATIVE TRAITS: blindly optimistic, extremist, prone to exaggeration, wasteful, vain, unbalanced belief system, irresponsible.

KEYWORDS: expansion, fortune, optimism, enthusiasm, philosophy.

When the Sun or Moon moves through Sagittarius, we are inspired, more philosophical and optimistic. We tend to feel adventurous and have a need for independence.

Harmonious aspects to the Sun or Moon in Sagittarius help you advance anything related to Sagittarius. Stressful aspects can trigger panic attacks when feeling restricted. You might be blunt and prone to exaggeration.

FORECAST FOR 2023 *by Narelle*

Your ruling planet, Jupiter, can put a fire in your belly and a thirst for adventure during the first five months of 2023 as it traverses through the firecracker sign of Aries. If you have anything you want to conquer, fears you want to challenge, or goals you want to smash, now is the time to do it!

Infused with a bold new sense of confidence, you can take on even the steepest of mountains and know you will climb to the top. When you have timed it right, you will be able to bask in the rewards of your efforts by the time Jupiter moves into the sign of Taurus in mid-May.

The second half of the year affords you a slower pace so you can take time to immerse your senses and soak in the splendid views from the summit of your achievements. Reflective periods include Venus retrograding through Leo during 23 July – 4 September to signal what is truly important so you can align with who and what most brings you joy and Mercury retrograding through your sign 23 December to the end of the year.

Original Artwork © Katarzyna Bruniewska-Gierczak, liscensed under Dreamstime

PEOPLE HAVE THE POWER

All we have to do is awaken the power in the people
By John Lennon

The new year dawns with Venus contacting Pluto on the first day of 2023; perhaps a celestial new year's resolution highlighting the need to restore the values, respect, reliability and integrity that have been eroded over these past years. Here is an invitation to value that which is deeply cherished and beloved, both personally and collectively.

As the last of their sixteen conjunctions in Capricorn, the celestial finale heralds the gradual exit of Pluto from Capricorn as it approaches its final degree of the sign. Established fiscal values and governmental standards dominant for the last sixteen years of its passage through Capricorn are yielding to the voices of revolution and innovation.

This year gives us a glimpse into the possibility of that future. Pluto ingresses into Aquarius on March 23. It spends less than three months in the sign before retrograding back into Capricorn on June 11th for the rest of the year.

The window of reform has opened, but can it stay open? This last half of the year, along with a few months in 2024, marks the ending of Pluto in Capricorn. Pluto's closing moments through the sign have a unique substructure.

Like with any ending, the focus is on the need for completion. With Pluto in Capricorn, the end focuses on relinquishing the policies and positions born of the misuse of political power. It is time to compact and consider the long-term effects of this transition. The cosmic question is, how do we end this passage well!

What is the residue from Pluto in Capricorn that needs to be cleared, and what needs to be transformed to take advantage of Pluto's passage through Aquarius?

Its entrance into Capricorn heralded the Global Financial Crisis. The GFC demonstrated that we live in a global economic environment where irresponsible and unethical fiscal policies and practices affect everyone.

Its exit from Capricorn leaves us with the distress of the pandemic, a virus not bound by borders, status, race, gender, religion, or age. Pluto's exodus exposes the anguish of misplaced values and principles, as well as the wasteland created by corruption. Yet it also reveals the awareness that our economies and our ecosystems are no longer contained by legislative borders or corporate commands.

Pluto turns retrograde May 2 at 0≈21, the degree where the 20-year Jupiter-Saturn cycle was seeded at the end of 2020. Both are powerful astrological images of establishing Aquarian ideals for the next 20 years.

On March 7 Saturn exits Aquarius, leaving Pluto to cultivate this growth. Saturn's entry into Pisces confirms the dissolution of structure and authority as we have known it. On a personal level, we are challenged with the reconstruction of what we imagined and idealised, what we had yearned for. Saturn's passage through Pisces synchronises with Neptune's last years in the sign, climaxing in their conjunction at the first degree of the zodiac (0♈) in 2026.

This year focuses on the social and governmental disbanding of what was once agreed upon, and the experts who determine this. The question is what is consensus –what is the collective agreement as we enter the post-pandemic revisioning of state.

A pandemic does not discriminate – its etymology reminds us that it means all people. The virtue of Aquarius is that it characterises the people, the demos. The community is stronger than the individual, yet each individual is of equal importance in the tapestry of the collective. It was out of this perception that the ancient Greeks forged a new age through their ideal of democracy.

As Pluto's gaze turns to Aquarius, the power of the people is potentiated. Astrologically it is not events that repeat but the archetypal images underpinning these.

The last time Pluto was in Aquarius was a time of rebellion and discovery, an archetypal possibility that arises once again. This time the revolutions and the innovations occur in the context of the times. 2023 will be a swelling of this new wave. But first, the conscious acknowledgement and redemption of the shadow cast by plutocratic structures need to be recognised.

With Pluto's first foray into Aquarius this year, I am reminded of Patti Smith's words: "People have the power to redeem the work of fools".

Pluto's passage marks out generations. As it enters Aquarius, it opposes Pluto in the generation now between 64 and 85, who are challenged to relinquish the reins of power.

The Pluto in Virgo generation are between 50 and 66, and with Saturn opposing their Plutos in the next three years, it is time for adjustment and refocusing.

With Pluto trining the Pluto in Libra generation (38 to 51), it is time for this generation to enter the driver's seat, holding the balance of power that helps reform and transform our planet's destiny.

The Pluto in Scorpio generation, mostly in their 30s, support the process, while the Pluto in Sagittarius generation (14 to 28) are the voices of vision and hope for the planet.

Pluto is power, personally and collectively, and its passage into Aquarius asks us individually and mutually how we can let go of our subjective views to be more mindful of inclusivity and diversity.

Jupiter ingresses into Taurus on May 17, joining Uranus in the sign. Social awareness of climate change, environmental devastation and annihilation of our planet's resources is rapidly growing, as we are impacted more and more physically and materially with the depletion of resources and lifestyle. Jupiter's square to Pluto on May 18 might highlight some of these shortages.

The question is how we can best mobilise the power of the populace for the best outcomes for our planet.

The lunar nodes shift into the Aries-Libra polarity, stressing personal action in the context of others does make a difference.

Perhaps focusing our will on the best outcomes for everyone, rather than solely on ourselves, is a way that benefits each one of us.

Brian Clark, www.astrosynthesis.com.au

Moon Void of Course (voc)

On her journey around the Earth, the Moon reflects not only the Sun's light but also interacts with other planets.

The Moon takes approximately 2.5 days to move through each zodiac sign. It forms aspects with other planets which energise the planets involved.

The time between the last aspect the Moon makes in a zodiac sign and the moment when it ingresses in the next sign is called Moon Void of Course (voc). This happens every two to three days and may take just a few minutes or several hours. Sometimes, however, it can take more than a day.

During voc times, we tend to make unrealistic decisions, and projects started will most likely encounter delays, shortages and fizzle out.

However, we can use this time constructively by focusing inward, recharging our batteries, consolidating and cleaning up clutter.

When the Moon ingresses into the next zodiac sign, it is time to move on, refreshed and ready for the next interaction.

Harmonious, easy and flowing aspects:

☌ Conjunction 0°: blends with

⚹ Sextile 60°: co-operates with

△ Trine 120°: energises

Challenging and opposing aspects:

☌ Conjunction 0°: intensifies

☐ Square 90°: internal tensions can bring rewards over time

☍ Opposition 180°: external opposition, confrontation.

Aspect Interpretations
☽ Moon Aspects

☽☌☽	Beginning of new lunar cycle. A harmonious time to enjoy.
☽⚹☽	Receptive, contentment, good perception. Use opportunities constructively.
☽☐☽	Impulsive actions, lessons to be learned, female issues. Overcome obstacles.
☽△☽	Good ability to express. Put plans and projects into action.
☽☍☽	Conflict caused by others, strong emotions, crises, issues with females.

☽☌☉	New beginnings. Male and female energies. Emotions and ego are harmonising.
☽⚹☉	Internal equilibrium. Use opportunities to create harmonious relationships.
☽☐☉	Internal tension between willpower and emotions, lessons to be learned.
☽△☉	Ability to express. Put plans and projects into action.
☽☍☉	Conflict through others. Emotions conflict with honourable responses.

☽☌☿	Emotions and mind are in harmony. Honest talks bring clarity.
☽⚹☿	Feelings are easily communicated. Make use of opportunities.
☽☐☿	Irritable, internal conflict of mind and emotions. Lessons to be learned.
☽△☿	Emotions and mind are in harmony. Good to progress projects.
☽☍☿	Opposition, too much pressure. No time for proper communication.

☽☌♀	Romantic feelings, nurturing and/or creativity are enhanced.
☽⚹♀	Expression of emotions, love, affection and nurturing.
☽☐♀	Feeling emotional needs. Appearance is important. Lessons to be learned.
☽△♀	Nurture beauty and feminine aspects. Good to progress projects.
☽☍♀	Tendency to be obsessed with other people. Indulgence in excessive feelings.

☽☌♂ Decisiveness and quick responses lead to good results.
☽⚹♂ Feelings and actions harmonise, plenty of energy, use opportunities.
☽□♂ Internal tension, excitable, accident–prone. Avoid being rash, lessons to be learned.
☽△♂ Urge to get things done, decisiveness and leadership comes easy.
☽☍♂ Pent–up emotions, irritable, conflicts with others, competition.

☽☌♃ Uplifting, optimistic, may be overemotional, benefit from women.
☽⚹♃ Use opportunity to present your case. Good for study, research, group work.
☽□♃ Over–emotional, excessive, opinionated. Learning through obstacles.
☽△♃ Feeling confident, optimistic, successful. Good to progress projects.
☽☍♃ Opposition, extravagant tendencies, exaggeration of emotions.

☽☌♄ Steadfastness, conservatism. Control of feelings.
☽⚹♄ A sensible, careful and thorough approach to daily duties and responsibilities.
☽□♄ Internal conflict. Feelings of loneliness, depression and separateness.
☽△♄ Tolerance and control of emotional impulses bring great results.
☽☍♄ Constraint through opposition. Frustration and judgement, lack of flexibility.

☽☌⚷ Sheltering the homeless, feeling secure, kindly listening to another's pain.
☽⚹⚷ Creating opportunity from injury, supporting the outsider, liberate past sorrows.
☽□⚷ Healing family wounds, dis/relocation, create a new home, emotional challenges.
☽△⚷ Hands–on, healing ability, sanctuary for the soul, acceptance of the unknown.
☽☍⚷ Engaging the foreign, confronting past wounds, mothering the inner child.

☽☌♅ Urge to explore feelings. Sudden changes, uncertainty, new beginnings.
☽⚹♅ Use opportunities to work on new ideas, experimenting is favoured.
☽□♅ Internal conflict, tension, wilfulness, obstacles. Lessons to be learned.
☽△♅ Be inventive. Share ideas and inspirations.
☽☍♅ Expect disruptions, obsessions and changing circumstances.

☽☌♆ Impressionable, emotional, dreamy, insightful, intuitive.
☽⚹♆ Use opportunities to be creative, artistic, sensitive, psychic, express oneness.
☽□♆ Daydreaming, weird messages, confusion. Feelings of uncertainty.
☽△♆ Creative inspiration, positive thinking and feeling. Express your visions.
☽☍♆ Confused feelings, deception, unclear messages, misunderstandings.

☽☌♇ Intense feelings can lead to emotional release and healing.
☽⚹♇ Deep–rooted feelings surface, use the opportunity to transform relationships.
☽□♇ Internal emotional power struggles, compulsive behaviour.
☽△♇ Strong feelings and emotional release can cause constructive transformation.
☽☍♇ Opposition causes tensions. Opportunity for transformation.

☽☌⚸ Intuition is strong. Connect with your inner world, self–nourishment.
☽⚹⚸ Psychic openness; turn within, rest and replenish. Honour the Divine Feminine.
☽□⚸ Strong conflicting emotions, uncomfortable feelings, children, family struggles.
☽△⚸ Deep rest, coming home, soul nourishment, internal prompting, prayer, ritual.
☽☍⚸ Standing strong in inner wisdom in the face of opposition.

☽☌☊ Connect on a deep instinctual level to feelings and memories of the past.
☽⚹☊ Easy access to emotional support and inner resources.
☽□☊ Oversensitivity. Feeling a lack of love. Take care of your emotional needs.
☽△☊ Positive relationships with women, emotional support from others.
☽☍☊ Tune into the healing powers of nature, release neediness and heal old wounds.

☉☌☉	Beginning of a new solar cycle. Harmony within, stability, integrity.
☉⚹☉	Strong ego and health. Good relations with males. Use opportunities.
☉□☉	Obstacles to overcome, lessons to be learned. Male issues.
☉△☉	Good for decision-making and relations with males. Progress projects.
☉☍☉	Conflict through opposition. Crises illuminate (mostly) male issues.

☉☌☿	Harmony of will and thought. Communication and writing is favoured.
☉⚹☿	Communication flows easily. Use opportunities for networking and socialising.
☉□☿	Internal conflict, restlessness, irritability. Lessons to be learned.
☉△☿	Harmonious self-expression and communication. Advance projects.
☉☍☿	Arguments and worry caused by opposing ideas.

☉☌♀	Friendly and romantic feelings, enhanced creativity, idealism.
☉⚹♀	Friendship, love, pleasure. Balanced judgement. Make use of opportunities.
☉□♀	Excessive indulgence in beauty and enjoyment.
☉△♀	Beautiful and artistic expression is favoured and appreciated.
☉☍♀	Excessive indulgence in beauty and pleasure. Honour obligations.

☉☌♂	Self-assertiveness. Creative energy. Good for new beginnings.
☉⚹♂	Vibrant energy, good for sport, new activities and projects. Use opportunities.
☉□♂	Power urge, impulsiveness, male issues. Reactions to inner conflict.
☉△♂	Leadership, drive and ambition. Build and advance your project.
☉☍♂	Physical injury, volatility and irritability. Conflicting interests cause arguments.

☉☌♃	New beginnings, optimistic, ambitious. Excess can be a problem.
☉⚹♃	Group work and studies, enthusiasm brings success. Great opportunities.
☉□♃	Pompousness and opinions cause internal tension.
☉△♃	Optimism, confidence, abundance. Inspiration for growth and expansion.
☉☍♃	Overconfident, extravagant. Moral or legal issues, huge effort.

☉☌♄	Concentrated, rational thought, good judgement. Beginning of a new cycle.
☉⚹♄	Steady, be thorough. Making use of opportunities leads to success.
☉□♄	Obstacles and limitations, low self-esteem. A need to prove oneself.
☉△♄	Accepting responsibilities brings success. Good to progress projects.
☉☍♄	Male authority, father figure. Limitation through opposition.

☉☌⚷	Fostering the underdog, maverick, individualist. Feeling the pain of the father.
☉⚹⚷	Healing the broken spirit, accepting what cannot be fixed, a helping hand.
☉□⚷	Confronting an outsider, a heroic challenge. Leaving the house of the father.
☉△⚷	One of a kind, success from courage to stand apart and promote alternatives.
☉☍⚷	The road less travelled, challenging the establishment, wisdom from the unwanted.

☉☌♅	Sudden impulses, new beginnings. Expression of individuality and ideas.
☉⚹♅	Use opportunities and act on inventive ideas to bring about change.
☉□♅	Overly reactive, craving for excitement. Lessons to be learned.
☉△♅	Express and share ideas and inspirations. Interesting new developments.
☉☍♅	Sudden changes, recklessness, awkward revelations, opposition.

☉☌♆	Impressionable, sensitive, strong intuition. Expression of beauty and empathy.
☉⚹♆	Use opportunities to be compassionate, creative and idealistic.
☉□♆	Things are not as they seem. Lessons to be learned.
☉△♆	Dreams, wishful thinking. Take your inspiration a step further.
☉☍♆	Opposition, confusion, deception, misunderstandings, errors in judgement.

☉☌♇	Intense feelings, personal power, determination. Beginning of a new cycle.
☉⚹♇	Personal, sexual and financial power, determination. Make use of opportunities.
☉□♇	Compulsive and unconscious behaviour reveals inner conflict.
☉△♇	Strong magnetism, power, determination. Take your project a step further.
☉☍♇	Stifled emotions, jealousy. Power struggles with others.

☉☌⚸	Strength of character, deep inner trust. Capacity to be true to who you are.
☉⚹⚸	Ease of self-reliance. A sense of purpose and creative power grows.
☉□⚸	Internal conflict between aspirations and outer goals. Passion, energy, action.
☉△⚸	Confidence in your capacity to dig deep and stand strong. Energy flows freely.
☉☍⚸	Opposition from those in authority challenge you to be true to yourself.

☉☌☊	Awakening, enlightenment, increased success, contentment and warmth.
☉⚹☊	Creative ease and purposeful self-expression.
☉□☊	A turning point on the path to self-identification. Find your true identity.
☉△☊	Easy flow of solar energy. Express your confidence with ease.
☉☍☊	Purposeful encounters with others that feel fated. Release of stagnant energies.

☿ Mercury Aspects

☿☌☿	Thoughts, planning, communication. New beginning of mercury cycle.
☿⚹☿	Effective communication, networking, transport and trade. Use opportunities.
☿□☿	Obstacles and troubleshooting. Make the extra effort.
☿△☿	Good communication, networking, trading agreements. Progress projects.
☿☍☿	Troubleshooting. Be flexible in your approach to others.

☿☌♀	Agreeable communication and interaction. Beginning of a new cycle.
☿⚹♀	Harmonious relationships, agreement. Use opportunities for participation.
☿□♀	Superficial social pleasantries. Internal conflict causes obstacles.
☿△♀	Harmonious interaction and agreement. Good to progress projects.
☿☍♀	Opposition. Superficial social pleasantries require more effort.

☿☌♂	Sharp mentality, decisive action, honesty, skills. Good for business dealings.
☿⚹♂	Emphasis on intellectual energy. Use opportunities to interact and resolve issues.
☿□♂	Internal tension, arguments, breakdowns. A need to overcome obstacles.
☿△♂	Good communication and decision-making. Get things done efficiently.
☿☍♂	Anger, conflicting interests, hostility, breakdowns, impulsiveness.

☿☌♃	Consider the whole picture. Good judgement. Beginning of a new cycle.
☿⚹♃	Interest in learning, good judgement. Use opportunities for interaction and study.
☿□♃	Internal conflict, rash decisions. Think before you act.
☿△♃	Quick and sharp mind. Teaching, learning and business are favoured.
☿☍♃	Mental over-stimulation, extravagant tendencies, opinionated, overconfidence.

☿☌♄	Rational and serious. Focus mental energy on long-term planning.
☿⚹♄	Thorough approach, good for goal setting, planning and problem-solving.
☿□♄	Negative thinking, limitations, loneliness. Lessons to be learned.
☿△♄	Keen perception, realistic outlook, mental focus. Take your project a step further.
☿☍♄	Narrow mindedness, limited transport. Confrontation with male authority.

☿☌⚷	Think outside the square, learn in unusual ways, guide to the inner dream world.
☿⚹⚷	Healing with humour, a kind word, a loving thought.
☿□⚷	Hearing what is not being said, healing negative thoughts.
☿△⚷	Communicate emphatically, healing message, teacher of inner intelligence.
☿☍⚷	Reading subtleties, curious connections; believe in your inner thoughts and intuition.

☿☌♅	Inventive ideas. Expression of radical and unusual points of view.
☿⚹♅	Experiment with inventive ideas or points of view. Make use of opportunities.
☿□♅	Disrupted communication. Mental tension around radical, unconventional views.
☿△♅	Inspiration, communication. Take your inventive ideas to another level.
☿☍♅	Inflexibility, erratic mind. Challenge through opposition.
☿☌♆	Mind and imagination are in harmony. Creative expression is favoured.
☿⚹♆	Intuitive and visionary thinking. Opportunity to perceive subtleties.
☿□♆	Confusion, self-deception. Lessons to be learned.
☿△♆	Intuitive, visionary. Express subtleties artistically.
☿☍♆	Nebulous, confused, deception. Mind and imagination are in opposition.
☿☌♇	Intense thoughts and powerful conversations.
☿⚹♇	Opportunity for awareness of sexual, death and power issues.
☿□♇	Inner conflict, troubled mind, intensity of speech, plotting and strategising.
☿△♇	Money, sex, power and communication. Good to progress developments.
☿☍♇	Intense communication, transformative arguments.
☿☌⚸	Speaking truths that have long been silenced. Buried knowledge surfaces.
☿⚹⚸	Easy to speak your mind and express deep thoughts. Having something to say.
☿□⚸	Communicate with power and honesty rather than talking over the top of others.
☿△⚸	The power of words can heal and release the hidden past.
☿☍⚸	Polarising and straight talk can cause conflict or bring new harmony with others.
☿☌☊	Unexpected changes, important discussions and negotiations. Travel plans.
☿⚹☊	Creative problem solving is possible.
☿□☊	Inability to express thoughts and feelings. Meditate on different realities.
☿△☊	Easy flow of communication. Navigate between different views and opinions.
☿☍☊	Habitual thinking and communication patterns are challenged. Feeling ineffective.

♀ Venus Aspects

♀☌♀	Harmonious interactions. The beginning of a new cycle.
♀⚹♀	Consent, friendship. Opportunity for harmonious participation.
♀□♀	Internal tension between appreciation and beauty.
♀△♀	Friendship, harmony, beauty. Co-operative interactions.
♀☍♀	Differences, opposition. Make effort to co-operate.
♀☌♂	Physical attraction, pleasurable activities. The beginning of a new cycle.
♀⚹♂	Flirtation, positive and co-operative interactions. Strong sexual attraction.
♀□♂	Wilful and passionate actions. Attraction causes inner tension and conflict.
♀△♂	Co-operation and creativity. Express your romantic and passionate feelings.
♀☍♂	Competition, opposition. Conflict between genders.
♀☌♃	Friendships, relationships, projects. Beginning of a new cycle.
♀⚹♃	Emphasis on friendliness, comfort and beauty, large get-togethers.
♀□♃	Exaggerated feelings and actions, too much pleasure takes its toll.
♀△♃	Enjoyable friendships, contentment, luck. Good to progress projects.
♀☍♃	Exaggeration, extravagant tendencies, over-valuing and over-indulging.
♀☌♄	Shared responsibility and commitment. New beginnings.
♀⚹♄	A sensible, careful and thorough approach. Feeling safe and secure.
♀□♄	Conflict between comfort and security. Limitations arise, reassess desires.
♀△♄	Good judgement. Progress personal, financial and business plans.
♀☍♄	Separation, inhibitions. Social and traditional matters oppose each other.

♀☌⚷	Valuing differences, finding love in unusual places, a beautiful sadness.
♀⚹⚷	Discover beauty in the beast, celebrate diversity, honour past relationships.
♀□⚷	Heal a relationship, love your abandoned self, appreciate the tension of opposites.
♀△⚷	The healing power of love, a sensitive artist, inner beauty.
♀☍⚷	Embracing the uninhibited, reuniting with what was relinquished, reconciliation.

♀☌♅	Unique expression of appreciation and affection. New, exciting beginnings.
♀⚹♅	Affections, excitement. Use opportunities to share artistic inspiration.
♀□♅	Intense excitement; rebellious, unconventional tendencies. Internal conflict.
♀△♅	Taste for the bizarre, artistic expression. Take inspirations a step further.
♀☍♅	Expect unusual disruptions and changes.

♀☌♆	Time for art, beauty and enjoyment. Beginning of a new cycle.
♀⚹♆	Sensitive, psychic and romantic liaisons. Use your imagination.
♀□♆	Unrealistic expectations, romantic fantasy, easily impressed. Internal conflict.
♀△♆	Ease, idealism, appreciation of art and beauty. Go with the flow.
♀☍♆	Confusion, deception, error of judgement. Conflicting interests.

♀☌♇	Intense feelings and interactions lead to new beginning.
♀⚹♇	Deep-rooted feelings of love and appreciation surface.
♀□♇	Compulsive behaviour, jealousy and sexual tensions. Inner conflict.
♀△♇	Express profound feelings, transformational change. Take things further.
♀☍♇	Obsession for power in relationships. Conflict through opposition.

♀☌⚸	Feminine wisdom expressed with confidence and grace. Pleasure, sensuality.
♀⚹⚸	Art can heal and soothe the heart. Express your natural sensuality and beauty.
♀□⚸	Conflicts and jealousies between women stir deep passions. Discover what is true.
♀△⚸	Enjoyment, pleasure, delight in your sexuality and inner light. Express yourself freely.
♀☍⚸	Others may challenge your feminine wisdom. Betrayal, relationship challenges.

♀☌☊	Times of pleasant events, celebrations and nurturing meetings with friends.
♀⚹☊	Opportunities for pleasant encounters with women.
♀□☊	Issues relating to appreciating partners and relationships need clarification.
♀△☊	It is easy to express appreciation for beauty and art.
♀☍☊	Karmic relationships, dependence on others. Reassess social contracts.

♂ Mars Aspects

♂☌♂	Constructive planning, desire for action. New beginning.
♂⚹♂	Strong survival instincts, drive. Good opportunity to be constructive and productive.
♂□♂	Self-preservation, assertive and aggressive behaviour, accident-prone.
♂△♂	Efficiency, productivity. Follow your urge to get things done well.
♂☍♂	Volatile emotions, conflicts and competition with others.

♂☌♃	Courage and confidence. Energy is expansive, uplifting and optimistic.
♂⚹♃	Confidence, optimism, good for sports. Opportunities bring success.
♂□♃	Internal conflict, frustration. Risk-taking can lead to mistakes and accidents.
♂△♃	Good for sports, co-operation. Express your confidence.
♂☍♃	Overconfidence, lack of consideration. Try and keep reactions in check.

♂☌♄	Discipline and endurance, fortunate delays. Accomplishment in business.
♂⚹♄	Sensible, thorough approach to duties. Good opportunity to progress matters.
♂□♄	Internal conflict, limitations, control issues. Persistence brings results.
♂△♄	Discipline, patience. Express your enthusiasm for best outcomes.
♂☍♄	Limitations imposed, anger, sickness, injury. Will meets resistance.

♂☌⚷ Spiritual warrior, breaking the pain threshold, heroic action.
♂✶⚷ Focus on spiritual aspirations, let go of negative patterns.
♂□⚷ Tame the shrew, overcome your fear of being hurt, resolve conflict.
♂△⚷ Employ your aggressive instinct therapeutically, strive to be healthy.
♂☍⚷ Align will with spirit, confront limitations, healthy competition.

♂☌♅ Ingenious ideas and individual decisions spark new inventions.
♂✶♅ Dynamic leadership, opportunities. Desire to make things happen.
♂□♅ Obstacles, challenges. Creative problem solving contributes to changes.
♂△♅ Abundance and flow of energy. Express your ingenious ideas and individuality.
♂☍♅ Unusual stresses illuminate conflict of interests.

♂☌♆ Strong impressions, beliefs and feelings of oneness.
♂✶♆ Powerful faith, belief and ideology, search for oneness.
♂□♆ Hidden conflicts, disappointment. Lack of physical strength.
♂△♆ Faith and ideology. Powerful drive inspires creativity.
♂☍♆ Confusion, subversiveness. Conflict of interest.

♂☌♇ Intense feelings lead to new emotional foundations.
♂✶♇ Opportunity to purify, unite and transform, share power.
♂□♇ Strong sexual desires, internal conflict. Sustain effort to achieve transformation.
♂△♇ Release of potent energy. Powerful drive to accomplish.
♂☍♇ Tensions, conflicts. Opposing interests.

♂☌⚸ Demanding action brings results. Take steps and claim your independence.
♂✶⚸ Vitality; dynamic, alive and forthright in doing your own thing. Move your body.
♂□⚸ Volatile, impulsive and headstrong. Battles of power. Feisty. Anger and fury.
♂△⚸ Feminine leadership is expressed easily, with confidence, daring, boldness.
♂☍⚸ Warring with others polarises. Provocation, frustration. Release tensions safely.

♂☌☊ Courage to follow through on new ideas. Careful with pushing too hard.
♂✶☊ Creative expression of physical energy is possible. Feeling energised.
♂□☊ Impulsiveness. Blocked energies that need positive outlets.
♂△☊ The right course of action. Easy progress.
♂☍☊ Instinctive reactions. Beware of accidents. Use pent-up energies creatively.

♃ Jupiter Aspects

♃☌♃ Beginning of a new twelve-year Jupiter cycle. Dream big and make plans.
♃✶♃ Opportunities, luck, optimism. Best time for travel and studies.
♃□♃ Overconfidence, exaggeration. Slow down and exercise caution.
♃△♃ Good luck, optimism. Express and develop opportunities.
♃☍♃ Over optimistic, idealistic. Avoid making important decisions now.

♃☌♄ Expansion, promotion, opportunity. Acknowledgement of ability and wisdom.
♃✶♄ Great business opportunity. Good judgement for long-term decisions.
♃□♄ Internal conflict, restrictions. Need for reassessment, new structure.
♃△♄ Confidence, wisdom, experience, good judgement. Great for deals and contracts.
♃☍♄ Lack of flexibility, constraint. Restriction through opposition.

♃☌⚷ The inner journey, spiritual mentoring, a healing vision.
♃✶⚷ Strengthen your spirit, a philosophy of healing, genuine hope.
♃□⚷ Gut feelings versus concepts, human versus divine justice; spiritual disappointment.
♃△⚷ Teaching the wisdom of the wound, faith in the inner world, spiritual healer.
♃☍⚷ Re-embrace your optimism. Abundance, hope for the future, healing journey.

♃☌♅ Excitement, strong psychic ability. The need for freedom.

♃⚹♅ Study, networking, advanced technologies. Make use of sudden opportunities.

♃□♅ Obstacles, restrictions, lack of good judgement. Best to restrain yourself.

♃△♅ Strong psychic ability, inspiration. Advance technological ideas.

♃☍♅ Ideological conflicts, obsessions. Expect disruptions.

♃☌♆ Heightened intuition, spiritual quest. Need for dreaming.

♃⚹♆ Empathy, spiritual fulfilment. Opportunities for internal or external travel.

♃□♆ Unrealistic or deceptive points of views. Avoid making important decisions.

♃△♆ Strong intuition and inspiration. Express yourself creatively.

♃☍♆ Exaggeration, confusion, deception. Avoid making important decisions.

♃☌♇ Start of a very powerful cycle. Initiate positive changes and growth.

♃⚹♇ Use intense power positively and be fair at all times.

♃□♇ Internal conflict, compulsive behaviour. Lack of tolerance and confidence.

♃△♇ Confidence, power, control. Sound judgement furthers positive changes.

♃☍♇ Abuse of power, legal battles. Avoid taking risks and oppositions.

♃☌⚸ Unmask falsehoods, quest for hidden truth. Powerful access to feminine wisdom.

♃⚹⚸ Feminine wisdom flows easily and is received well. Deep inner journeying.

♃□⚸ Challenge beliefs about women. Exposing secrets brings freedom.

♃△⚸ Stand up for what is right, don't hold back. Expand knowledge of deep wisdom.

♃☍⚸ Growing awareness of false teachers, propaganda, false news. Big energy.

♃☌☊ Fortunate encounters of philosophical nature. A generous heart brings success.

♃⚹☊ Expand your horizon. Opportunity to break free from habits and conventions.

♃□☊ Exaggeration and over–enthusiasm. A broad vision that lacks realism.

♃△☊ Feeling protected and having faith in oneself.

♃♂☊ Unrealistic expectations. Drive to fulfil one's destiny.

♄ Saturn Aspects

♄☌♄ 'Saturn Return', the beginning of a new 29–year Saturn cycle.

♄⚹♄ Opportunity to use the wisdom you have gained and follow your purpose.

♄□♄ Internal conflict, restructuring. Reassessment of plans and situations.

♄△♄ Sound decision–making. Follow your purpose.

♄☍♄ Lack of flexibility, constraint, opposition. Accept your responsibilities.

♄☌⚷ Spiritual awakenings, unlock alternate realities, healing the system.

♄⚹⚷ New traditions emerge to heal the past, a spiritual authority.

♄□⚷ Confronting the wound of authority, reconciling the use of power and control.

♄△⚷ Merging of the mundane and the sacred. Timelessness, spiritual discipline and order.

♄☍⚷ Reconcile tradition with the spirit of the times, healing limitations and fears.

♄☌♅ Beginning of new cycle, build stability. Use your own inner resources.

♄⚹♅ Inventive ideas, breakthroughs. Make the most of exciting opportunities.

♄□♅ Internal conflict between responsibilities and rebellious feelings.

♄△♅ Feeling at ease with new responsibilities and new understanding.

♄☍♅ Disruptions of routines and sudden changes reflect the need for freedom.

♄☌♆ Loneliness, lack of hope, depression. Contemplate the beginning of a new cycle.

♄⚹♆ Disciplined and dreamy. Use opportunities and move into a new direction.

♄□♆ Depression, confusion, internal conflict. Best to reflect and re–assess.

♄△♆ Heightened intuition. Express your creative and spiritual inspiration.

♄☍♆ Solitude, studies. Soothe yourself and avoid harsh environments.

♄☌♇ Start of a new cycle. Clear out the old to make space for the new.
♄⚹♇ Approach projects with a mix of discipline and compromise.
♄□♇ Challenging circumstances are opportunities in disguise.
♄△♇ Discipline and compromise. Express your insight and wisdom.
♄☍♇ Limitations, restrictions, opposition. React carefully and with consideration.

♄☌⚸ Stand strong, inner authority, confront oppressive conditions. Self-respect.
♄⚹⚸ Use established structures to support your growth in responsibility and maturity.
♄□⚸ Depressive energies. Pressure. Draw on innate integrity and strength.
♄△⚸ Create new forms based on deep inner wisdom and self-knowledge. Dignity.
♄☍⚸ Oppression. Confrontations with established authority. Challenging the status quo.

♄☌☊ Encounters with elders bring insights and guidance. Self-sufficiency.
♄⚹☊ Connecting with people from the past can give guidance and insight.
♄□☊ Duties and obligations of authority figures might distract from one's path.
♄△☊ Traditional values help stabilise. Meetings with authority figures bring progress.
♄☍☊ Isolation and depression. Accept imperfections and overcome feelings of guilt.

⚷ Chiron Aspects

⚷☌⚷ Time for healing and honouring the authentic self, integration.
⚷⚹⚷ Accepting what we cannot change. A supportive mentor.
⚷□⚷ Encountering the shadow, accepting our wounds and limits.
⚷△⚷ Being at ease with disease, spiritual evolution, healing others.
⚷☍⚷ A helping hand, a spiritual breakthrough, a wise partner.

⚷☌♅ Uncommon in natal charts. By transit it is a spiritual initiation for young and old.
⚷⚹♅ Rare aspect, unusual souls who are spiritually sympathetic to traumatic transitions.
⚷□♅ In the second half of 21st C, challenges souls to adopt future possibilities.
⚷△♅ A rare aspect which helps align the wheels of karma.
⚷☍♅ Contrasts spiritual solidarity with individual rights and freedoms.

⚷☌♆ Once, sometimes twice a century this conjunction heralds a spiritual emergence.
⚷⚹♆ A rare opportunity for a healing reconciliation.
⚷□♆ An uncommon aspect which challenges our spiritual perceptions and ideals.
⚷△♆ Spiritual awakening, soul images and dreams expressed through art.
⚷☍♆ Spiritual crossroads, the soul is mirrored in suffering, healing reflections.

⚷☌♇ At extraordinary moments, the healing power of the soul emerges.
⚷⚹♇ A re-emergence of healing, the power of spirit, therapeutic imagery.
⚷□♇ Recognising the inner saboteur, exorcising the ghosts.
⚷△♇ Transformative healing, soul repair and renewal.
⚷☍♇ The restless dead, the power of death, befriending the unknown.

⚷☌☊ Emphasis on healing and mentoring. Tap into your powers of healing.
⚷⚹☊ Contact with people who need an opportunity to heal old wounds.
⚷□☊ Self-doubt and lack of self-acceptance brings uncertainty.
⚷△☊ Attraction to people or situations for healing purposes.
⚷☍☊ Encounter with karmic wounds. Pay attention to transgenerational issues.

⚸ Black Moon Lilith Aspects

⚸☌⚸ Endings and beginning of a nine-year cycle. Deep feminine wisdom, power.
⚸⚹⚸ Feeling attuned to deep instincts. Time for rest and emotional balance.
⚸□⚸ Tension, difficult choices. Unknown forces pushing issues to the surface.
⚸△⚸ Deep inner harmony between emotional needs and power. Rest in the dark.
⚸☍⚸ Conflicting energies between males and females. Frustration and tension.

⚸☌⚷ Ancient wounds surface to be healed, a profound healing journey begins.
⚸⚹⚷ Wisdom and insight are easily available. Trusting your intuition brings healing.
⚸□⚷ Strong conflicting emotions. A crisis brings buried wounds to the surface. Release.
⚸△⚷ Rest and quiet are needed. Turning inwards, letting go of struggle. Soul healing.
⚸☍⚷ Trying to please everyone else is painful and takes you further away from yourself.

⚸☌♅ Radical revealing of hidden truths. Rebellious outbursts. Outrageous, wild and free.
⚸⚹♅ Tap into deep inner intelligence and consciousness, inspiration brings liberation.
⚸□♅ Build up of stress causes seismic reactions. Urge to rebel, volatile, unpredictable.
⚸△♅ Visionary insights flow. Knowledge of hidden cosmic mysteries is available.
⚸☍♅ Reactive against oppressive forces. Breaking free from bondage. Refusing to obey.

⚸☌♆ Loss, fathomless depths. Sacrifice. The Void. Deep letting go opens to trust.
⚸⚹♆ Intuition and inspiration come from the deep. Prayer and silence bring healing.
⚸□♆ Emotional overwhelm. Painful resistance; letting go of control brings redemption.
⚸△♆ Psychic knowing, natural communion with the Divine Mother. Rest. Silence.
⚸☍♆ Confusion, doubt, subversive interactions. Irrational fears of the dark void.

⚸☌♇ Powerful transitions. Death, endings. Journey into the Dark Mysteries. Intensity.
⚸⚹♇ Restorative power of deep rest, stillness, silence. Hold your own sacred space.
⚸□♇ Volcanic eruptions. Resist temptations for revenge; battle inner demons.
⚸△♇ Regeneration, shedding of old layers of identity. Healing old traumas. Tantra.
⚸☍♇ Powerful opposing forces challenge you, dig deep and hold your ground. Death.

⚸☌☊ Connect to your authentic self. Challenging encounters can break taboos.
⚸⚹☊ Creative energies that feel liberating and challenging.
⚸□☊ Living your truth is a challenge. Cannot compromise; important insights.
⚸△☊ Authentic living comes easy. Meetings with women bring feelings of liberation.
⚸☍☊ Powerful feminine energies. Addressing gender equality goes against the norm.

☊ North Node Aspects

☊☌☊ Beginning of a new 18–year cycle; a fortunate time of forming relationships.
☊⚹☊ Opportunities for making purposeful connections.
☊□☊ A turning point that feels fated. Redefine your purpose.
☊△☊ Helpful encounters with others.
☊☍☊ Opportunity to detach from and release old relationships and past events.

☊☌♅ Unusual events and meetings can be liberating. Release of blocked energy.
☊⚹♅ Think out of the square. Liberating thoughts are exciting or provocative.
☊□♅ Sudden events challenge what feels familiar. Fragmentation.
☊△♅ Embrace the new. Encounters with unusual, inspiring people.
☊☍♅ Events alienate and isolate. Fragmentation, accidents.

☊☌♆ Access to one's spiritual path; soul connection. Meeting with a spiritual leader.
☊⚹♆ Creative inspiration. Paint, dance, sing or write poetry. Meditate.
☊□♆ Confusion, deception; misplaced trust. Idealisation leads to disappointment.
☊△♆ Compassion, sensitivity, inspiration. Creation of great artworks.
☊☍♆ Unfocused action; disillusionment. Pay attention to dreams.

☊☌♇ Permanent changes in life situations. Transformation.
☊⚹♇ Opportunities for soul growth and making life–altering changes.
☊□♇ Compulsiveness and over–identification. A too–narrow focus.
☊△♇ Self–empowerment. Overcoming fear is easy.
☊☍♇ Intensity and desires that need releasing. Karmic residues need clearing.

Date Year	Day	Moon ☽	Sun ☉	Mercury ☿	Venus ♀	Mars ♂	Jupiter ♃	Saturn ♄	Uranus ♅	Neptune ♆	Pluto ♇	Chiron ⚷	N Node ☊	Lilith ⚸
Jan 1 2023	Sun	03°Ta39'	10°Cp17'	23°Cp42' R	27°Cp23'	09°Ge03' R	01°Ar11'	22°Aq25'	15°Ta08' R	22°Pi52'	27°Cp39'	11°Ar58'	11°Ta45'	29°Cn09'
Jan 2 2023	Mon	16°Ta14'	11°Cp18'	23°Cp05'	28°Cp38'	08°Ge54'	01°Ar18'	22°Aq31'	15°Ta07'	22°Pi53'	27°Cp41'	11°Ar58'	11°Ta45' R	29°Cn15'
Jan 3 2023	Tue	28°Ta36'	12°Cp19'	22°Cp18'	29°Cp53'	08°Ge46'	01°Ar26'	22°Aq37'	15°Ta06'	22°Pi54'	27°Cp43'	11°Ar59'	11°Ta43'	29°Cn22'
Jan 4 2023	Wed	10°Ge48'	13°Cp20'	21°Cp19'	01°Aq08'	08°Ge38'	01°Ar34'	22°Aq43'	15°Ta05'	22°Pi55'	27°Cp45'	11°Ar59'	11°Ta39'	29°Cn29'
Jan 5 2023	Thu	22°Ge53'	14°Cp21'	20°Cp12'	02°Aq23'	08°Ge32'	01°Ar41'	22°Aq49'	15°Ta04'	22°Pi56'	27°Cp47'	12°Ar00'	11°Ta32'	29°Cn35'
Jan 6 2023	Fri	04°Cn52'	15°Cp22'	18°Cp58'	03°Aq38'	08°Ge26'	01°Ar49'	22°Aq55'	15°Ta03'	22°Pi57'	27°Cp49'	12°Ar01'	11°Ta23'	29°Cn42'
Jan 7 2023	Sat	16°Cn48'	16°Cp23'	17°Cp40'	04°Aq53'	08°Ge21'	01°Ar57'	23°Aq01'	15°Ta03'	22°Pi58'	27°Cp50'	12°Ar01'	11°Ta11'	29°Cn49'
Jan 8 2023	Sun	28°Cn41'	17°Cp25'	16°Cp19'	06°Aq08'	08°Ge17'	02°Ar06'	23°Aq08'	15°Ta02'	22°Pi59'	27°Cp52'	12°Ar02'	10°Ta58'	29°Cn56'
Jan 9 2023	Mon	10°Le33'	18°Cp26'	14°Cp59'	07°Aq23'	08°Ge13'	02°Ar14'	23°Aq14'	15°Ta01'	23°Pi00'	27°Cp54'	12°Ar03'	10°Ta44'	00°Le02'
Jan 10 2023	Tue	22°Le26'	19°Cp27'	13°Cp42'	08°Aq38'	08°Ge10'	02°Ar22'	23°Aq21'	15°Ta00'	23°Pi02'	27°Cp56'	12°Ar04'	10°Ta32'	00°Le09'
Jan 11 2023	Wed	04°Vi21'	20°Cp28'	12°Cp30'	09°Aq53'	08°Ge09'	02°Ar31'	23°Aq27'	15°Ta00'	23°Pi03'	27°Cp58'	12°Ar05'	10°Ta21'	00°Le16'
Jan 12 2023	Thu	16°Vi21'	21°Cp29'	11°Cp25'	11°Aq08'	08°Ge08'	02°Ar40'	23°Aq34'	14°Ta59'	23°Pi04'	28°Cp00'	12°Ar06'	10°Ta13'	00°Le23'
Jan 13 2023	Fri	28°Vi30'	22°Cp30'	10°Cp29'	12°Aq23'	08°Ge07' D	02°Ar49'	23°Aq40'	14°Ta59'	23°Pi05'	28°Cp02'	12°Ar07'	10°Ta07'	00°Le29'
Jan 14 2023	Sat	10°Li51'	23°Cp31'	09°Cp42'	13°Aq38'	08°Ge08'	02°Ar58'	23°Aq47'	14°Ta58'	23°Pi07'	28°Cp04'	12°Ar08'	10°Ta05'	00°Le36'
Jan 15 2023	Sun	23°Li29'	24°Cp32'	09°Cp04'	14°Aq53'	08°Ge09'	03°Ar07'	23°Aq53'	14°Ta58'	23°Pi08'	28°Cp06'	12°Ar10'	10°Ta04'	00°Le43'
Jan 16 2023	Mon	06°Sc28'	25°Cp33'	08°Cp36'	16°Aq08'	08°Ge11'	03°Ar17'	24°Aq00'	14°Ta57'	23°Pi10'	28°Cp08'	12°Ar11'	10°Ta04' D	00°Le49'
Jan 17 2023	Tue	19°Sc53'	26°Cp35'	08°Cp18'	17°Aq23'	08°Ge14'	03°Ar26'	24°Aq07'	14°Ta57'	23°Pi11'	28°Cp10'	12°Ar12'	10°Ta04' R	00°Le56'
Jan 18 2023	Wed	03°Sg47'	27°Cp36'	08°Cp09'	18°Aq38'	08°Ge17'	03°Ar36'	24°Aq13'	14°Ta57'	23°Pi12'	28°Cp12'	12°Ar14'	10°Ta02'	01°Le03'
Jan 19 2023	Thu	18°Sg10'	28°Cp37'	08°Cp08' D	19°Aq53'	08°Ge21'	03°Ar45'	24°Aq20'	14°Ta56'	23°Pi14'	28°Cp14'	12°Ar15'	09°Ta58'	01°Le10'
Jan 20 2023	Fri	03°Cp01'	29°Cp38'	08°Cp16'	21°Aq08'	08°Ge26'	03°Ar55'	24°Aq27'	14°Ta56'	23°Pi15'	28°Cp16'	12°Ar16'	09°Ta50'	01°Le16'
Jan 21 2023	Sat	18°Cp11'	00°Aq39'	08°Cp31'	22°Aq23'	08°Ge32'	04°Ar05'	24°Aq34'	14°Ta56'	23°Pi17'	28°Cp18'	12°Ar18'	09°Ta41'	01°Le23'
Jan 22 2023	Sun	03°Aq33'	01°Aq40'	08°Cp53'	23°Aq38'	08°Ge38'	04°Ar15'	24°Aq41'	14°Ta56'	23°Pi18'	28°Cp20'	12°Ar19'	09°Ta29'	01°Le30'
Jan 23 2023	Mon	18°Aq53'	02°Aq41'	09°Cp21'	24°Aq53'	08°Ge45'	04°Ar26'	24°Aq47'	14°Ta56' D	23°Pi20'	28°Cp22'	12°Ar21'	09°Ta18'	01°Le37'
Jan 24 2023	Tue	04°Pi01'	03°Aq42'	09°Cp55'	26°Aq07'	08°Ge53'	04°Ar36'	24°Aq54'	14°Ta56'	23°Pi22'	28°Cp24'	12°Ar23'	09°Ta07'	01°Le43'
Jan 25 2023	Wed	18°Pi46'	04°Aq43'	10°Cp34'	27°Aq22'	09°Ge01'	04°Ar46'	25°Aq01'	14°Ta56'	23°Pi23'	28°Cp26'	12°Ar24'	08°Ta59'	01°Le50'
Jan 26 2023	Thu	03°Ar04'	05°Aq44'	11°Cp18'	28°Aq37'	09°Ge10'	04°Ar57'	25°Aq08'	14°Ta56'	23°Pi25'	28°Cp28'	12°Ar26'	08°Ta53'	01°Le57'
Jan 27 2023	Fri	16°Ar51'	06°Aq45'	12°Cp06'	29°Aq52'	09°Ge20'	05°Ar08'	25°Aq15'	14°Ta56'	23°Pi27'	28°Cp30'	12°Ar28'	08°Ta50'	02°Le03'
Jan 28 2023	Sat	00°Ta10'	07°Aq46'	12°Cp58'	01°Pi06'	09°Ge30'	05°Ar18'	25°Aq22'	14°Ta57'	23°Pi28'	28°Cp32'	12°Ar30'	08°Ta49'	02°Le10'
Jan 29 2023	Sun	13°Ta03'	08°Aq47'	13°Cp53'	02°Pi21'	09°Ge40'	05°Ar29'	25°Aq29'	14°Ta57'	23°Pi30'	28°Cp34'	12°Ar32'	08°Ta49'	02°Le17'
Jan 30 2023	Mon	25°Ta35'	09°Aq48'	14°Cp52'	03°Pi36'	09°Ge52'	05°Ar40'	25°Aq36'	14°Ta57'	23°Pi32'	28°Cp35'	12°Ar34'	08°Ta49'	02°Le24'
Jan 31 2023	Tue	07°Ge52'	10°Aq49'	15°Cp53'	04°Pi50'	10°Ge04'	05°Ar52'	25°Aq43'	14°Ta58'	23°Pi34'	28°Cp37'	12°Ar36'	08°Ta47'	02°Le30'

PLANETARY TABLE FEBRUARY 2023 ~ 0:01 AM GMT

Date Year	Day	Moon ☽	Sun ☉	Mercury ☿	Venus ♀	Mars ♂	Jupiter ♃	Saturn ♄	Uranus ♅	Neptune ♆	Pluto ♇	Chiron ⚷	N Node ☊	Lilith ⚸
Feb 1 2023	Wed	19°Ge56'	11°Aq50'	16°Cp57'	06°Pi05'	10°Ge16'	06°Ar03'	25°Aq51'	14°Ta58'	23°Pi35'	28°Cp39'	12°Ar38'	08°Ta42' R	02°Le37'
Feb 2 2023	Thu	01°Cn54'	12°Aq51'	18°Cp03'	07°Pi19'	10°Ge29'	06°Ar14'	25°Aq58'	14°Ta59'	23°Pi37'	28°Cp41'	12°Ar40'	08°Ta34'	02°Le44'
Feb 3 2023	Fri	13°Cn47'	13°Aq52'	19°Cp11'	08°Pi34'	10°Ge43'	06°Ar26'	26°Aq05'	14°Ta59'	23°Pi39'	28°Cp43'	12°Ar42'	08°Ta24'	02°Le50'
Feb 4 2023	Sat	25°Cn39'	14°Aq53'	20°Cp22'	09°Pi48'	10°Ge57'	06°Ar37'	26°Aq12'	15°Ta00'	23°Pi41'	28°Cp45'	12°Ar44'	08°Ta10'	02°Le57'
Feb 5 2023	Sun	07°Le31'	15°Aq54'	21°Cp34'	11°Pi03'	11°Ge11'	06°Ar49'	26°Aq19'	15°Ta00'	23°Pi43'	28°Cp47'	12°Ar46'	07°Ta56'	03°Le04'
Feb 6 2023	Mon	19°Le26'	16°Aq54'	22°Cp48'	12°Pi17'	11°Ge27'	07°Ar00'	26°Aq26'	15°Ta01'	23°Pi45'	28°Cp49'	12°Ar48'	07°Ta41'	03°Le11'
Feb 7 2023	Tue	01°Vi23'	17°Aq55'	24°Cp04'	13°Pi32'	11°Ge42'	07°Ar12'	26°Aq34'	15°Ta02'	23°Pi47'	28°Cp51'	12°Ar51'	07°Ta27'	03°Le17'
Feb 8 2023	Wed	13°Vi25'	18°Aq56'	25°Cp21'	14°Pi46'	11°Ge58'	07°Ar24'	26°Aq41'	15°Ta03'	23°Pi49'	28°Cp53'	12°Ar53'	07°Ta15'	03°Le24'
Feb 9 2023	Thu	25°Vi32'	19°Aq57'	26°Cp40'	16°Pi00'	12°Ge15'	07°Ar36'	26°Aq48'	15°Ta04'	23°Pi50'	28°Cp55'	12°Ar55'	07°Ta05'	03°Le31'
Feb 10 2023	Fri	07°Li48'	20°Aq57'	28°Cp00'	17°Pi15'	12°Ge31'	07°Ar48'	26°Aq55'	15°Ta04'	23°Pi52'	28°Cp56'	12°Ar58'	06°Ta59'	03°Le38'
Feb 11 2023	Sat	20°Li14'	21°Aq58'	29°Cp21'	18°Pi29'	12°Ge49'	08°Ar00'	27°Aq02'	15°Ta05'	23°Pi54'	28°Cp58'	13°Ar00'	06°Ta56'	03°Le44'
Feb 12 2023	Sun	02°Sc53'	22°Aq59'	00°Aq43'	19°Pi43'	13°Ge07'	08°Ar12'	27°Aq10'	15°Ta06'	23°Pi56'	29°Cp00'	13°Ar03'	06°Ta55'	03°Le51'
Feb 13 2023	Mon	15°Sc50'	23°Aq59'	02°Aq07'	20°Pi57'	13°Ge25'	08°Ar25'	27°Aq17'	15°Ta08'	23°Pi58'	29°Cp02'	13°Ar05'	06°Ta55' D	03°Le58'
Feb 14 2023	Tue	29°Sc09'	25°Aq00'	03°Aq31'	22°Pi11'	13°Ge43'	08°Ar37'	27°Aq24'	15°Ta09'	24°Pi00'	29°Cp04'	13°Ar08'	06°Ta55' R	04°Le04'
Feb 15 2023	Wed	12°Sg52'	26°Aq01'	04°Aq57'	23°Pi25'	14°Ge02'	08°Ar50'	27°Aq31'	15°Ta10'	24°Pi03'	29°Cp05'	13°Ar10'	06°Ta54'	04°Le11'
Feb 16 2023	Thu	27°Sg00'	27°Aq01'	06°Aq24'	24°Pi39'	14°Ge22'	09°Ar02'	27°Aq39'	15°Ta11'	24°Pi05'	29°Cp07'	13°Ar13'	06°Ta50'	04°Le18'
Feb 17 2023	Fri	11°Cp34'	28°Aq02'	07°Aq52'	25°Pi53'	14°Ge42'	09°Ar15'	27°Aq46'	15°Ta12'	24°Pi07'	29°Cp09'	13°Ar16'	06°Ta45'	04°Le25'
Feb 18 2023	Sat	26°Cp30'	29°Aq03'	09°Aq21'	27°Pi07'	15°Ge02'	09°Ar28'	27°Aq53'	15°Ta14'	24°Pi09'	29°Cp11'	13°Ar18'	06°Ta36'	04°Le31'
Feb 19 2023	Sun	11°Aq39'	00°Pi03'	10°Aq50'	28°Pi21'	15°Ge22'	09°Ar40'	28°Aq00'	15°Ta15'	24°Pi11'	29°Cp13'	13°Ar21'	06°Ta26'	04°Le38'
Feb 20 2023	Mon	26°Aq53'	01°Pi04'	12°Aq21'	29°Pi35'	15°Ge43'	09°Ar53'	28°Aq08'	15°Ta16'	24°Pi13'	29°Cp14'	13°Ar24'	06°Ta16'	04°Le45'
Feb 21 2023	Tue	12°Pi00'	02°Pi04'	13°Aq53'	00°Ar49'	16°Ge05'	10°Ar06'	28°Aq15'	15°Ta18'	24°Pi15'	29°Cp16'	13°Ar27'	06°Ta07'	04°Le51'
Feb 22 2023	Wed	26°Pi49'	03°Pi05'	15°Aq26'	02°Ar03'	16°Ge26'	10°Ar19'	28°Aq22'	15°Ta19'	24°Pi17'	29°Cp18'	13°Ar30'	05°Ta59'	04°Le58'
Feb 23 2023	Thu	11°Ar15'	04°Pi05'	16°Aq59'	03°Ar17'	16°Ge48'	10°Ar32'	28°Aq29'	15°Ta21'	24°Pi19'	29°Cp19'	13°Ar32'	05°Ta54'	05°Le05'
Feb 24 2023	Fri	25°Ar11'	05°Pi06'	18°Aq34'	04°Ar30'	17°Ge10'	10°Ar45'	28°Aq37'	15°Ta23'	24°Pi22'	29°Cp21'	13°Ar35'	05°Ta51'	05°Le12'
Feb 25 2023	Sat	08°Ta39'	06°Pi06'	20°Aq10'	05°Ar44'	17°Ge33'	10°Ar58'	28°Aq44'	15°Ta24'	24°Pi24'	29°Cp23'	13°Ar38'	05°Ta51' D	05°Le18'
Feb 26 2023	Sun	21°Ta40'	07°Pi06'	21°Aq46'	06°Ar57'	17°Ge56'	11°Ar12'	28°Aq51'	15°Ta26'	24°Pi26'	29°Cp24'	13°Ar41'	05°Ta52'	05°Le25'
Feb 27 2023	Mon	04°Ge17'	08°Pi07'	23°Aq24'	08°Ar11'	18°Ge19'	11°Ar25'	28°Aq58'	15°Ta28'	24°Pi28'	29°Cp26'	13°Ar44'	05°Ta52'	05°Le32'
Feb 28 2023	Tue	16°Ge35'	09°Pi07'	25°Aq03'	09°Ar24'	18°Ge42'	11°Ar38'	29°Aq06'	15°Ta29'	24°Pi30'	29°Cp28'	13°Ar47'	05°Ta52' R	05°Le39'

Date Year	Day	Moon ☽	Sun ☉	Mercury ☿	Venus ♀	Mars ♂	Jupiter ♃	Saturn ♄	Uranus ♅	Neptune ♆	Pluto ♇	Chiron ⚷	N Node ☊	Lilith ⚸
Mar 1 2023	Wed	28°Ge40'	10°Pi07'	26°Aq42'	10°Ar38'	19°Ge06'	11°Ar52'	29°Aq13'	15°Ta31'	24°Pi33'	29°Cp29'	13°Ar50'	05°Ta50' R	05°Le45'
Mar 2 2023	Thu	10°Cn36'	11°Pi07'	28°Aq23'	11°Ar51'	19°Ge30'	12°Ar05'	29°Aq20'	15°Ta33'	24°Pi35'	29°Cp31'	13°Ar53'	05°Ta46'	05°Le52'
Mar 3 2023	Fri	22°Cn28'	12°Pi08'	00°Pi04'	13°Ar05'	19°Ge54'	12°Ar19'	29°Aq27'	15°Ta35'	24°Pi37'	29°Cp32'	13°Ar56'	05°Ta39'	05°Le59'
Mar 4 2023	Sat	04°Le19'	13°Pi08'	01°Pi47'	14°Ar18'	20°Ge19'	12°Ar32'	29°Aq34'	15°Ta37'	24°Pi39'	29°Cp34'	14°Ar00'	05°Ta30'	06°Le05'
Mar 5 2023	Sun	16°Le13'	14°Pi08'	03°Pi31'	15°Ar31'	20°Ge44'	12°Ar46'	29°Aq41'	15°Ta39'	24°Pi42'	29°Cp35'	14°Ar03'	05°Ta21'	06°Le12'
Mar 6 2023	Mon	28°Le11'	15°Pi08'	05°Pi16'	16°Ar44'	21°Ge09'	12°Ar59'	29°Aq48'	15°Ta41'	24°Pi44'	29°Cp37'	14°Ar06'	05°Ta11'	06°Le19'
Mar 7 2023	Tue	10°Vi15'	16°Pi08'	07°Pi02'	17°Ar57'	21°Ge34'	13°Ar13'	29°Aq56'	15°Ta43'	24°Pi46'	29°Cp38'	14°Ar09'	05°Ta01'	06°Le26'
Mar 8 2023	Wed	22°Vi27'	17°Pi08'	08°Pi49'	19°Ar10'	22°Ge00'	13°Ar27'	00°Pi03'	15°Ta45'	24°Pi48'	29°Cp40'	14°Ar12'	04°Ta53'	06°Le32'
Mar 9 2023	Thu	04°Li47'	18°Pi08'	10°Pi37'	20°Ar23'	22°Ge25'	13°Ar41'	00°Pi10'	15°Ta47'	24°Pi51'	29°Cp41'	14°Ar15'	04°Ta47'	06°Le39'
Mar 10 2023	Fri	17°Li17'	19°Pi08'	12°Pi26'	21°Ar36'	22°Ge51'	13°Ar54'	00°Pi17'	15°Ta50'	24°Pi53'	29°Cp43'	14°Ar19'	04°Ta43'	06°Le46'
Mar 11 2023	Sat	29°Li57'	20°Pi08'	14°Pi16'	22°Ar49'	23°Ge18'	14°Ar08'	00°Pi24'	15°Ta52'	24°Pi55'	29°Cp44'	14°Ar22'	04°Ta41'	06°Le53'
Mar 12 2023	Sun	12°Sc50'	21°Pi08'	16°Pi08'	24°Ar01'	23°Ge44'	14°Ar22'	00°Pi31'	15°Ta54'	24°Pi57'	29°Cp45'	14°Ar25'	04°Ta41' D	06°Le59'
Mar 13 2023	Mon	25°Sc56'	22°Pi08'	18°Pi00'	25°Ar14'	24°Ge11'	14°Ar36'	00°Pi38'	15°Ta57'	25°Pi00'	29°Cp47'	14°Ar29'	04°Ta43'	07°Le06'
Mar 14 2023	Tue	09°Sg19'	23°Pi08'	19°Pi54'	26°Ar27'	24°Ge38'	14°Ar50'	00°Pi44'	15°Ta59'	25°Pi02'	29°Cp48'	14°Ar32'	04°Ta44'	07°Le13'
Mar 15 2023	Wed	23°Sg00'	24°Pi08'	21°Pi49'	27°Ar39'	25°Ge05'	15°Ar04'	00°Pi51'	16°Ta01'	25°Pi04'	29°Cp49'	14°Ar35'	04°Ta45'	07°Le19'
Mar 16 2023	Thu	06°Cp59'	25°Pi07'	23°Pi45'	28°Ar51'	25°Ge32'	15°Ar18'	00°Pi58'	16°Ta04'	25°Pi07'	29°Cp51'	14°Ar39'	04°Ta44' R	07°Le26'
Mar 17 2023	Fri	21°Cp17'	26°Pi07'	25°Pi41'	00°Ta04'	25°Ge59'	15°Ar32'	01°Pi05'	16°Ta06'	25°Pi09'	29°Cp52'	14°Ar42'	04°Ta42'	07°Le33'
Mar 18 2023	Sat	05°Aq51'	27°Pi07'	27°Pi39'	01°Ta16'	26°Ge27'	15°Ar46'	01°Pi12'	16°Ta09'	25°Pi11'	29°Cp53'	14°Ar45'	04°Ta38'	07°Le40'
Mar 19 2023	Sun	20°Aq36'	28°Pi07'	29°Pi38'	02°Ta28'	26°Ge55'	16°Ar01'	01°Pi19'	16°Ta11'	25°Pi13'	29°Cp54'	14°Ar49'	04°Ta33'	07°Le46'
Mar 20 2023	Mon	05°Pi27'	29°Pi06'	01°Ar37'	03°Ta41'	27°Ge23'	16°Ar15'	01°Pi25'	16°Ta14'	25°Pi16'	29°Cp56'	14°Ar52'	04°Ta27'	07°Le53'
Mar 21 2023	Tue	20°Pi14'	00°Ar06'	03°Ar37'	04°Ta53'	27°Ge51'	16°Ar29'	01°Pi32'	16°Ta17'	25°Pi18'	29°Cp57'	14°Ar56'	04°Ta22'	08°Le00'
Mar 22 2023	Wed	04°Ar50'	01°Ar06'	05°Ar38'	06°Ta05'	28°Ge19'	16°Ar43'	01°Pi39'	16°Ta19'	25°Pi20'	29°Cp58'	14°Ar59'	04°Ta18'	08°Le06'
Mar 23 2023	Thu	19°Ar08'	02°Ar05'	07°Ar39'	07°Ta17'	28°Ge48'	16°Ar58'	01°Pi45'	16°Ta22'	25°Pi22'	29°Cp59'	15°Ar03'	04°Ta16'	08°Le13'
Mar 24 2023	Fri	03°Ta03'	03°Ar05'	09°Ar40'	08°Ta28'	29°Ge16'	17°Ar12'	01°Pi52'	16°Ta25'	25°Pi25'	00°Aq00'	15°Ar06'	04°Ta15'	08°Le20'
Mar 25 2023	Sat	16°Ta33'	04°Ar04'	11°Ar41'	09°Ta40'	29°Ge45'	17°Ar26'	01°Pi58'	16°Ta27'	25°Pi27'	00°Aq01'	15°Ar09'	04°Ta15' D	08°Le27'
Mar 26 2023	Sun	29°Ta38'	05°Ar04'	13°Ar41'	10°Ta52'	00°Cn14'	17°Ar40'	02°Pi05'	16°Ta30'	25°Pi29'	00°Aq02'	15°Ar13'	04°Ta17'	08°Le33'
Mar 27 2023	Mon	12°Ge20'	06°Ar03'	15°Ar41'	12°Ta03'	00°Cn44'	17°Ar55'	02°Pi11'	16°Ta33'	25°Pi31'	00°Aq03'	15°Ar16'	04°Ta18'	08°Le40'
Mar 28 2023	Tue	24°Ge44'	07°Ar03'	17°Ar40'	13°Ta15'	01°Cn13'	18°Ar09'	02°Pi18'	16°Ta36'	25°Pi34'	00°Aq04'	15°Ar20'	04°Ta20'	08°Le47'
Mar 29 2023	Wed	06°Cn52'	08°Ar02'	19°Ar37'	14°Ta26'	01°Cn42'	18°Ar24'	02°Pi24'	16°Ta39'	25°Pi36'	00°Aq05'	15°Ar23'	04°Ta20'	08°Le54'
Mar 30 2023	Thu	18°Cn51'	09°Ar01'	21°Ar33'	15°Ta38'	02°Cn12'	18°Ar38'	02°Pi31'	16°Ta41'	25°Pi38'	00°Aq06'	15°Ar27'	04°Ta20' R	09°Le00'
Mar 31 2023	Fri	00°Le44'	10°Ar01'	23°Ar26'	16°Ta49'	02°Cn42'	18°Ar52'	02°Pi37'	16°Ta44'	25°Pi40'	00°Aq07'	15°Ar31'	04°Ta18'	09°Le07'

Planetary Table April 2023 ~ 0:01 AM GMT

Date Year	Day	Moon ☽	Sun ☉	Mercury ☿	Venus ♀	Mars ♂	Jupiter ♃	Saturn ♄	Uranus ♅	Neptune ♆	Pluto ♇	Chiron ⚷	N Node ☊	Lilith ⚸
Apr 1 2023	Sat	12°Le36'	11°Ar00'	25°Ar17'	18°Ta00'	03°Cn12'	19°Ar07'	02°Pi43'	16°Ta47'	25°Pi43'	00°Aq08'	15°Ar34'	04°Ta16' R	09°Le14'
Apr 2 2023	Sun	24°Le32'	11°Ar59'	27°Ar06'	19°Ta11'	03°Cn42'	19°Ar21'	02°Pi49'	16°Ta50'	25°Pi45'	00°Aq09'	15°Ar38'	04°Ta12'	09°Le20'
Apr 3 2023	Mon	05°Vi33'	12°Ar58'	28°Ar50'	20°Ta22'	04°Cn12'	19°Ar36'	02°Pi55'	16°Ta53'	25°Pi47'	00°Aq10'	15°Ar41'	04°Ta09'	09°Le27'
Apr 4 2023	Tue	18°Vi45'	13°Ar57'	00°Ta31'	21°Ta33'	04°Cn42'	19°Ar50'	03°Pi01'	16°Ta56'	25°Pi49'	00°Aq10'	15°Ar45'	04°Ta06'	09°Le34'
Apr 5 2023	Wed	01°Li07'	14°Ar57'	02°Ta08'	22°Ta44'	05°Cn12'	20°Ar05'	03°Pi08'	16°Ta59'	25°Pi51'	00°Aq11'	15°Ar48'	04°Ta03'	09°Le41'
Apr 6 2023	Thu	13°Li42'	15°Ar56'	03°Ta41'	23°Ta54'	05°Cn43'	20°Ar19'	03°Pi14'	17°Ta02'	25°Pi54'	00°Aq12'	15°Ar52'	04°Ta01'	09°Le47'
Apr 7 2023	Fri	26°Li30'	16°Ar55'	05°Ta08'	25°Ta05'	06°Cn14'	20°Ar33'	03°Pi19'	17°Ta06'	25°Pi56'	00°Aq13'	15°Ar55'	04°Ta00'	09°Le54'
Apr 8 2023	Sat	09°Sc32'	17°Ar54'	06°Ta31'	26°Ta15'	06°Cn44'	20°Ar48'	03°Pi25'	17°Ta09'	25°Pi58'	00°Aq13'	15°Ar59'	04°Ta00' D	10°Le01'
Apr 9 2023	Sun	22°Sc46'	18°Ar53'	07°Ta49'	27°Ta25'	07°Cn15'	21°Ar02'	03°Pi31'	17°Ta12'	26°Pi00'	00°Aq14'	16°Ar02'	04°Ta00'	10°Le07'
Apr 10 2023	Mon	06°Sg14'	19°Ar52'	09°Ta01'	28°Ta36'	07°Cn46'	21°Ar17'	03°Pi37'	17°Ta15'	26°Pi02'	00°Aq15'	16°Ar06'	04°Ta01'	10°Le14'
Apr 11 2023	Tue	19°Sg53'	20°Ar51'	10°Ta07'	29°Ta46'	08°Cn17'	21°Ar31'	03°Pi43'	17°Ta18'	26°Pi04'	00°Aq15'	16°Ar09'	04°Ta03'	10°Le21'
Apr 12 2023	Wed	03°Cp45'	21°Ar49'	11°Ta08'	00°Ge56'	08°Cn48'	21°Ar46'	03°Pi48'	17°Ta21'	26°Pi06'	00°Aq16'	16°Ar13'	04°Ta03'	10°Le28'
Apr 13 2023	Thu	17°Cp47'	22°Ar48'	12°Ta02'	02°Ge05'	09°Cn20'	22°Ar00'	03°Pi54'	17°Ta25'	26°Pi08'	00°Aq16'	16°Ar16'	04°Ta04'	10°Le34'
Apr 14 2023	Fri	01°Aq58'	23°Ar47'	12°Ta51'	03°Ge15'	09°Cn51'	22°Ar15'	04°Pi00'	17°Ta28'	26°Pi11'	00°Aq17'	16°Ar20'	04°Ta04' R	10°Le41'
Apr 15 2023	Sat	16°Aq16'	24°Ar46'	13°Ta33'	04°Ge25'	10°Cn23'	22°Ar29'	04°Pi05'	17°Ta31'	26°Pi13'	00°Aq17'	16°Ar23'	04°Ta03'	10°Le48'
Apr 16 2023	Sun	00°Pi38'	25°Ar45'	14°Ta09'	05°Ge34'	10°Cn54'	22°Ar44'	04°Pi10'	17°Ta34'	26°Pi15'	00°Aq18'	16°Ar27'	04°Ta03'	10°Le55'
Apr 17 2023	Mon	15°Pi01'	26°Ar43'	14°Ta39'	06°Ge44'	11°Cn26'	22°Ar58'	04°Pi16'	17°Ta38'	26°Pi17'	00°Aq18'	16°Ar30'	04°Ta02'	11°Le01'
Apr 18 2023	Tue	29°Pi19'	27°Ar42'	15°Ta03'	07°Ge53'	11°Cn58'	23°Ar13'	04°Pi21'	17°Ta41'	26°Pi19'	00°Aq19'	16°Ar34'	04°Ta01'	11°Le08'
Apr 19 2023	Wed	13°Ar29'	28°Ar41'	15°Ta20'	09°Ge02'	12°Cn30'	23°Ar27'	04°Pi26'	17°Ta44'	26°Pi21'	00°Aq19'	16°Ar37'	04°Ta00'	11°Le15'
Apr 20 2023	Thu	27°Ar25'	29°Ar39'	15°Ta31'	10°Ge11'	13°Cn02'	23°Ar42'	04°Pi31'	17°Ta48'	26°Pi23'	00°Aq19'	16°Ar41'	04°Ta00'	11°Le21'
Apr 21 2023	Fri	11°Ta05'	00°Ta38'	15°Ta36'	11°Ge20'	13°Cn34'	23°Ar56'	04°Pi37'	17°Ta51'	26°Pi25'	00°Aq20'	16°Ar44'	04°Ta00' D	11°Le28'
Apr 22 2023	Sat	24°Ta26'	01°Ta37'	15°Ta36' R	12°Ge28'	14°Cn06'	24°Ar10'	04°Pi42'	17°Ta54'	26°Pi27'	00°Aq20'	16°Ar48'	04°Ta00'	11°Le35'
Apr 23 2023	Sun	07°Ge28'	02°Ta35'	15°Ta29'	13°Ge37'	14°Cn38'	24°Ar25'	04°Pi47'	17°Ta58'	26°Pi29'	00°Aq20'	16°Ar51'	04°Ta00'	11°Le42'
Apr 24 2023	Mon	20°Ge10'	03°Ta34'	15°Ta17'	14°Ge45'	15°Cn11'	24°Ar39'	04°Pi52'	18°Ta01'	26°Pi30'	00°Aq20'	16°Ar55'	04°Ta01'	11°Le48'
Apr 25 2023	Tue	02°Cn35'	04°Ta32'	15°Ta00'	15°Ge54'	15°Cn43'	24°Ar54'	04°Pi56'	18°Ta04'	26°Pi32'	00°Aq21'	16°Ar58'	04°Ta01' R	11°Le55'
Apr 26 2023	Wed	14°Cn46'	05°Ta31'	14°Ta38'	17°Ge02'	16°Cn16'	25°Ar08'	05°Pi01'	18°Ta08'	26°Pi34'	00°Aq21'	17°Ar01'	04°Ta00'	12°Le02'
Apr 27 2023	Thu	26°Cn46'	06°Ta29'	14°Ta12'	18°Ge10'	16°Cn48'	25°Ar22'	05°Pi06'	18°Ta11'	26°Pi36'	00°Aq21'	17°Ar05'	04°Ta00'	12°Le09'
Apr 28 2023	Fri	08°Le41'	07°Ta27'	13°Ta42'	19°Ge18'	17°Cn21'	25°Ar37'	05°Pi10'	18°Ta15'	26°Pi38'	00°Aq21'	17°Ar08'	04°Ta00' D	12°Le15'
Apr 29 2023	Sat	20°Le34'	08°Ta26'	13°Ta09'	20°Ge25'	17°Cn54'	25°Ar51'	05°Pi15'	18°Ta18'	26°Pi40'	00°Aq21'	17°Ar11'	04°Ta00'	12°Le22'
Apr 30 2023	Sun	02°Vi30'	09°Ta24'	12°Ta34'	21°Ge33'	18°Cn26'	26°Ar05'	05°Pi19'	18°Ta22'	26°Pi42'	00°Aq21'	17°Ar15'	04°Ta01'	12°Le29'

PLANETARY TABLE MAY 2023 ~ 0:01 AM GMT

Date Year	Day	Moon ☽	Sun ☉	Mercury ☿	Venus ♀	Mars ♂	Jupiter ♃	Saturn ♄	Uranus ♅	Neptune ♆	Pluto ♇	Chiron ⚷	N Node ☊	Lilith ⚸
May 1 2023	Mon	14°Vi34'	10°Ta22'	11°Ta57' R	22°Ge40'	18°Cn59'	26°Ar19'	05°Pi24'	18°Ta25'	26°Pi43'	00°Aq21'	17°Ar18'	04°Ta01'	12°Le35'
May 2 2023	Tue	26°Vi49'	11°Ta21'	11°Ta18' R	23°Ge47'	19°Cn32'	26°Ar34'	05°Pi28'	18°Ta29'	26°Pi45'	00°Aq21' R	17°Ar21'	04°Ta02'	12°Le42'
May 3 2023	Wed	09°Li20'	12°Ta19'	10°Ta40'	24°Ge54'	20°Cn05'	26°Ar48'	05°Pi32'	18°Ta32'	26°Pi47'	00°Aq21'	17°Ar25'	04°Ta03'	12°Le49'
May 4 2023	Thu	22°Li07'	13°Ta17'	10°Ta01'	26°Ge01'	20°Cn39'	27°Ar02'	05°Pi36'	18°Ta35'	26°Pi49'	00°Aq21'	17°Ar28'	04°Ta03'	12°Le56'
May 5 2023	Fri	05°Sc12'	14°Ta15'	09°Ta23'	27°Ge07'	21°Cn12'	27°Ar16'	05°Pi41'	18°Ta39'	26°Pi50'	00°Aq21'	17°Ar31'	04°Ta03' R	13°Le02'
May 6 2023	Sat	18°Sc35'	15°Ta13'	08°Ta47'	28°Ge14'	21°Cn45'	27°Ar30'	05°Pi45'	18°Ta42'	26°Pi52'	00°Aq21'	17°Ar34'	04°Ta03'	13°Le09'
May 7 2023	Sun	02°Sg16'	16°Ta11'	08°Ta13'	29°Ge20'	22°Cn18'	27°Ar44'	05°Pi48'	18°Ta46'	26°Pi54'	00°Aq21'	17°Ar38'	04°Ta02'	13°Le16'
May 8 2023	Mon	16°Sg10'	17°Ta09'	07°Ta42'	00°Cn26'	22°Cn52'	27°Ar58'	05°Pi52'	18°Ta49'	26°Pi55'	00°Aq21'	17°Ar41'	04°Ta01'	13°Le22'
May 9 2023	Tue	00°Cp16'	18°Ta08'	07°Ta14'	01°Cn32'	23°Cn25'	28°Ar12'	05°Pi56'	18°Ta53'	26°Pi57'	00°Aq21'	17°Ar44'	03°Ta59'	13°Le29'
May 10 2023	Wed	14°Cp29'	19°Ta06'	06°Ta50'	02°Cn37'	23°Cn59'	28°Ar26'	06°Pi00'	18°Ta56'	26°Pi58'	00°Aq20'	17°Ar47'	03°Ta57'	13°Le36'
May 11 2023	Thu	28°Cp46'	20°Ta04'	06°Ta29'	03°Cn43'	24°Cn32'	28°Ar40'	06°Pi03'	19°Ta00'	27°Pi00'	00°Aq20'	17°Ar50'	03°Ta56'	13°Le43'
May 12 2023	Fri	13°Aq02'	21°Ta02'	06°Ta13'	04°Cn48'	25°Cn06'	28°Ar54'	06°Pi07'	19°Ta03'	27°Pi01'	00°Aq20'	17°Ar53'	03°Ta55'	13°Le49'
May 13 2023	Sat	27°Aq15'	21°Ta59'	06°Ta01'	05°Cn53'	25°Cn40'	29°Ar08'	06°Pi10'	19°Ta07'	27°Pi03'	00°Aq20'	17°Ar56'	03°Ta55' D	13°Le56'
May 14 2023	Sun	11°Pi23'	22°Ta57'	05°Ta53'	06°Cn57'	26°Cn13'	29°Ar22'	06°Pi14'	19°Ta10'	27°Pi04'	00°Aq19'	17°Ar59'	03°Ta56'	14°Le03'
May 15 2023	Mon	25°Pi24'	23°Ta55'	05°Ta51'	08°Cn02'	26°Cn47'	29°Ar36'	06°Pi17'	19°Ta14'	27°Pi06'	00°Aq19'	18°Ar02'	03°Ta57'	14°Le10'
May 16 2023	Tue	09°Ar16'	24°Ta53'	05°Ta52' D	09°Cn06'	27°Cn21'	29°Ar50'	06°Pi20'	19°Ta17'	27°Pi07'	00°Aq19'	18°Ar05'	03°Ta58'	14°Le16'
May 17 2023	Wed	22°Ar58'	25°Ta51'	05°Ta59'	10°Cn10'	27°Cn55'	00°Ta03'	06°Pi23'	19°Ta21'	27°Pi09'	00°Aq18'	18°Ar08'	03°Ta59'	14°Le23'
May 18 2023	Thu	06°Ta28'	26°Ta49'	06°Ta09'	11°Cn14'	28°Cn29'	00°Ta17'	06°Pi26'	19°Ta24'	27°Pi10'	00°Aq18'	18°Ar11'	04°Ta00' R	14°Le30'
May 19 2023	Fri	19°Ta45'	27°Ta47'	06°Ta25'	12°Cn17'	29°Cn03'	00°Ta31'	06°Pi29'	19°Ta27'	27°Pi11'	00°Aq17'	18°Ar14'	03°Ta59'	14°Le36'
May 20 2023	Sat	02°Ge49'	28°Ta45'	06°Ta45'	13°Cn20'	29°Cn37'	00°Ta44'	06°Pi32'	19°Ta31'	27°Pi13'	00°Aq17'	18°Ar17'	03°Ta57'	14°Le43'
May 21 2023	Sun	15°Ge38'	29°Ta42'	07°Ta09'	14°Cn23'	00°Le12'	00°Ta58'	06°Pi35'	19°Ta34'	27°Pi14'	00°Aq16'	18°Ar20'	03°Ta54'	14°Le50'
May 22 2023	Mon	28°Ge12'	00°Ge40'	07°Ta37'	15°Cn26'	00°Le46'	01°Ta11'	06°Pi37'	19°Ta38'	27°Pi15'	00°Aq16'	18°Ar23'	03°Ta49'	14°Le57'
May 23 2023	Tue	10°Cn33'	01°Ge38'	08°Ta10'	16°Cn28'	01°Le20'	01°Ta25'	06°Pi40'	19°Ta41'	27°Pi16'	00°Aq15'	18°Ar25'	03°Ta45'	15°Le03'
May 24 2023	Wed	22°Cn42'	02°Ge36'	08°Ta46'	17°Cn30'	01°Le55'	01°Ta38'	06°Pi42'	19°Ta45'	27°Pi18'	00°Aq15'	18°Ar28'	03°Ta40'	15°Le10'
May 25 2023	Thu	04°Le42'	03°Ge33'	09°Ta27'	18°Cn32'	02°Le29'	01°Ta51'	06°Pi45'	19°Ta48'	27°Pi19'	00°Aq14'	18°Ar31'	03°Ta36'	15°Le17'
May 26 2023	Fri	16°Le36'	04°Ge31'	10°Ta11'	19°Cn33'	03°Le03'	02°Ta05'	06°Pi47'	19°Ta51'	27°Pi20'	00°Aq13'	18°Ar34'	03°Ta34'	15°Le23'
May 27 2023	Sat	28°Le28'	05°Ge29'	10°Ta58'	20°Cn34'	03°Le38'	02°Ta18'	06°Pi49'	19°Ta55'	27°Pi21'	00°Aq13'	18°Ar36'	03°Ta32'	15°Le30'
May 28 2023	Sun	10°Vi24'	06°Ge26'	11°Ta50'	21°Cn35'	04°Le13'	02°Ta31'	06°Pi51'	19°Ta58'	27°Pi22'	00°Aq12'	18°Ar39'	03°Ta32' D	15°Le37'
May 29 2023	Mon	22°Vi27'	07°Ge24'	12°Ta45'	22°Cn35'	04°Le47'	02°Ta44'	06°Pi53'	20°Ta02'	27°Pi23'	00°Aq11'	18°Ar41'	03°Ta33'	15°Le44'
May 30 2023	Tue	04°Li43'	08°Ge21'	13°Ta43'	23°Cn35'	05°Le22'	02°Ta57'	06°Pi55'	20°Ta05'	27°Pi24'	00°Aq10'	18°Ar44'	03°Ta34'	15°Le50'
May 31 2023	Wed	17°Li15'	09°Ge19'	14°Ta44'	24°Cn35'	05°Le57'	03°Ta10'	06°Pi57'	20°Ta08'	27°Pi25'	00°Aq10'	18°Ar46'	03°Ta36'	15°Le57'

PLANETARY TABLE JUNE 2023 ~ 0:01 AM GMT

Date Year	Day	Moon ☽	Sun ☉	Mercury ☿	Venus ♀	Mars ♂	Jupiter ♃	Saturn ♄	Uranus ♅	Neptune ♆	Pluto ♇	Chiron ⚷	N Node ☊	Lilith ⚸
Jun 1 2023	Thu	00°Sc08'	10°Ge16'	15°Ta49'	25°Cn34'	06°Le31'	03°Ta23'	06°Pi58'	20°Ta12'	27°Pi26'	00°Aq09' R	18°Ar49'	03°Ta37'	16°Le04'
Jun 2 2023	Fri	13°Sc25'	11°Ge14'	16°Ta57'	26°Cn33'	07°Le06'	03°Ta36'	07°Pi00'	20°Ta15'	27°Pi27'	00°Aq08'	18°Ar51'	03°Ta37' R	16°Le10'
Jun 3 2023	Sat	27°Sc05'	12°Ge11'	18°Ta07'	27°Cn31'	07°Le41'	03°Ta49'	07°Pi01'	20°Ta18'	27°Pi28'	00°Aq07'	18°Ar54'	03°Ta35'	16°Le17'
Jun 4 2023	Sun	11°Sg07'	13°Ge09'	19°Ta21'	28°Cn29'	08°Le16'	04°Ta02'	07°Pi03'	20°Ta21'	27°Pi29'	00°Aq06'	18°Ar56'	03°Ta31'	16°Le24'
Jun 5 2023	Mon	25°Sg28'	14°Ge06'	20°Ta38'	29°Cn27'	08°Le51'	04°Ta14'	07°Pi04'	20°Ta25'	27°Pi30'	00°Aq06'	18°Ar58'	03°Ta26'	16°Le31'
Jun 6 2023	Tue	10°Cp02'	15°Ge04'	21°Ta57'	00°Le24'	09°Le26'	04°Ta27'	07°Pi05'	20°Ta28'	27°Pi31'	00°Aq05'	19°Ar01'	03°Ta19'	16°Le37'
Jun 7 2023	Wed	24°Cp41'	16°Ge01'	23°Ta20'	01°Le20'	10°Le01'	04°Ta40'	07°Pi06'	20°Ta31'	27°Pi31'	00°Aq04'	19°Ar03'	03°Ta13'	16°Le44'
Jun 8 2023	Thu	09°Aq20'	16°Ge58'	24°Ta45'	02°Le16'	10°Le36'	04°Ta52'	07°Pi07'	20°Ta34'	27°Pi32'	00°Aq03'	19°Ar05'	03°Ta08'	16°Le51'
Jun 9 2023	Fri	23°Aq52'	17°Ge56'	26°Ta13'	03°Le12'	11°Le11'	05°Ta04'	07°Pi08'	20°Ta38'	27°Pi33'	00°Aq02'	19°Ar07'	03°Ta04'	16°Le58'
Jun 10 2023	Sat	08°Pi12'	18°Ge53'	27°Ta44'	04°Le07'	11°Le46'	05°Ta17'	07°Pi09'	20°Ta41'	27°Pi34'	00°Aq01'	19°Ar10'	03°Ta02'	17°Le04'
Jun 11 2023	Sun	22°Pi17'	19°Ge51'	29°Ta18'	05°Le02'	12°Le22'	05°Ta29'	07°Pi10'	20°Ta44'	27°Pi34'	00°Aq00'	19°Ar12'	03°Ta01' D	17°Le11'
Jun 12 2023	Mon	06°Ar07'	20°Ge48'	00°Ge54'	05°Le56'	12°Le57'	05°Ta41'	07°Pi11'	20°Ta47'	27°Pi35'	29°Cp59'	19°Ar14'	03°Ta02'	17°Le18'
Jun 13 2023	Tue	19°Ar41'	21°Ge45'	02°Ge34'	06°Le49'	13°Le32'	05°Ta53'	07°Pi11'	20°Ta50'	27°Pi36'	29°Cp58'	19°Ar16'	03°Ta03'	17°Le24'
Jun 14 2023	Wed	03°Ta02'	22°Ge43'	04°Ge16'	07°Le42'	14°Le08'	06°Ta05'	07°Pi11'	20°Ta53'	27°Pi36'	29°Cp57'	19°Ar18'	03°Ta04'	17°Le31'
Jun 15 2023	Thu	16°Ta09'	23°Ge40'	06°Ge00'	08°Le34'	14°Le43'	06°Ta17'	07°Pi12'	20°Ta56'	27°Pi37'	29°Cp56'	19°Ar20'	03°Ta03' R	17°Le38'
Jun 16 2023	Fri	29°Ta04'	24°Ge37'	07°Ge47'	09°Le26'	15°Le18'	06°Ta29'	07°Pi12'	20°Ta59'	27°Pi37'	29°Cp55'	19°Ar21'	03°Ta00'	17°Le45'
Jun 17 2023	Sat	11°Ge47'	25°Ge35'	09°Ge37'	10°Le17'	15°Le54'	06°Ta41'	07°Pi12'	21°Ta02'	27°Pi38'	29°Cp54'	19°Ar23'	02°Ta55'	17°Le51'
Jun 18 2023	Sun	24°Ge20'	26°Ge32'	11°Ge30'	11°Le07'	16°Le29'	06°Ta53'	07°Pi12' R	21°Ta05'	27°Pi38'	29°Cp52'	19°Ar25'	02°Ta47'	17°Le58'
Jun 19 2023	Mon	06°Cn42'	27°Ge29'	13°Ge25'	11°Le57'	17°Le05'	07°Ta04'	07°Pi12'	21°Ta08'	27°Pi38'	29°Cp51'	19°Ar27'	02°Ta38'	18°Le05'
Jun 20 2023	Tue	18°Cn54'	28°Ge27'	15°Ge22'	12°Le46'	17°Le41'	07°Ta16'	07°Pi12'	21°Ta11'	27°Pi39'	29°Cp50'	19°Ar28'	02°Ta28'	18°Le11'
Jun 21 2023	Wed	00°Le58'	29°Ge24'	17°Ge22'	13°Le34'	18°Le16'	07°Ta27'	07°Pi12'	21°Ta14'	27°Pi39'	29°Cp49'	19°Ar30'	02°Ta17'	18°Le18'
Jun 22 2023	Thu	12°Le55'	00°Cn21'	19°Ge23'	14°Le21'	18°Le52'	07°Ta39'	07°Pi11'	21°Ta17'	27°Pi39'	29°Cp48'	19°Ar32'	02°Ta08'	18°Le25'
Jun 23 2023	Fri	24°Le47'	01°Cn18'	21°Ge27'	15°Le08'	19°Le28'	07°Ta50'	07°Pi11'	21°Ta20'	27°Pi40'	29°Cp47'	19°Ar33'	02°Ta00'	18°Le32'
Jun 24 2023	Sat	06°Vi37'	02°Cn16'	23°Ge32'	15°Le53'	20°Le04'	08°Ta01'	07°Pi10'	21°Ta23'	27°Pi40'	29°Cp45'	19°Ar35'	01°Ta55'	18°Le38'
Jun 25 2023	Sun	18°Vi31'	03°Cn13'	25°Ge40'	16°Le38'	20°Le39'	08°Ta12'	07°Pi10'	21°Ta25'	27°Pi40'	29°Cp44'	19°Ar36'	01°Ta52'	18°Le45'
Jun 26 2023	Mon	00°Li32'	04°Cn10'	27°Ge48'	17°Le22'	21°Le15'	08°Ta23'	07°Pi09'	21°Ta28'	27°Pi40'	29°Cp43'	19°Ar38'	01°Ta50'	18°Le52'
Jun 27 2023	Tue	12°Li45'	05°Cn07'	29°Ge57'	18°Le05'	21°Le51'	08°Ta34'	07°Pi08'	21°Ta31'	27°Pi40'	29°Cp42'	19°Ar39'	01°Ta50' D	18°Le58'
Jun 28 2023	Wed	25°Li16'	06°Cn05'	02°Cn08'	18°Le47'	22°Le27'	08°Ta45'	07°Pi07'	21°Ta34'	27°Pi41'	29°Cp40'	19°Ar40'	01°Ta51'	19°Le05'
Jun 29 2023	Thu	08°Sc08'	07°Cn02'	04°Cn19'	19°Le28'	23°Le03'	08°Ta55'	07°Pi06'	21°Ta36'	27°Pi41'	29°Cp39'	19°Ar42'	01°Ta51' R	19°Le12'
Jun 30 2023	Fri	21°Sc27'	07°Cn59'	06°Cn30'	20°Le07'	23°Le39'	09°Ta06'	07°Pi05'	21°Ta39'	27°Pi41'	29°Cp38'	19°Ar43'	01°Ta49'	19°Le19'

PLANETARY TABLE JULY 2023 ~ 0:01 AM GMT

Date Year	Day	Moon ☽	Sun ☉	Mercury ☿	Venus ♀	Mars ♂	Jupiter ♃	Saturn ♄	Uranus ♅	Neptune ♆	Pluto ♇	Chiron ⚷	N Node ☊	Lilith ⚸
Jul 1 2023	Sat	05°Sg14'	08°Cn56'	08°Cn41'	20°Le46'	24°Le15'	09°Ta16'	07°Pi03' R	21°Ta42'	27°Pi41' R	29°Cp36' R	19°Ar44'	01°Ta46' R	19°Le25'
Jul 2 2023	Sun	19°Sg28'	09°Cn53'	10°Cn51'	21°Le24'	24°Le51'	09°Ta27'	07°Pi02'	21°Ta44'	27°Pi41'	29°Cp35'	19°Ar45'	01°Ta39'	19°Le32'
Jul 3 2023	Mon	04°Cp06'	10°Cn51'	13°Cn01'	22°Le00'	25°Le28'	09°Ta37'	07°Pi01'	21°Ta47'	27°Pi41'	29°Cp34'	19°Ar46'	01°Ta31'	19°Le39'
Jul 4 2023	Tue	19°Cp02'	11°Cn48'	15°Cn11'	22°Le35'	26°Le04'	09°Ta47'	06°Pi59'	21°Ta49'	27°Pi41'	29°Cp32'	19°Ar47'	01°Ta21'	19°Le45'
Jul 5 2023	Wed	04°Aq05'	12°Cn45'	17°Cn19'	23°Le09'	26°Le40'	09°Ta57'	06°Pi58'	21°Ta52'	27°Pi40'	29°Cp31'	19°Ar48'	01°Ta11'	19°Le52'
Jul 6 2023	Thu	19°Aq07'	13°Cn42'	19°Cn26'	23°Le41'	27°Le16'	10°Ta07'	06°Pi56'	21°Ta54'	27°Pi40'	29°Cp30'	19°Ar49'	01°Ta02'	19°Le59'
Jul 7 2023	Fri	03°Pi59'	14°Cn39'	21°Cn32'	24°Le12'	27°Le53'	10°Ta17'	06°Pi54'	21°Ta57'	27°Pi40'	29°Cp28'	19°Ar50'	00°Ta55'	20°Le06'
Jul 8 2023	Sat	18°Pi32'	15°Cn36'	23°Cn36'	24°Le42'	28°Le29'	10°Ta27'	06°Pi52'	21°Ta59'	27°Pi40'	29°Cp27'	19°Ar51'	00°Ta51'	20°Le12'
Jul 9 2023	Sun	02°Ar45'	16°Cn34'	25°Cn39'	25°Le10'	29°Le05'	10°Ta36'	06°Pi50'	22°Ta01'	27°Pi40'	29°Cp26'	19°Ar52'	00°Ta48'	20°Le19'
Jul 10 2023	Mon	16°Ar35'	17°Cn31'	27°Cn40'	25°Le37'	29°Le42'	10°Ta46'	06°Pi48'	22°Ta04'	27°Pi39'	29°Cp24'	19°Ar52'	00°Ta48'	20°Le26'
Jul 11 2023	Tue	00°Ta03'	18°Cn28'	29°Cn39'	26°Le02'	00°Vi18'	10°Ta55'	06°Pi46'	22°Ta06'	27°Pi39'	29°Cp23'	19°Ar53'	00°Ta48' D	20°Le32'
Jul 12 2023	Wed	13°Ta12'	19°Cn25'	01°Le36'	26°Le25'	00°Vi55'	11°Ta04'	06°Pi44'	22°Ta08'	27°Pi39'	29°Cp21'	19°Ar54'	00°Ta47' R	20°Le39'
Jul 13 2023	Thu	26°Ta04'	20°Cn23'	03°Le32'	26°Le47'	01°Vi31'	11°Ta13'	06°Pi41'	22°Ta10'	27°Pi38'	29°Cp20'	19°Ar54'	00°Ta45'	20°Le46'
Jul 14 2023	Fri	08°Ge42'	21°Cn20'	05°Le26'	27°Le06'	02°Vi08'	11°Ta22'	06°Pi39'	22°Ta13'	27°Pi38'	29°Cp19'	19°Ar55'	00°Ta41'	20°Le53'
Jul 15 2023	Sat	21°Ge10'	22°Cn17'	07°Le18'	27°Le24'	02°Vi45'	11°Ta31'	06°Pi36'	22°Ta15'	27°Pi38'	29°Cp17'	19°Ar55'	00°Ta33'	20°Le59'
Jul 16 2023	Sun	03°Cn28'	23°Cn14'	09°Le08'	27°Le41'	03°Vi21'	11°Ta40'	06°Pi34'	22°Ta17'	27°Pi37'	29°Cp16'	19°Ar56'	00°Ta23'	21°Le06'
Jul 17 2023	Mon	15°Cn37'	24°Cn11'	10°Le56'	27°Le55'	03°Vi58'	11°Ta49'	06°Pi31'	22°Ta19'	27°Pi37'	29°Cp14'	19°Ar56'	00°Ta11'	21°Le13'
Jul 18 2023	Tue	27°Cn40'	25°Cn09'	12°Le42'	28°Le07'	04°Vi35'	11°Ta57'	06°Pi28'	22°Ta21'	27°Pi36'	29°Cp13'	19°Ar56'	29°Ar57'	21°Le19'
Jul 19 2023	Wed	09°Le38'	26°Cn06'	14°Le27'	28°Le17'	05°Vi12'	12°Ta05'	06°Pi26'	22°Ta23'	27°Pi35'	29°Cp12'	19°Ar57'	29°Ar43'	21°Le26'
Jul 20 2023	Thu	21°Le31'	27°Cn03'	16°Le10'	28°Le25'	05°Vi48'	12°Ta14'	06°Pi23'	22°Ta25'	27°Pi35'	29°Cp10'	19°Ar57'	29°Ar31'	21°Le33'
Jul 21 2023	Fri	03°Vi21'	28°Cn01'	17°Le50'	28°Le31'	06°Vi25'	12°Ta22'	06°Pi20'	22°Ta27'	27°Pi34'	29°Cp09'	19°Ar57'	29°Ar20'	21°Le40'
Jul 22 2023	Sat	15°Vi11'	28°Cn58'	19°Le29'	28°Le34'	07°Vi02'	12°Ta29'	06°Pi17'	22°Ta28'	27°Pi34'	29°Cp07'	19°Ar57'	29°Ar12'	21°Le46'
Jul 23 2023	Sun	27°Vi04'	29°Cn55'	21°Le06'	28°Le36'	07°Vi39'	12°Ta37'	06°Pi14'	22°Ta30'	27°Pi33'	29°Cp06'	19°Ar57'	29°Ar06'	21°Le53'
Jul 24 2023	Mon	09°Li04'	00°Le52'	22°Le41'	28°Le35' R	08°Vi16'	12°Ta45'	06°Pi10'	22°Ta32'	27°Pi32'	29°Cp04'	19°Ar57' R	29°Ar03'	22°Le00'
Jul 25 2023	Tue	21°Li15'	01°Le50'	24°Le14'	28°Le31'	08°Vi53'	12°Ta52'	06°Pi07'	22°Ta34'	27°Pi31'	29°Cp03'	19°Ar57'	29°Ar03'	22°Le06'
Jul 26 2023	Wed	03°Sc43'	02°Le47'	25°Le46'	28°Le26'	09°Vi30'	13°Ta00'	06°Pi04'	22°Ta35'	27°Pi31'	29°Cp02'	19°Ar57'	29°Ar02'	22°Le13'
Jul 27 2023	Thu	16°Sc32'	03°Le44'	27°Le15'	28°Le17'	10°Vi07'	13°Ta07'	06°Pi00'	22°Ta37'	27°Pi30'	29°Cp00'	19°Ar57'	29°Ar02'	22°Le20'
Jul 28 2023	Fri	29°Sc47'	04°Le42'	28°Le43'	28°Le07'	10°Vi45'	13°Ta14'	05°Pi57'	22°Ta39'	27°Pi29'	28°Cp59'	19°Ar57'	29°Ar00'	22°Le27'
Jul 29 2023	Sat	13°Sg31'	05°Le39'	00°Vi08'	27°Le54'	11°Vi22'	13°Ta21'	05°Pi53'	22°Ta40'	27°Pi28'	28°Cp57'	19°Ar57'	28°Ar57'	22°Le33'
Jul 30 2023	Sun	27°Sg45'	06°Le36'	01°Vi32'	27°Le39'	11°Vi59'	13°Ta27'	05°Pi50'	22°Ta42'	27°Pi27'	28°Cp56'	19°Ar56'	28°Ar50'	22°Le40'
Jul 31 2023	Mon	12°Cp26'	07°Le34'	02°Vi54'	27°Le21'	12°Vi36'	13°Ta34'	05°Pi46'	22°Ta43'	27°Pi26'	28°Cp55'	19°Ar56'	28°Ar42'	22°Le47'

PLANETARY TABLE AUGUST 2023 ~ 0:01 AM GMT

Date Year	Day	Moon ☽	Sun ☉	Mercury ☿	Venus ♀	Mars ♂	Jupiter ♃	Saturn ♄	Uranus ♅	Neptune ♆	Pluto ♇	Chiron ⚷	N Node ☊	Lilith ⚸
Aug 1 2023	Tue	27°Cp30'	08°Le31'	04°Vi13'	27°Le01' R	13°Vi14'	13°Ta40'	05°Pi42' R	22°Ta44'	27°Pi26' R	28°Cp53' R	19°Ar55' R	28°Ar31' R	22°Le53'
Aug 2 2023	Wed	12°Aq45'	09°Le28'	05°Vi31'	26°Le39'	13°Vi51'	13°Ta47'	05°Pi38'	22°Ta46'	27°Pi25'	28°Cp52'	19°Ar55'	28°Ar21'	23°Le00'
Aug 3 2023	Thu	28°Aq03'	10°Le26'	06°Vi46'	26°Le14'	14°Vi28'	13°Ta53'	05°Pi35'	22°Ta47'	27°Pi24'	28°Cp50'	19°Ar54'	28°Ar11'	23°Le07'
Aug 4 2023	Fri	13°Pi10'	11°Le23'	08°Vi00'	25°Le48'	15°Vi06'	13°Ta59'	05°Pi31'	22°Ta48'	27°Pi23'	28°Cp49'	19°Ar54'	28°Ar03'	23°Le14'
Aug 5 2023	Sat	27°Pi59'	12°Le21'	09°Vi11'	25°Le20'	15°Vi43'	14°Ta05'	05°Pi27'	22°Ta50'	27°Pi22'	28°Cp48'	19°Ar53'	27°Ar58'	23°Le20'
Aug 6 2023	Sun	12°Ar23'	13°Le18'	10°Vi19'	24°Le50'	16°Vi21'	14°Ta10'	05°Pi23'	22°Ta51'	27°Pi21'	28°Cp46'	19°Ar53'	27°Ar56'	23°Le27'
Aug 7 2023	Mon	26°Ar21'	14°Le16'	11°Vi26'	24°Le18'	16°Vi58'	14°Ta16'	05°Pi19'	22°Ta52'	27°Pi19'	28°Cp45'	19°Ar52'	27°Ar55'	23°Le34'
Aug 8 2023	Tue	09°Ta52'	15°Le13'	12°Vi30'	23°Le45'	17°Vi36'	14°Ta21'	05°Pi15'	22°Ta53'	27°Pi18'	28°Cp43'	19°Ar51'	27°Ar55' D	23°Le40'
Aug 9 2023	Wed	23°Ta00'	16°Le11'	13°Vi31'	23°Le11'	18°Vi14'	14°Ta26'	05°Pi11'	22°Ta54'	27°Pi17'	28°Cp42'	19°Ar50'	27°Ar55' R	23°Le47'
Aug 10 2023	Thu	05°Ge47'	17°Le08'	14°Vi29'	22°Le35'	18°Vi51'	14°Ta31'	05°Pi06'	22°Ta55'	27°Pi16'	28°Cp41'	19°Ar49'	27°Ar53'	23°Le54'
Aug 11 2023	Fri	18°Ge17'	18°Le06'	15°Vi25'	21°Le59'	19°Vi29'	14°Ta36'	05°Pi02'	22°Ta56'	27°Pi15'	28°Cp39'	19°Ar49'	27°Ar50'	24°Le01'
Aug 12 2023	Sat	00°Cn35'	19°Le03'	16°Vi18'	21°Le22'	20°Vi07'	14°Ta40'	04°Pi58'	22°Ta57'	27°Pi14'	28°Cp38'	19°Ar48'	27°Ar43'	24°Le07'
Aug 13 2023	Sun	12°Cn43'	20°Le01'	17°Vi07'	20°Le45'	20°Vi44'	14°Ta45'	04°Pi54'	22°Ta58'	27°Pi12'	28°Cp37'	19°Ar47'	27°Ar35'	24°Le14'
Aug 14 2023	Mon	24°Cn43'	20°Le58'	17°Vi53'	20°Le08'	21°Vi22'	14°Ta49'	04°Pi49'	22°Ta58'	27°Pi11'	28°Cp35'	19°Ar45'	27°Ar24'	24°Le21'
Aug 15 2023	Tue	06°Le39'	21°Le56'	18°Vi36'	19°Le31'	22°Vi00'	14°Ta53'	04°Pi45'	22°Ta59'	27°Pi10'	28°Cp34'	19°Ar44'	27°Ar12'	24°Le27'
Aug 16 2023	Wed	18°Le32'	22°Le54'	19°Vi15'	18°Le54'	22°Vi38'	14°Ta57'	04°Pi41'	23°Ta00'	27°Pi09'	28°Cp33'	19°Ar43'	27°Ar00'	24°Le34'
Aug 17 2023	Thu	00°Vi23'	23°Le51'	19°Vi51'	18°Le18'	23°Vi16'	15°Ta01'	04°Pi36'	23°Ta00'	27°Pi07'	28°Cp32'	19°Ar42'	26°Ar48'	24°Le41'
Aug 18 2023	Fri	12°Vi13'	24°Le49'	20°Vi22'	17°Le42'	23°Vi54'	15°Ta04'	04°Pi32'	23°Ta01'	27°Pi06'	28°Cp30'	19°Ar41'	26°Ar39'	24°Le48'
Aug 19 2023	Sat	24°Vi06'	25°Le47'	20°Vi49'	17°Le08'	24°Vi32'	15°Ta07'	04°Pi27'	23°Ta01'	27°Pi05'	28°Cp29'	19°Ar39'	26°Ar32'	24°Le54'
Aug 20 2023	Sun	06°Li02'	26°Le44'	21°Vi11'	16°Le34'	25°Vi10'	15°Ta10'	04°Pi23'	23°Ta02'	27°Pi03'	28°Cp28'	19°Ar38'	26°Ar27'	25°Le01'
Aug 21 2023	Mon	18°Li06'	27°Le42'	21°Vi29'	16°Le03'	25°Vi48'	15°Ta13'	04°Pi18'	23°Ta02'	27°Pi02'	28°Cp27'	19°Ar37'	26°Ar25'	25°Le08'
Aug 22 2023	Tue	00°Sc20'	28°Le40'	21°Vi41'	15°Le32'	26°Vi27'	15°Ta16'	04°Pi14'	23°Ta03'	27°Pi01'	28°Cp26'	19°Ar35'	26°Ar25' D	25°Le14'
Aug 23 2023	Wed	12°Sc48'	29°Le38'	21°Vi49'	15°Le04'	27°Vi05'	15°Ta19'	04°Pi09'	23°Ta03'	26°Pi59'	28°Cp24'	19°Ar34'	26°Ar25'	25°Le21'
Aug 24 2023	Thu	25°Sc35'	00°Vi36'	21°Vi51' R	14°Le37'	27°Vi43'	15°Ta21'	04°Pi05'	23°Ta03'	26°Pi58'	28°Cp23'	19°Ar32'	26°Ar26'	25°Le28'
Aug 25 2023	Fri	08°Sg46'	01°Vi33'	21°Vi47'	14°Le12'	28°Vi21'	15°Ta23'	04°Pi00'	23°Ta04'	26°Pi56'	28°Cp22'	19°Ar31'	26°Ar26' R	25°Le34'
Aug 26 2023	Sat	22°Sg23'	02°Vi31'	21°Vi37'	13°Le50'	29°Vi00'	15°Ta25'	03°Pi56'	23°Ta04'	26°Pi55'	28°Cp21'	19°Ar29'	26°Ar24'	25°Le41'
Aug 27 2023	Sun	06°Cp28'	03°Vi29'	21°Vi22'	13°Le30'	29°Vi38'	15°Ta27'	03°Pi51'	23°Ta04'	26°Pi53'	28°Cp20'	19°Ar27'	26°Ar20'	25°Le48'
Aug 28 2023	Mon	21°Cp00'	04°Vi27'	21°Vi00'	13°Le12'	00°Li17'	15°Ta29'	03°Pi47'	23°Ta04'	26°Pi52'	28°Cp19'	19°Ar26'	26°Ar15'	25°Le55'
Aug 29 2023	Tue	05°Aq56'	05°Vi25'	20°Vi32'	12°Le56'	00°Li55'	15°Ta30'	03°Pi42'	23°Ta04'	26°Pi50'	28°Cp18'	19°Ar24'	26°Ar08'	26°Le01'
Aug 30 2023	Wed	21°Aq08'	06°Vi23'	19°Vi59'	12°Le42'	01°Li34'	15°Ta31'	03°Pi38'	23°Ta04' R	26°Pi49'	28°Cp17'	19°Ar22'	26°Ar00'	26°Le08'
Aug 31 2023	Thu	06°Pi25'	07°Vi21'	19°Vi20'	12°Le31'	02°Li12'	15°Ta32'	03°Pi33'	23°Ta04'	26°Pi47'	28°Cp16'	19°Ar20'	25°Ar53'	26°Le15'

PLANETARY TABLE SEPTEMBER 2023 ~ 0:01 AM GMT

Date Year	Day	Moon ☽	Sun ☉	Mercury ☿	Venus ♀	Mars ♂	Jupiter ♃	Saturn ♄	Uranus ♅	Neptune ♆	Pluto ♇	Chiron ⚷	N Node ☊	Lilith ⚸
Sep 1 2023	Fri	21°Pi37'	08°Vi19'	18°Vi36' R	12°Le23' R	02°Li51'	15°Ta33'	03°Pi29' R	23°Ta04' R	26°Pi46' R	28°Cp15' R	19°Ar18' R	25°Ar48' R	26°Le21'
Sep 2 2023	Sat	06°Ar33'	09°Vi17'	17°Vi47'	12°Le17'	03°Li29'	15°Ta34'	03°Pi24'	23°Ta04'	26°Pi44'	28°Cp14'	19°Ar17'	25°Ar44'	26°Le28'
Sep 3 2023	Sun	21°Ar08'	10°Vi15'	16°Vi55'	12°Le13'	04°Li08'	15°Ta34'	03°Pi19'	23°Ta03'	26°Pi43'	28°Cp13'	19°Ar15'	25°Ar43'	26°Le35'
Sep 4 2023	Mon	05°Ta15'	11°Vi13'	15°Vi59'	12°Le12'	04°Li47'	15°Ta34'	03°Pi15'	23°Ta03'	26°Pi41'	28°Cp12'	19°Ar13'	25°Ar43' D	26°Le42'
Sep 5 2023	Tue	18°Ta54'	12°Vi11'	15°Vi02'	12°Le13' D	05°Li26'	15°Ta34' R	03°Pi11'	23°Ta03'	26°Pi39'	28°Cp11'	19°Ar11'	25°Ar44'	26°Le48'
Sep 6 2023	Wed	02°Ge07'	13°Vi09'	14°Vi03'	12°Le16'	06°Li04'	15°Ta34'	03°Pi06'	23°Ta02'	26°Pi38'	28°Cp10'	19°Ar09'	25°Ar46'	26°Le55'
Sep 7 2023	Thu	14°Ge56'	14°Vi08'	13°Vi05'	12°Le22'	06°Li43'	15°Ta33'	03°Pi02'	23°Ta02'	26°Pi36'	28°Cp09'	19°Ar06'	25°Ar46' R	27°Le02'
Sep 8 2023	Fri	27°Ge26'	15°Vi06'	12°Vi09'	12°Le30'	07°Li22'	15°Ta33'	02°Pi57'	23°Ta02'	26°Pi35'	28°Cp08'	19°Ar04'	25°Ar45'	27°Le08'
Sep 9 2023	Sat	09°Cn41'	16°Vi04'	11°Vi16'	12°Le40'	08°Li01'	15°Ta32'	02°Pi53'	23°Ta01'	26°Pi33'	28°Cp07'	19°Ar02'	25°Ar43'	27°Le15'
Sep 10 2023	Sun	21°Cn44'	17°Vi02'	10°Vi27'	12°Le52'	08°Li40'	15°Ta31'	02°Pi49'	23°Ta00'	26°Pi31'	28°Cp06'	19°Ar00'	25°Ar38'	27°Le22'
Sep 11 2023	Mon	03°Le40'	18°Vi01'	09°Vi43'	13°Le06'	09°Li19'	15°Ta30'	02°Pi44'	23°Ta00'	26°Pi30'	28°Cp05'	18°Ar58'	25°Ar33'	27°Le28'
Sep 12 2023	Tue	15°Le32'	18°Vi59'	09°Vi06'	13°Le22'	09°Li58'	15°Ta29'	02°Pi40'	22°Ta59'	26°Pi28'	28°Cp05'	18°Ar56'	25°Ar26'	27°Le35'
Sep 13 2023	Wed	27°Le23'	19°Vi57'	08°Vi37'	13°Le41'	10°Li37'	15°Ta27'	02°Pi36'	22°Ta58'	26°Pi27'	28°Cp04'	18°Ar53'	25°Ar19'	27°Le42'
Sep 14 2023	Thu	09°Vi15'	20°Vi56'	08°Vi15'	14°Le01'	11°Li17'	15°Ta26'	02°Pi32'	22°Ta58'	26°Pi25'	28°Cp03'	18°Ar51'	25°Ar13'	27°Le49'
Sep 15 2023	Fri	21°Vi09'	21°Vi54'	08°Vi03'	14°Le23'	11°Li56'	15°Ta24'	02°Pi27'	22°Ta57'	26°Pi23'	28°Cp02'	18°Ar49'	25°Ar08'	27°Le55'
Sep 16 2023	Sat	03°Li08'	22°Vi53'	08°Vi00' D	14°Le46'	12°Li35'	15°Ta21'	02°Pi23'	22°Ta56'	26°Pi22'	28°Cp02'	18°Ar46'	25°Ar04'	28°Le02'
Sep 17 2023	Sun	15°Li13'	23°Vi51'	08°Vi06'	15°Le12'	13°Li14'	15°Ta19'	02°Pi19'	22°Ta55'	26°Pi20'	28°Cp01'	18°Ar44'	25°Ar02'	28°Le09'
Sep 18 2023	Mon	27°Li27'	24°Vi50'	08°Vi22'	15°Le38'	13°Li54'	15°Ta16'	02°Pi15'	22°Ta54'	26°Pi18'	28°Cp00'	18°Ar41'	25°Ar02' D	28°Le15'
Sep 19 2023	Tue	09°Sc51'	25°Vi48'	08°Vi47'	16°Le07'	14°Li33'	15°Ta14'	02°Pi11'	22°Ta53'	26°Pi17'	28°Cp00'	18°Ar39'	25°Ar03'	28°Le22'
Sep 20 2023	Wed	22°Sc28'	26°Vi47'	09°Vi21'	16°Le37'	15°Li13'	15°Ta11'	02°Pi07'	22°Ta52'	26°Pi15'	27°Cp59'	18°Ar36'	25°Ar04'	28°Le29'
Sep 21 2023	Thu	05°Sg21'	27°Vi45'	10°Vi03'	17°Le09'	15°Li52'	15°Ta07'	02°Pi03'	22°Ta51'	26°Pi13'	27°Cp59'	18°Ar34'	25°Ar06'	28°Le35'
Sep 22 2023	Fri	18°Sg33'	28°Vi44'	10°Vi54'	17°Le42'	16°Li32'	15°Ta04'	02°Pi00'	22°Ta50'	26°Pi12'	27°Cp58'	18°Ar31'	25°Ar07'	28°Le42'
Sep 23 2023	Sat	02°Cp06'	29°Vi43'	11°Vi53'	18°Le16'	17°Li11'	15°Ta00'	01°Pi56'	22°Ta49'	26°Pi10'	27°Cp58'	18°Ar29'	25°Ar07' R	28°Le49'
Sep 24 2023	Sun	16°Cp01'	00°Li42'	12°Vi59'	18°Le52'	17°Li51'	14°Ta57'	01°Pi52'	22°Ta48'	26°Pi08'	27°Cp57'	18°Ar26'	25°Ar07'	28°Le56'
Sep 25 2023	Mon	00°Aq19'	01°Li40'	14°Vi12'	19°Le29'	18°Li31'	14°Ta53'	01°Pi48'	22°Ta46'	26°Pi07'	27°Cp57'	18°Ar24'	25°Ar05'	29°Le02'
Sep 26 2023	Tue	14°Aq56'	02°Li39'	15°Vi30'	20°Le07'	19°Li10'	14°Ta49'	01°Pi45'	22°Ta45'	26°Pi05'	27°Cp56'	18°Ar21'	25°Ar02'	29°Le09'
Sep 27 2023	Wed	29°Aq49'	03°Li38'	16°Vi54'	20°Le46'	19°Li50'	14°Ta44'	01°Pi41'	22°Ta44'	26°Pi03'	27°Cp56'	18°Ar19'	24°Ar59'	29°Le16'
Sep 28 2023	Thu	14°Pi50'	04°Li37'	18°Vi22'	21°Le26'	20°Li30'	14°Ta40'	01°Pi38'	22°Ta42'	26°Pi02'	27°Cp55'	18°Ar16'	24°Ar57'	29°Le22'
Sep 29 2023	Fri	29°Pi50'	05°Li36'	19°Vi54'	22°Le08'	21°Li10'	14°Ta35'	01°Pi35'	22°Ta41'	26°Pi00'	27°Cp55'	18°Ar13'	24°Ar55'	29°Le29'
Sep 30 2023	Sat	14°Ar40'	06°Li34'	21°Vi29'	22°Le51'	21°Li50'	14°Ta31'	01°Pi31'	22°Ta39'	25°Pi58'	27°Cp55'	18°Ar11'	24°Ar53'	29°Le36'

Planetary Table October 2023 ~ 0:01 AM GMT

Date Year	Day	Moon ☽	Sun ☉	Mercury ☿	Venus ♀	Mars ♂	Jupiter ♃	Saturn ♄	Uranus ♅	Neptune ♆	Pluto ♇	Chiron ⚷	N Node ☊	Lilith ⚸
Oct 1 2023	Sun	29°Ar13'	07°Li33'	23°Vi08'	23°Le34'	22°Li30'	14°Ta26' R	01°Pi28' R	22°Ta38' R	25°Pi57' R	27°Cp54' R	18°Ar08' R	24°Ar53'	29°Le42'
Oct 2 2023	Mon	13°Ta24'	08°Li32'	24°Vi48'	24°Le19'	23°Li10'	14°Ta20'	01°Pi25'	22°Ta36'	25°Pi55'	27°Cp54'	18°Ar05'	24°Ar54'	29°Le49'
Oct 3 2023	Tue	27°Ta10'	09°Li31'	26°Vi30'	25°Le05'	23°Li50'	14°Ta15'	01°Pi22'	22°Ta35'	25°Pi54'	27°Cp54'	18°Ar03'	24°Ar55'	29°Le56'
Oct 4 2023	Wed	10°Ge29'	10°Li30'	28°Vi14'	25°Le51'	24°Li30'	14°Ta10'	01°Pi19'	22°Ta33'	25°Pi52'	27°Cp54'	18°Ar00'	24°Ar56'	00°Vi03'
Oct 5 2023	Thu	23°Ge24'	11°Li29'	29°Vi59'	26°Le39'	25°Li10'	14°Ta04'	01°Pi16'	22°Ta31'	25°Pi50'	27°Cp54'	17°Ar57'	24°Ar57'	00°Vi09'
Oct 6 2023	Fri	05°Cn58'	12°Li28'	01°Li45'	27°Le27'	25°Li50'	13°Ta58'	01°Pi13'	22°Ta30'	25°Pi49'	27°Cp53'	17°Ar55'	24°Ar57'	00°Vi16'
Oct 7 2023	Sat	18°Cn14'	13°Li28'	03°Li31'	28°Le16'	26°Li31'	13°Ta52'	01°Pi10'	22°Ta28'	25°Pi47'	27°Cp53'	17°Ar52'	24°Ar58' R	00°Vi23'
Oct 8 2023	Sun	00°Le18'	14°Li27'	05°Li17'	29°Le06'	27°Li11'	13°Ta46'	01°Pi08'	22°Ta26'	25°Pi46'	27°Cp53'	17°Ar49'	24°Ar57'	00°Vi29'
Oct 9 2023	Mon	12°Le13'	15°Li26'	07°Li03'	29°Le57'	27°Li51'	13°Ta40'	01°Pi05'	22°Ta24'	25°Pi44'	27°Cp53'	17°Ar46'	24°Ar56'	00°Vi36'
Oct 10 2023	Tue	24°Le04'	16°Li25'	08°Li50'	00°Vi49'	28°Li32'	13°Ta34'	01°Pi02'	22°Ta22'	25°Pi43'	27°Cp53'	17°Ar44'	24°Ar55'	00°Vi43'
Oct 11 2023	Wed	05°Vi55'	17°Li25'	10°Li36'	01°Vi41'	29°Li12'	13°Ta27'	01°Pi00'	22°Ta21'	25°Pi41'	27°Cp53'	17°Ar41'	24°Ar54'	00°Vi49'
Oct 12 2023	Thu	17°Vi49'	18°Li24'	12°Li22'	02°Vi34'	29°Li53'	13°Ta20'	00°Pi58'	22°Ta19'	25°Pi40'	27°Cp53' D	17°Ar38'	24°Ar53'	00°Vi56'
Oct 13 2023	Fri	29°Vi49'	19°Li23'	14°Li07'	03°Vi27'	00°Sc33'	13°Ta14'	00°Pi55'	22°Ta17'	25°Pi38'	27°Cp53'	17°Ar36'	24°Ar52'	01°Vi03'
Oct 14 2023	Sat	11°Li57'	20°Li23'	15°Li52'	04°Vi21'	01°Sc14'	13°Ta07'	00°Pi53'	22°Ta15'	25°Pi37'	27°Cp53'	17°Ar33'	24°Ar52'	01°Vi10'
Oct 15 2023	Sun	24°Li16'	21°Li22'	17°Li37'	05°Vi16'	01°Sc54'	13°Ta00'	00°Pi51'	22°Ta13'	25°Pi35'	27°Cp53'	17°Ar30'	24°Ar52'	01°Vi16'
Oct 16 2023	Mon	06°Sc46'	22°Li22'	19°Li21'	06°Vi11'	02°Sc35'	12°Ta53'	00°Pi49'	22°Ta11'	25°Pi34'	27°Cp53'	17°Ar27'	24°Ar52' D	01°Vi23'
Oct 17 2023	Tue	19°Sc28'	23°Li21'	21°Li04'	07°Vi07'	03°Sc16'	12°Ta45'	00°Pi47'	22°Ta09'	25°Pi32'	27°Cp54'	17°Ar25'	24°Ar52'	01°Vi30'
Oct 18 2023	Wed	02°Sg23'	24°Li21'	22°Li47'	08°Vi04'	03°Sc57'	12°Ta38'	00°Pi46'	22°Ta06'	25°Pi31'	27°Cp54'	17°Ar22'	24°Ar52'	01°Vi36'
Oct 19 2023	Thu	15°Sg32'	25°Li20'	24°Li29'	09°Vi01'	04°Sc38'	12°Ta31'	00°Pi44'	22°Ta04'	25°Pi30'	27°Cp54'	17°Ar19'	24°Ar52' R	01°Vi43'
Oct 20 2023	Fri	28°Sg56'	26°Li20'	26°Li10'	09°Vi59'	05°Sc19'	12°Ta23'	00°Pi42'	22°Ta02'	25°Pi28'	27°Cp54'	17°Ar17'	24°Ar52'	01°Vi50'
Oct 21 2023	Sat	12°Cp34'	27°Li20'	27°Li51'	10°Vi57'	05°Sc59'	12°Ta15'	00°Pi41'	22°Ta00'	25°Pi27'	27°Cp55'	17°Ar14'	24°Ar52'	01°Vi56'
Oct 22 2023	Sun	26°Cp26'	28°Li19'	29°Li31'	11°Vi55'	06°Sc40'	12°Ta08'	00°Pi39'	21°Ta58'	25°Pi25'	27°Cp55'	17°Ar11'	24°Ar52'	02°Vi03'
Oct 23 2023	Mon	10°Aq33'	29°Li19'	01°Sc11'	12°Vi54'	07°Sc21'	12°Ta00'	00°Pi38'	21°Ta56'	25°Pi24'	27°Cp55'	17°Ar09'	24°Ar52' D	02°Vi10'
Oct 24 2023	Tue	24°Aq52'	00°Sc19'	02°Sc50'	13°Vi54'	08°Sc03'	11°Ta52'	00°Pi37'	21°Ta53'	25°Pi23'	27°Cp55'	17°Ar06'	24°Ar52'	02°Vi16'
Oct 25 2023	Wed	09°Pi20'	01°Sc18'	04°Sc28'	14°Vi54'	08°Sc44'	11°Ta44'	00°Pi36'	21°Ta51'	25°Pi22'	27°Cp56'	17°Ar03'	24°Ar53'	02°Vi23'
Oct 26 2023	Thu	23°Pi55'	02°Sc18'	06°Sc06'	15°Vi54'	09°Sc25'	11°Ta36'	00°Pi35'	21°Ta49'	25°Pi20'	27°Cp56'	17°Ar01'	24°Ar53'	02°Vi30'
Oct 27 2023	Fri	08°Ar29'	03°Sc18'	07°Sc43'	16°Vi55'	10°Sc06'	11°Ta28'	00°Pi34'	21°Ta46'	25°Pi19'	27°Cp57'	16°Ar58'	24°Ar54'	02°Vi37'
Oct 28 2023	Sat	22°Ar59'	04°Sc18'	09°Sc20'	17°Vi56'	10°Sc47'	11°Ta20'	00°Pi33'	21°Ta44'	25°Pi18'	27°Cp57'	16°Ar55'	24°Ar54'	02°Vi43'
Oct 29 2023	Sun	07°Ta17'	05°Sc18'	10°Sc56'	18°Vi58'	11°Sc29'	11°Ta12'	00°Pi33'	21°Ta42'	25°Pi17'	27°Cp58'	16°Ar53'	24°Ar54' R	02°Vi50'
Oct 30 2023	Mon	21°Ta19'	06°Sc18'	12°Sc32'	20°Vi00'	12°Sc10'	11°Ta04'	00°Pi32'	21°Ta39'	25°Pi16'	27°Cp58'	16°Ar50'	24°Ar53'	02°Vi57'
Oct 31 2023	Tue	05°Ge02'	07°Sc17'	14°Sc07'	21°Vi02'	12°Sc52'	10°Ta56'	00°Pi31'	21°Ta37'	25°Pi14'	27°Cp59'	16°Ar48'	24°Ar52'	03°Vi03'

PLANETARY TABLE NOVEMBER 2023 ~ 0:01 AM GMT

Date Year	Day	Moon ☽	Sun ☉	Mercury ☿	Venus ♀	Mars ♂	Jupiter ♃	Saturn ♄	Uranus ♅	Neptune ♆	Pluto ♇	Chiron ⚷	N Node ☊	Lilith ⚸
Nov 1 2023	Wed	18°Ge22'	08°Sc17'	15°Sc42'	22°Vi05'	13°Sc33'	10°Ta48'R	00°Pi31'R	21°Ta35'R	25°Pi13'R	27°Cp59'	16°Ar45'R	24°Ar50'R	03°Vi10'
Nov 2 2023	Thu	01°Cn20'	09°Sc17'	17°Sc16'	23°Vi08'	14°Sc15'	10°Ta40'	00°Pi31'	21°Ta32'	25°Pi12'	28°Cp00'	16°Ar43'	24°Ar48'	03°Vi17'
Nov 3 2023	Fri	13°Cn57'	10°Sc17'	18°Sc50'	24°Vi12'	14°Sc56'	10°Ta32'	00°Pi30'	21°Ta30'	25°Pi11'	28°Cp01'	16°Ar40'	24°Ar46'	03°Vi23'
Nov 4 2023	Sat	26°Cn17'	11°Sc18'	20°Sc23'	25°Vi15'	15°Sc38'	10°Ta24'	00°Pi30'	21°Ta27'	25°Pi10'	28°Cp01'	16°Ar38'	24°Ar45'	03°Vi30'
Nov 5 2023	Sun	08°Le22'	12°Sc18'	21°Sc56'	26°Vi19'	16°Sc20'	10°Ta15'	00°Pi30'D	21°Ta25'	25°Pi09'	28°Cp02'	16°Ar36'	24°Ar44'	03°Vi37'
Nov 6 2023	Mon	20°Le18'	13°Sc18'	23°Sc29'	27°Vi24'	17°Sc01'	10°Ta07'	00°Pi30'	21°Ta22'	25°Pi08'	28°Cp03'	16°Ar33'	24°Ar44'D	03°Vi44'
Nov 7 2023	Tue	02°Vi09'	14°Sc18'	25°Sc01'	28°Vi29'	17°Sc43'	09°Ta59'	00°Pi31'	21°Ta20'	25°Pi07'	28°Cp04'	16°Ar31'	24°Ar45'	03°Vi50'
Nov 8 2023	Wed	14°Vi00'	15°Sc18'	26°Sc33'	29°Vi34'	18°Sc25'	09°Ta51'	00°Pi31'	21°Ta17'	25°Pi06'	28°Cp04'	16°Ar28'	24°Ar47'	03°Vi57'
Nov 9 2023	Thu	25°Vi56'	16°Sc18'	28°Sc04'	00°Li39'	19°Sc07'	09°Ta43'	00°Pi31'	21°Ta15'	25°Pi05'	28°Cp05'	16°Ar26'	24°Ar48'	04°Vi04'
Nov 10 2023	Fri	08°Li00'	17°Sc19'	29°Sc35'	01°Li45'	19°Sc49'	09°Ta35'	00°Pi32'	21°Ta13'	25°Pi04'	28°Cp06'	16°Ar24'	24°Ar50'	04°Vi10'
Nov 11 2023	Sat	20°Li17'	18°Sc19'	01°Sg06'	02°Li51'	20°Sc31'	09°Ta27'	00°Pi33'	21°Ta10'	25°Pi04'	28°Cp07'	16°Ar22'	24°Ar51'R	04°Vi17'
Nov 12 2023	Sun	02°Sc49'	19°Sc19'	02°Sg36'	03°Li57'	21°Sc13'	09°Ta19'	00°Pi33'	21°Ta08'	25°Pi03'	28°Cp08'	16°Ar20'	24°Ar51'R	04°Vi24'
Nov 13 2023	Mon	15°Sc37'	20°Sc20'	04°Sg06'	05°Li03'	21°Sc55'	09°Ta11'	00°Pi34'	21°Ta05'	25°Pi02'	28°Cp09'	16°Ar17'	24°Ar49'	04°Vi30'
Nov 14 2023	Tue	28°Sc41'	21°Sc20'	05°Sg36'	06°Li10'	22°Sc37'	09°Ta03'	00°Pi35'	21°Ta03'	25°Pi01'	28°Cp10'	16°Ar15'	24°Ar46'	04°Vi37'
Nov 15 2023	Wed	12°Sg02'	22°Sc20'	07°Sg05'	07°Li17'	23°Sc19'	08°Ta56'	00°Pi36'	21°Ta00'	25°Pi01'	28°Cp11'	16°Ar13'	24°Ar43'	04°Vi44'
Nov 16 2023	Thu	25°Sg36'	23°Sc21'	08°Sg34'	08°Li24'	24°Sc02'	08°Ta48'	00°Pi37'	20°Ta58'	25°Pi00'	28°Cp12'	16°Ar11'	24°Ar38'	04°Vi50'
Nov 17 2023	Fri	09°Cp23'	24°Sc21'	10°Sg02'	09°Li31'	24°Sc44'	08°Ta40'	00°Pi39'	20°Ta55'	24°Pi59'	28°Cp13'	16°Ar09'	24°Ar33'	04°Vi57'
Nov 18 2023	Sat	23°Cp19'	25°Sc22'	11°Sg30'	10°Li38'	25°Sc26'	08°Ta33'	00°Pi40'	20°Ta53'	24°Pi59'	28°Cp14'	16°Ar07'	24°Ar29'	05°Vi04'
Nov 19 2023	Sun	07°Aq21'	26°Sc22'	12°Sg57'	11°Li46'	26°Sc09'	08°Ta25'	00°Pi42'	20°Ta50'	24°Pi58'	28°Cp15'	16°Ar05'	24°Ar26'	05°Vi10'
Nov 20 2023	Mon	21°Aq28'	27°Sc23'	14°Sg24'	12°Li54'	26°Sc51'	08°Ta18'	00°Pi43'	20°Ta48'	24°Pi57'	28°Cp16'	16°Ar03'	24°Ar25'	05°Vi17'
Nov 21 2023	Tue	05°Pi37'	28°Sc24'	15°Sg50'	14°Li02'	27°Sc34'	08°Ta11'	00°Pi45'	20°Ta45'	24°Pi57'	28°Cp17'	16°Ar01'	24°Ar25'D	05°Vi24'
Nov 22 2023	Wed	19°Pi47'	29°Sc24'	17°Sg16'	15°Li11'	28°Sc16'	08°Ta04'	00°Pi47'	20°Ta43'	24°Pi56'	28°Cp18'	16°Ar00'	24°Ar26'	05°Vi31'
Nov 23 2023	Thu	03°Ar56'	00°Sg25'	18°Sg40'	16°Li19'	28°Sc59'	07°Ta57'	00°Pi49'	20°Ta40'	24°Pi56'	28°Cp19'	15°Ar58'	24°Ar28'	05°Vi37'
Nov 24 2023	Fri	18°Ar02'	01°Sg25'	20°Sg04'	17°Li28'	29°Sc41'	07°Ta50'	00°Pi51'	20°Ta38'	24°Pi55'	28°Cp21'	15°Ar56'	24°Ar29'	05°Vi44'
Nov 25 2023	Sat	02°Ta03'	02°Sg26'	21°Sg27'	18°Li37'	00°Sg24'	07°Ta43'	00°Pi53'	20°Ta35'	24°Pi55'	28°Cp22'	15°Ar54'	24°Ar29'R	05°Vi51'
Nov 26 2023	Sun	15°Ta56'	03°Sg27'	22°Sg49'	19°Li46'	01°Sg07'	07°Ta37'	00°Pi55'	20°Ta33'	24°Pi55'	28°Cp23'	15°Ar53'	24°Ar27'	05°Vi57'
Nov 27 2023	Mon	29°Ta38'	04°Sg27'	24°Sg10'	20°Li55'	01°Sg50'	07°Ta30'	00°Pi57'	20°Ta31'	24°Pi54'	28°Cp24'	15°Ar51'	24°Ar23'	06°Vi04'
Nov 28 2023	Tue	13°Ge05'	05°Sg28'	25°Sg29'	22°Li04'	02°Sg32'	07°Ta24'	00°Pi59'	20°Ta28'	24°Pi54'	28°Cp26'	15°Ar50'	24°Ar17'	06°Vi11'
Nov 29 2023	Wed	26°Ge16'	06°Sg29'	26°Sg47'	23°Li14'	03°Sg15'	07°Ta18'	01°Pi02'	20°Ta26'	24°Pi54'	28°Cp27'	15°Ar48'	24°Ar10'	06°Vi17'
Nov 30 2023	Thu	09°Cn10'	07°Sg29'	28°Sg02'	24°Li24'	03°Sg58'	07°Ta12'	01°Pi05'	20°Ta23'	24°Pi54'	28°Cp28'	15°Ar47'	24°Ar02'	06°Vi24'

PLANETARY TABLE DECEMBER 2023 ~ 0:01 AM GMT

Date Year	Day	Moon ☽	Sun ☉	Mercury ☿	Venus ♀	Mars ♂	Jupiter ♃	Saturn ♄	Uranus ♅	Neptune ♆	Pluto ♇	Chiron ⚷	N Node ☊	Lilith ⚸
Dec 1 2023	Fri	21°Cn45'	08°Sg30'	29°Sg16'	25°Li34'	04°Sg41'	07°Ta06' R	01°Pi07'	20°Ta21' R	24°Pi53' R	28°Cp30'	15°Ar45' R	23°Ar54' R	06°Vi31'
Dec 2 2023	Sat	04°Le05'	09°Sg31'	00°Cp27'	26°Li44'	05°Sg24'	07°Ta00'	01°Pi10'	20°Ta19'	24°Pi53'	28°Cp31'	15°Ar44'	23°Ar47'	06°Vi37'
Dec 3 2023	Sun	16°Le10'	10°Sg32'	01°Cp36'	27°Li54'	06°Sg07'	06°Ta54'	01°Pi13'	20°Ta16'	24°Pi53'	28°Cp33'	15°Ar43'	23°Ar42'	06°Vi44'
Dec 4 2023	Mon	28°Le06'	11°Sg33'	02°Cp41'	29°Li04'	06°Sg50'	06°Ta49'	01°Pi16'	20°Ta14'	24°Pi53'	28°Cp34'	15°Ar41'	23°Ar39'	06°Vi51'
Dec 5 2023	Tue	09°Vi57'	12°Sg34'	03°Cp43'	00°Sc15'	07°Sg34'	06°Ta44'	01°Pi19'	20°Ta12'	24°Pi53'	28°Cp35'	15°Ar40'	23°Ar38'	06°Vi57'
Dec 6 2023	Wed	21°Vi47'	13°Sg34'	04°Cp41'	01°Sc25'	08°Sg17'	06°Ta39'	01°Pi22'	20°Ta10'	24°Pi53'	28°Cp37'	15°Ar39'	23°Ar38' D	07°Vi04'
Dec 7 2023	Thu	03°Li42'	14°Sg35'	05°Cp33'	02°Sc36'	09°Sg00'	06°Ta34'	01°Pi25'	20°Ta07'	24°Pi53' D	28°Cp38'	15°Ar38'	23°Ar39'	07°Vi11'
Dec 8 2023	Fri	15°Li48'	15°Sg35'	06°Cp21'	03°Sc47'	09°Sg44'	06°Ta29'	01°Pi29'	20°Ta05'	24°Pi53'	28°Cp40'	15°Ar37'	23°Ar40'	07°Vi18'
Dec 9 2023	Sat	28°Li08'	16°Sg36'	07°Cp02'	04°Sc58'	10°Sg27'	06°Ta25'	01°Pi32'	20°Ta03'	24°Pi53'	28°Cp41'	15°Ar36'	23°Ar40' R	07°Vi24'
Dec 10 2023	Sun	10°Sc48'	17°Sg38'	07°Cp36'	06°Sc09'	11°Sg10'	06°Ta20'	01°Pi36'	20°Ta01'	24°Pi53'	28°Cp43'	15°Ar35'	23°Ar39'	07°Vi31'
Dec 11 2023	Mon	23°Sc49'	18°Sg39'	08°Cp03'	07°Sc20'	11°Sg54'	06°Ta16'	01°Pi39'	19°Ta59'	24°Pi53'	28°Cp45'	15°Ar34'	23°Ar35'	07°Vi38'
Dec 12 2023	Tue	07°Sg12'	19°Sg40'	08°Cp20'	08°Sc32'	12°Sg37'	06°Ta12'	01°Pi43'	19°Ta57'	24°Pi53'	28°Cp46'	15°Ar33'	23°Ar28'	07°Vi44'
Dec 13 2023	Wed	20°Sg57'	20°Sg41'	08°Cp28'	09°Sc43'	13°Sg21'	06°Ta08'	01°Pi47'	19°Ta55'	24°Pi54'	28°Cp48'	15°Ar32'	23°Ar20'	07°Vi51'
Dec 14 2023	Thu	05°Cp00'	21°Sg42'	08°Cp26' R	10°Sc55'	14°Sg05'	06°Ta05'	01°Pi51'	19°Ta53'	24°Pi54'	28°Cp49'	15°Ar31'	23°Ar10'	07°Vi58'
Dec 15 2023	Fri	19°Cp16'	22°Sg43'	08°Cp13'	12°Sc06'	14°Sg48'	06°Ta01'	01°Pi55'	19°Ta51'	24°Pi54'	28°Cp51'	15°Ar31'	23°Ar00'	08°Vi04'
Dec 16 2023	Sat	03°Aq39'	23°Sg44'	07°Cp48'	13°Sc18'	15°Sg32'	05°Ta58'	01°Pi59'	19°Ta49'	24°Pi54'	28°Cp53'	15°Ar30'	22°Ar50'	08°Vi11'
Dec 17 2023	Sun	18°Aq03'	24°Sg45'	07°Cp12'	14°Sc30'	16°Sg16'	05°Ta55'	02°Pi03'	19°Ta47'	24°Pi55'	28°Cp54'	15°Ar29'	22°Ar43'	08°Vi18'
Dec 18 2023	Mon	02°Pi24'	25°Sg46'	06°Cp24'	15°Sc42'	17°Sg00'	05°Ta52'	02°Pi07'	19°Ta45'	24°Pi55'	28°Cp56'	15°Ar29'	22°Ar38'	08°Vi24'
Dec 19 2023	Tue	16°Pi38'	26°Sg48'	05°Cp26'	16°Sc54'	17°Sg44'	05°Ta50'	02°Pi11'	19°Ta43'	24°Pi56'	28°Cp58'	15°Ar28'	22°Ar36'	08°Vi31'
Dec 20 2023	Wed	0C°Ar43'	27°Sg49'	04°Cp19'	18°Sc06'	18°Sg27'	05°Ta47'	02°Pi16'	19°Ta41'	24°Pi56'	28°Cp59'	15°Ar28'	22°Ar36' D	08°Vi38'
Dec 21 2023	Thu	14°Ar38'	28°Sg50'	03°Cp04'	19°Sc18'	19°Sg11'	05°Ta45'	02°Pi20'	19°Ta40'	24°Pi56'	29°Cp01'	15°Ar28'	22°Ar36'	08°Vi44'
Dec 22 2023	Fri	28°Ar23'	29°Sg51'	01°Cp44'	20°Sc30'	19°Sg55'	05°Ta43'	02°Pi25'	19°Ta38'	24°Pi57'	29°Cp03'	15°Ar27'	22°Ar36' R	08°Vi51'
Dec 23 2023	Sat	11°Ta59'	00°Cp52'	00°Cp21'	21°Sc42'	20°Sg40'	05°Ta41'	02°Pi29'	19°Ta36'	24°Pi58'	29°Cp05'	15°Ar27'	22°Ar35'	08°Vi58'
Dec 24 2023	Sun	25°Ta25'	01°Cp53'	28°Sg59'	22°Sc55'	21°Sg24'	05°Ta40'	02°Pi34'	19°Ta34'	24°Pi58'	29°Cp06'	15°Ar27'	22°Ar30'	09°Vi04'
Dec 25 2023	Mon	08°Ge42'	02°Cp54'	27°Sg40'	24°Sc07'	22°Sg08'	05°Ta38'	02°Pi39'	19°Ta33'	24°Pi59'	29°Cp08'	15°Ar27'	22°Ar23'	09°Vi11'
Dec 26 2023	Tue	21°Ge47'	03°Cp55'	26°Sg26'	25°Sc20'	22°Sg52'	05°Ta37'	02°Pi44'	19°Ta31'	24°Pi59'	29°Cp10'	15°Ar27'	22°Ar13'	09°Vi18'
Dec 27 2023	Wed	04°Cn41'	04°Cp56'	25°Sg20'	26°Sc32'	23°Sg36'	05°Ta36'	02°Pi48'	19°Ta30'	25°Pi00'	29°Cp12'	15°Ar27'	22°Ar01'	09°Vi25'
Dec 28 2023	Thu	17°Cn21'	05°Cp57'	24°Sg22'	27°Sc45'	24°Sg20'	05°Ta35'	02°Pi53'	19°Ta28'	25°Pi01'	29°Cp14'	15°Ar27' D	21°Ar48'	09°Vi31'
Dec 29 2023	Fri	25°Cn48'	06°Cp58'	23°Sg35'	28°Sc58'	25°Sg05'	05°Ta35'	02°Pi59'	19°Ta27'	25°Pi02'	29°Cp15'	15°Ar27'	21°Ar34'	09°Vi38'
Dec 30 2023	Sat	12°Le03'	08°Cp00'	22°Sg58'	00°Sg11'	25°Sg49'	05°Ta34'	03°Pi04'	19°Ta25'	25°Pi02'	29°Cp17'	15°Ar27'	21°Ar22'	09°Vi45'
Dec 31 2023	Sun	24°Le05'	09°Cp01'	22°Sg32'	01°Sg23'	26°Sg34'	05°Ta34'	03°Pi09'	19°Ta24'	25°Pi03'	29°Cp19'	15°Ar27'	21°Ar12'	09°Vi51'

MON 26   waxing Moon in Aquarius ♒ voc from 6:18 pm   air/ flower/ fat

☽✶⚷ ☽□♌ ☽□♅ ☽☌♄
- favourable day to start weaning babies (until next full Moon)
- great time to connect with friends and meet new people

Boxing Day

TUE 27   voc to 7:33 am ingress into Pisces ♓   water/ leaf/ carbo

☽☌♓ ☽✶☉ ☽□♂
- a warm Epsom Salts foot soak helps you sleep
- attend to and water indoor plants

Christmas Day observed

WED 28   waxing Moon in Pisces ♓   water/ leaf/ carbo

☽✶♌ ☽✶♅ ☽☌♆ ☽✶♀ ♀✶♆
- excellent time to refine and restock your shop display today
- improve your digestive system by drinking bitter teas

THU 29   voc from 6:19 am to 10:36 am ingress into Aries ♈   fire/ fruit/ protein

☽✶☿ ☽✶♇ ☽△⚷ ☽☌♈ ☽☌♃ ☿☌♀
- avoid alcohol and stimulants to prevent headaches and migraines
- perfect day for a nurturing foot soak and pedicure

FRI 30   waxing Moon in Aries ♈   fire/ fruit/ protein

☽□☉   ☽⚹♂   ☽♂♄

• all things nourishing and regenerative for body and mind are beneficial
• good days for hair colouring and streaks, shorter application time

Mercury ☿ retrograde until 18 Jan.

SAT 31   voc from 12:42 pm to 5:08 pm ingress into Taurus ♉   earth/ root/ salt

☽⚹♄   ☽□♃   ☽□♀   ☽□♆   ☽□♆   ☽♂♉

• beware of impulsiveness and overindulgence tonight
• the new year brings what you bring to the new year

New Year's Eve

SUN 1   waxing Moon in Taurus ♉   earth/ root/ salt

☽△☉   ☽♂♌   ☽♂♅   ♀♂♆

• excellent time to think about how you can make the most of the year ahead
• we at Moontime Diary wish you a healthy and successful Year 2023

New Year's Day

☉ rise 8:05 am

*"What you think about and what you thank about,
you will bring about."*

John Demartini

M	T	W	T	F	S	S	
D				1	2	3	4	◗
E	5	6	7	8	9	10	11	○
C	12	13	14	15	16	17	18	◐
	19	20	21	22	23	24	25	●
	26	27	28	29	30	31		◗

M	T	W	T	F	S	S	
	30	31					1	
J	2	3	4	5	6	7	8	○
A	9	10	11	12	13	14	15	◐
N	16	17	18	19	20	21	22	●
	23	24	25	26	27	28	29	◗

M	T	W	T	F	S	S	
F			1	2	3	4	5	○
E	6	7	8	9	10	11	12	
B	13	14	15	16	17	18	19	◐
	20	21	22	23	24	25	26	●
	27	28						◗

MON 2 waxing Moon in Taurus ♉ earth/ root/ salt

☽□♄ ☽△☿ ☽⚹Ψ ☽△♇ ☉△☊ ☉□♅ ☿⚹Ψ ♀♂☾
- be aware of your own and others' needs for comfort and security
- work on projects which need persistence, structure and stability

TUE 3 voc from 2:09 am to 2:43 am ingress into Gemini ♊ air/ flower/ fat

☽⚹☾ ☽♂ ♊ ☽△♀ ☽⚹♃ ☽♂♂ ♀♂≈
- excellent day to attend to indoor flowering plants and vines
- great time to start growing sprouts for salads

Quadrantids Meteor Shower

WED 4 waxing Moon in Gemini ♊ air/ flower/ fat

☽⚹♅ ☽△♄ ♀⚹♃
- stretches and exercises for neck and shoulders have a strengthening effect
- opportune day to spend time with your siblings and friends

THU 5 voc from 0:07 am to 2:14 pm ingress into Cancer ♋ water/ leaf/ carbo

☽□Ψ ☽♂☊ ☽□♃ ☉△♅
- higher retention of fluids, good absorption and use of carbohydrates, weight gain
- avoid paint solvents and paint strip jobs

FRI   **6**   full Moon in Cancer ♋ 11:07 pm 16° 21′   water/ leaf/ carbo

☽✶♌   ☽□♄   ☽✶♅   ☽☌☉

• great evening for a full Moon ritual read more about Moon in Cancer on page 33

• favourable day to focus on home and family

SAT   **7**   waning Moon in Cancer ♋ voc from 10:22 pm   water/ leaf/ carbo

☽☌☿   ☽△♆   ☽☌♇   ☉☌☿

• improve your digestive system with bitter tasting teas or 'Swedish Bitters'

• eat light and leafy meals today

SUN   **8**   voc to 2:39 am ingress into Leo ♌   fire/ fruit/ protein

☽☌☽   ☽☌♌   ☽△♃   ☽☌♀   ☽✶♂   ☿△♅   ☾☌♌

• good time for any creatively inspired endeavour or performance

• avoid anything troubling or irritating to the heart

"Leaders think and talk about the solutions.
Followers think and talk about the problems."

Brian Tracy 5 January 1944

	M	T	W	T	F	S	S		
D					1	2	3	4	☽
E	5	6	7	8	9	10	11		○
C	12	13	14	15	16	17	18		☽
	19	20	21	22	23	24	25		●
	26	27	28	29	30	31			☽

	M	T	W	T	F	S	S	
		30	31				1	
J	2	3	4	5	6	7	8	○
A								
N	9	10	11	12	13	14	15	☽
	16	17	18	19	20	21	22	●
	23	24	25	26	27	28	29	☽

	M	T	W	T	F	S	S	
			1	2	3	4	5	○
F	6	7	8	9	10	11	12	
E	13	14	15	16	17	18	19	☽
B	20	21	22	23	24	25	26	●
	27	28						☽

MON 9 waning Moon in Leo ♌ fire/ fruit/ protein

)□♌)△♏)□♅ ♀△♂
• a back massage is wonderfully relaxing today
• good day for hair cuts, colouring and streaks

TUE 10 voc from 1:52 am to 3:14 pm ingress into Virgo ♍ earth/ root/ salt

)☍♄)♂♍
• deep cleansing skin and hair treatments are very effective today
• excellent time to make yourself and others feel special

WED 11 waning Moon in Virgo ♍ earth/ root/ salt

)□♂)△♐)△☿)△♅ ☿□♐ ♀□♌
• take care of private mail, email and messages
• great day to focus, analyse and structure

THU 12 waning Moon in Virgo ♍ voc from 11:06 pm earth/ root/ salt

)△☉)☍♆)△♇ ♀⚹♏
• favourable days for maintenance and sorting jobs
• good time for bookkeeping

FRI 13 voc to 2:56 am ingress into Libra ♎ air/ flower/ fat

☽☌♎ ☽⚹⚸ ☽☍♃ ☽△♂ ☽□☿ ☉⚹♆ ☿△☊

• go for a relaxing walk with your partner, family or friends
• good day for consolidating business networks

Mars ♂ direct

SAT 14 waning Moon in Libra ♎ air/ flower/ fat

☽☍⚷ ☽△♀

• great for projects requiring team work and co-operation
• excellent time to beautify your surroundings

SUN 15 voc from 8:39 am to 12:08 pm ingress into Scorpio ♏ water/ leaf/ carbo

☽△♄ ☽□☉ ☽□♇ ☽☌♏ ☽□⚸ ♀□♅

• favourable evening to detoxify in the sauna or have a hot Lavender bath
• drink teas that support the kidneys, e.g. Stinging Nettle

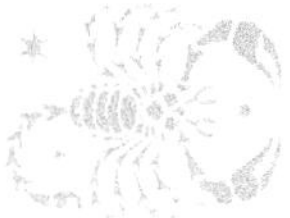

*"Smart people learn from everything and everyone.
Average people learn from their experiences.
Stupid people already have all the answers."*

Socrates

DEC	M	T	W	T	F	S	S	
				1	2	3	4	◗
	5	6	7	8	9	10	11	○
	12	13	14	15	16	17	18	◖
	19	20	21	22	23	24	25	●
	26	27	28	29	30	31		◗

JAN	M	T	W	T	F	S	S	
	30	31					1	
	2	3	4	5	6	7	8	○
	9	10	11	12	13	14	15	◖
	16	17	18	19	20	21	22	●
	23	24	25	26	27	28	29	◗

FEB	M	T	W	T	F	S	S	
			1	2	3	4	5	○
	6	7	8	9	10	11	12	
	13	14	15	16	17	18	19	◖
	20	21	22	23	24	25	26	●
	27	28						◗

MON 16 · waning Moon in Scorpio ♏ · water/ leaf/ carbo

☽✶☿ ☽☍♌ ☽☍♅ ☽□♀
- a coffee body scrub helps to firm and tighten your skin
- an intense day, nourish and soothe your soul

TUE 17 · voc from 2:26 pm to 5:32 pm ingress into Sagittarius ♐ · fire/ fruit/ protein

☽△♆ ☽□♄ ☽✶☉ ☽✶♆ ☽♂♐ ☽△☾ ☽△♃
- a lymphatic drainage massage is very beneficial
- eat light and simple meals today

WED 18 · waning Moon in Sagittarius ♐ · fire/ fruit/ protein

☽♂♂ ☽△☾ ☉♂♆
- good day to clean windows and mirrors and tiles
- dry brush your skin to remove old skin cells

THU 19 · voc from 10:08 am to 7:11 pm ingress into Capricorn ♑ · fire/ fruit/ protein

☽✶♀ ☽□♆ ☽✶♄ ☽♂♑
- good time for a spontaneous outing to meet friends and new people
- excellent days to set timber fence posts and install wooden floors

Mercury ☿ direct

☽Moon ☉Sun ☿Mercury ♀Venus ♂Mars ♃Jupiter ♄Saturn ♅Uranus ♆Neptune ♇Pluto ⚷Chiron
☊North Node ☾Lilth ♂Conjunction, Ingress ✶Sextile □Square ☍Opposition △Trine (page 46)

FRI **20** waning Moon in Capricorn ♑   earth/ root/ salt

☽□♃ ☽☌☿ ☽△♅ ☽□♂ ☽△♆ ☉☌≈
- best days of the year to harvest timber for building purposes, until new moon tomorrow
- excellent for earth works, paving and rendering

SAT **21** voc from 3:51 pm to 6:28 pm into Aquarius ≈ new Moon 8:53 pm 1° ≈ 32'

☽✶♆ ☽☌♆ ☽☌≈ ☽☍♄ ☽☌☉ ☉☍♄
- favourable time for sorting out and letting go of things you don't need any more
- read more about Sun and Moon in Aquarius on page 23

SUN **22** waxing Moon in Aquarius ≈   air/ flower/ fat

☽✶♃ ☽△♂ ☽□♄ ☽✶♄ ☽□♅ ☿△♄ ♀☌♄
- great time to do do something inspiring tonight like stargazing
- brainstorm, take note of and collect good ideas today

Chinese New Year

'The ability to read, write and analyse, the confidence to stand up and demand justice and equality; the qualifications and connections to get your foot in that door and take your seat at that table   all that starts with education."   Michelle Obama, 17 January 1964

	M	T	W	T	F	S	S
					1	2	3	4
D E C	5	6	7	8	9	10	11
	12	13	14	15	16	17	18
	19	20	21	22	23	24	25
	26	27	28	29	30	31	

	M	T	W	T	F	S	S
	30	31					1
J A N	2	3	4	5	6	7	8
	9	10	11	12	13	14	15
	16	17	18	19	20	21	22
	23	24	25	26	27	28	29

	M	T	W	T	F	S	S
			1	2	3	4	5
F E B	6	7	8	9	10	11	12
	13	14	15	16	17	18	19
	20	21	22	23	24	25	26
	27	28					

MON 23   voc from 10:18 am to 5:35 pm ingress into Pisces ♓   water/ leaf/ carbo

☽♂♄   ☽♂♀   ☽♂♓

• analytical thinking helps to structure your plans
• favourable time to pursue online endeavours

Uranus ♅ direct

TUE 24   waxing Moon in Pisces ♓   water/ leaf/ carbo

☽□♂   ☽⚹♌   ☽⚹☿   ☽⚹♅

• excellent day to refine and restock your shop display
• water, fertilise and tend to your indoor plants

International Day of Education

WED 25   voc from 4:11 pm to 6:47 pm ingress into Aries ♈   fire/ fruit/ protein

☽♂♆   ☽⚹♅   ☽♂♈   ☽△⚸   ☉⚹♃

• avoid haircuts and washing hair, encourages dandruff
• a foot reflexology massage is invigorating today

THU 26   waxing Moon in Aries ♈   fire/ fruit/ protein

☽♂♃   ☽⚹☉   ☽⚹♂   ☽□☿   ☽♂⚷

• all things nourishing and regenerative for body and mind are beneficial
• great day for a spontaneous outing

FRI   **27**   voc from 9:00 pm to 11:42 pm ingress into Taurus ♉   earth/ root/ salt

☽✶♄ ☽☐♆ ☽♂♉ ☿☐♀ ♀♂♓
- avoid alcohol and stimulants to prevent headaches and migraines
- relax your eyes under warm Chamomile tea bags

SAT   **28**   waxing Moon in Taurus ♉   earth/ root/ salt

☽✶♀ ☽☐♁ ☽☐☉ ☽♂♌
- good day to think out of the box, be inventive and resourceful
- be aware of your and others' need for comfort and security

SUN   **29**   waxing Moon in Taurus ♉   earth/ root/ salt

☽△☿ ☽♂♅ ☽✶♆ ☉☐♌
- be easy on your throat and voice, avoid drafts and noisy areas
- great time to practise any desirable skills

"You have to know what sparks the light in you so that you, in your own way, can illuminate the world."

Oprah Winfrey , 29 January 1954

	M	T	W	T	F	S	S	
					1	2	3	4 ☽
D	5	6	7	8	9	10	11	○
E	12	13	14	15	16	17	18	☽
C	19	20	21	22	23	24	25	●
	26	27	28	29	30	31		☽

	M	T	W	T	F	S	S	
	30	31					1	
J	2	3	4	5	6	7	8	○
A	9	10	11	12	13	14	15	☽
N	16	17	18	19	20	21	22	●
	23	24	25	26	27	28	29	☽

	M	T	W	T	F	S	S	
			1	2	3	4	5	○
F	6	7	8	9	10	11	12	
E	13	14	15	16	17	18	19	☽
B	20	21	22	23	24	25	26	●
	27	28						☽

MON 30   voc from 5:51 am to 8:34 am ingress into Gemini ♊   air/ flower/ fat

☽□♄ ☽△♆ ☽♂♊ ☽⚹♆ ☽□♀ ☽⚹♃ ☉△♂ ☿△♅
- stretches and exercise for shoulders have a strengthening effect
- avoid paint solvents and paint strip jobs

Look for Mercury low in the eastern sky just before sunrise

TUE 31   waxing Moon in Gemini ♊   air/ flower/ fat

☽♂♂ ☽△☉ ☽⚹♄
- good time to develop a product or advertising campaign
- great day for socialising and meeting new people

WED 1   voc from 11: 57 am to 8:11 pm ingress into Cancer ♋   water/ leaf/ carbo

☽□♆ ☽△♄ ☽♂♋ ☉⚹♄
- practice breathing, singing and playing music
- start growing sprouts for salads

Imbolc (see page 13)

THU 2   waxing Moon in Cancer ♋   water/ leaf/ carbo

☽□♃ ☽△♀ ☽⚹♌ ☽□♄ ♀♌
- improve your digestive system by drinking bitter teas for liver, stomach and bile flow
- nurture and spend time with loved ones

FRI   **3**   waxing Moon in Cancer ♋   water/ leaf/ carbo

☽⚹♅ ☽⚼☿ ☽△♆
- water, fertilise indoor plants with liquid seaweed
- good day to potter around the home and kitchen

SAT   **4**   voc from 6:18 am to 8:48 am ingress into Leo ♌   fire/ fruit/ protein

☽⚼♆ ☽♂♌ ☽♂⚶ ☽△♃ ☉□♅
- nourishing and regenerative cosmetics are very effective today
- fresh fruit is especially nutritious now

SUN   **5**   full Moon in Leo ♌ 6:28 pm 16° 40'   fire/ fruit/ protein

☽□♌ ☽⚹♂ ☽△⚶ ☽□♅ ☽⚼☉ ♀□♂
- great evening for a full Moon ritual, read more about Moon in Leo on page 35
- all creative and fun endeavours are favoured now

"There is no gate, no lock, no bolt that you can set upon the freedom of my mind."

Virginia Woolf 25 January 1882

	M	T	W	T	F	S	S			M	T	W	T	F	S	S			M	T	W	T	F	S	S	
	30	31					1					1	2	3	4	5	○			1	2	3	4	5	
J	2	3	4	5	6	7	8	○	F	6	7	8	9	10	11	12		M	6	7	8	9	10	11	12	○
A	9	10	11	12	13	14	15	☾	E	13	14	15	16	17	18	19	☾	A	13	14	15	16	17	18	19	☾
N	16	17	18	19	20	21	22	●	B	20	21	22	23	24	25	26	●	R	20	21	22	23	24	25	26	●
	23	24	25	26	27	28	29	☽		27	28						☽		27	28	29	30	31			☽

MON 6   voc from 2:15 pm to 9:13 pm ingress into Virgo ♍   earth/ root/ salt

☽☌♄ ☽☌♍ ☿⚹♆
- a back massage is wonderfully relaxing today
- good days for haircuts, colouring and streaks

TUE 7   waning Moon in Virgo ♍   earth/ root/ salt

☽△♌ ☽□♂
- perfect days for working on home, building and renovating projects
- time to focus on your health and daily routine

WED 8   waning Moon in Virgo ♍   earth/ root/ salt

☽☍♀ ☽△♅ ☽☍♆ ♀⚹♅
- good time to take care of private email and correspondence
- great day for bookkeeping and administrative jobs

THU 9   voc from 6:39 am to 8:46 am ingress into Libra ♎   air/ flower/ fat

☽△☿ ☽△♆ ☽☌♎ ☽⚹⚸
- a very favourable opportunity for any communication and diplomatic endeavour
- excellent time to beautify your surroundings

FRI 10   waning Moon in Libra ♎   air/ flower/ fat

☽☍♃   ☽△♂   ☽☍♄   ☿♂♆
- drink teas that support the kidneys, e.g. Stinging Nettle
- painting jobs turn out well

SAT 11   voc from 4:41 pm to 6:34 pm ingress into Scorpio ♏   water/ leaf/ carbo

☽△☉   ☽△♄   ☽☐♀   ☽♂♏   ☽☐☿   ☿♂♒   ♂⚹♄
- great day for projects requiring team work and cooperation
- good time to treat mould until next new Moon

Day of Women and Girls in Science

SUN 12   waning Moon in Scorpio ♏   water/ leaf/ carbo

☽☐♆   ☽☍♌   ☽☍♅
- good day to start treating warts and calluses (until next new Moon)
- a coffee scrub tightens your skin and helps repair sun damage

"I am so lucky.
I have such a great support system.
All I have to do is run."

Cathy Freeman, 16 February 1973

	M	T	W	T	F	S	S
J	30	31					1
A	2	3	4	5	6	7	8
N	9	10	11	12	13	14	15
	16	17	18	19	20	21	22
	23	24	25	26	27	28	29

	M	T	W	T	F	S	S
			1	2	3	4	5
F	6	7	8	9	10	11	12
E	13	14	15	16	17	18	19
B	20	21	22	23	24	25	26
	27	28					

	M	T	W	T	F	S	S
			1	2	3	4	5
M	6	7	8	9	10	11	12
A	13	14	15	16	17	18	19
R	20	21	22	23	24	25	26
	27	28	29	30	31		

MON 13 waning Moon in Scorpio ♏ voc from 11:51 pm — water/ leaf/ carbo

☽△♀ ☽△♆ ☽□☉ ☽□♄ ☽✱♇

• appreciate yourself with a nourishing Lavender bath tonight
• improve your digestive system by taking 'Swedish Bitters'

World Radio Day

TUE 14 voc to 1:30 am ingress into Sagittarius ♐ — fire/ fruit/ protein

☽☌♐ ☽✱☿ ☽△⚸ ☽△♃ ☿☍⚸

• great day for dry brushing your skin to remove old skin cells
• go for a relaxing walk with your partner, family or friends

Valentine's Day

WED 15 waning Moon in Sagittarius ♐ — fire/ fruit/ protein

☽△⚷ ☽☍♂ ☽□♆ ☽□♀ ♀☌♆

• excellent day for cleaning windows, mirrors and tiles
• cleansing and toning cosmetics are very effective

THU 16 voc from 1:05 am to 4:59 am ingress into Capricorn ♑ — earth/ root/ salt

☽✱☉ ☽✱♄ ☽☌♑ ☽△☊ ☽□♃ ☉☌♄ ☿□☊

• great opportunity to patiently practise any desired skills
• good time to air your bedding

☽Moon ☉Sun ☿Mercury ♀Venus ♂Mars ♃Jupiter ♄Saturn ♅Uranus ♆Neptune ♇Pluto ⚷Chiron
☊North Node ⚸Lilth ☌Conjunction, Ingress ✱Sextile □Square ☍Opposition △Trine (page 46)

FRI 17 waning Moon in Capricorn ♑   earth/ root/ salt

☽□♄ ☽△♅ ☽⚹♆
- avoid stress on bones and joints, particularly knees
- great day for earthworks, paving and rendering

SAT 18 voc from 4:17 am to 5:34 am ingress into Aquarius ♒   air/ flower/ fat

☽⚹♀ ☽♂♆ ☽♂♒ ☽♂☋ ☽□♌ ☽⚹♃ ☽♂☿ ☉♂♓ ☿⚹♃
- cleansing packs for hair, skin and nails bring great results
- great day for paint and glue jobs around the house

SUN 19 waning Moon in Aquarius ♒   air/ flower/ fat

☽⚹♄ ☽□♅ ☽△♂ ♀⚹♆
- excellent time to consolidate projects, sort out and release surplus
- good day for deep cleansing skin and hair

"You may think I am small, but
I have a universe inside my mind."

Yoko Ono, 18 February 1933

	M	T	W	T	F	S	S			M	T	W	T	F	S	S			M	T	W	T	F	S	S	
	30	31					1					1	2	3	4	5	○				1	2	3	4	5	
J	2	3	4	5	6	7	8	○	F	6	7	8	9	10	11	12		M	6	7	8	9	10	11	12	○
A	9	10	11	12	13	14	15	◐	E	13	14	15	16	17	18	19	◐	A	13	14	15	16	17	18	19	◐
N	16	17	18	19	20	21	22	●	B	20	21	22	23	24	25	26	●	R	20	21	22	23	24	25	26	●
	23	24	25	26	27	28	29	◑		27	28						◑		27	28	29	30	31			◑

MON 20   voc from 2:00 am to 4:55 am ingress into Pisces ♓ new Moon 7:05 am 1° 22′

☽☌♄ ☽☌♅ ☽☌☉ ☽⚹♌ ☿⚹♃ ♀☌♈

• great day to set new goals and work out steps to implement
• for more info about Sun and Moon in Pisces see page 25
World Day of Social Justice

TUE 21   waxing Moon in Pisces ♓ water/ leaf/ carbo

☽⚹♅ ☽□♂ ☽☌♆ ☿□♅

• excellent evening to watch a romantic or visionary movie
• great time to restock your shop display

WED 22   voc from 4:05 am to 5:13 am ingress into Aries ♈ fire/ fruit/ protein

☽⚹♆ ☽☌♈ ☽☌♀ ☽△♌ ☽☌♃ ☿△♂

• all things nourishing and regenerative for body and mind are beneficial
• good day for a pioneering outing

THU 23   waxing Moon in Aries ♈ fire/ fruit/ protein

☽☌♌ ☽⚹♂ ☽⚹☿

• eyes benefit from relaxation under cotton wool pads soaked in almond milk
• excellent day for hair colouring and streaks

FRI 24   voc from 7:21 am to 8:28 am ingress into Taurus ♉   earth/ root/ salt

☽⚹♄ ☽☐♆ ☽♂♉ ☽☐⚸ ☽♂♌ ☽⚹☉ ☉⚹♌ ♀△⚸

- prepare and eat root vegetables, use less salt today
- favourable time for focusing on dental hygiene

SAT 25   waxing Moon in Taurus ♉   earth/ root/ salt

☽♂♅

- be gentle with your voice and throat, for sore throats gargle with sage or chamomile
- be aware of your own as well as others' needs for comfort and security

SUN 26   voc from 2:42 pm to 3:47 pm ingress into Gemini ♊   air/ flower/ fat

☽☐☿ ☽⚹♆ ☽☐♄ ☽△♆ ☽♂♊

- healing and soothing baths, creams and packs are particularly effective
- a relaxing neck and shoulder massage is very beneficent today

"They say a person needs just three things to be truly happy in this world: something to love, something to do and something to hope for."

Thomas Edward Bodett, 23 February 1955

	M	T	W	T	F	S	S	
	30	31					1	
J	2	3	4	5	6	7	8	○
A	9	10	11	12	13	14	15	◗
N	16	17	18	19	20	21	22	●
	23	24	25	26	27	28	29	◖

	M	T	W	T	F	S	S	
			1	2	3	4	5	○
F	6	7	8	9	10	11	12	
E	13	14	15	16	17	18	19	◗
B	20	21	22	23	24	25	26	●
	27	28						◖

	M	T	W	T	F	S	S	
			1	2	3	4	5	
M	6	7	8	9	10	11	12	○
A	13	14	15	16	17	18	19	◗
R	20	21	22	23	24	25	26	●
	27	28	29	30	31			◖

MON 27   waxing Moon in Gemini ♊   air/ flower/ fat

☽⚹⚷ ☽□☉ ☽⚹♀ ☽⚹♃ ☽⚹♅

- excellent days for communication and networking
- start growing sprouts for salads

TUE 28   waxing Moon in Gemini ♊   air/ flower/ fat

☽♂♂ ☽□♆ ☽△☿

- gentle stretches and exercise for shoulders and arms have a strengthening effect
- avoid paint solvents and paint stripping jobs

WED 1   voc from 1:06 am to 2:39 am ingress into Cancer ♋   water/ leaf/ carbo

☽△♄ ☽♂♋ ☽⚹☊ ☊□⚷

- good day to spend time with family and friends
- favourable time to pursue online marketing

Zero Discrimination Day

THU 2   waxing Moon in Cancer ♋   water/ leaf/ carbo

☽△☉ ☽□♀ ☽□♃ ☽□♂ ☽⚹♅ ☿♂♄ ☽♂⚷ ♀♂♃

- fresh leafy salads, herbs and sprouts are very nutritious
- avoid washing hair, it becomes unruly

☽Moon ☉Sun ☿Mercury ♀Venus ♂Mars ♃Jupiter ♄Saturn ♅Uranus ♆Neptune ♇Pluto ⚷Chiron ☊North Node ⚸Lilth ♂Conjunction, Ingress ⚹Sextile □Square ☍Opposition △Trine (page 46)

FRI 3   voc from 2:22 pm to 3:15 pm ingress into Leo ♌   fire/ fruit/ protein

☽△♆ ☽⚌♆ ☽ ♂♌ ♀♂♊
- anything nourishing and regenerative to the heart and back is very effective
- nourishing and regenerative cosmetics are very beneficient today

World Wildlife Day

SAT 4   waxing Moon in Leo ♌   fire/ fruit/ protein

☽□♌ ☽♂☽ ☽△♃ ☽△♊ ☽△♀ ☽□♅
- avoid removal of unwanted body hair, strong re-growth
- great day for hair cuts, colouring and streaks

SUN 5   waxing Moon in Leo ♌   fire/ fruit/ protein

☽✳♂ ☿✳♌
- excellent day to make yourself and others feel special
- all creative and fun endeavours are favoured now

"In times of pain, when the future is too terrifying to contemplate and the past too painful to remember, I have learned to pay attention to right now. The precise moment I was in was always the only safe place for me." Julia Cameron, 4 March 1948

M	T	W	T	F	S	S	
		1	2	3	4	_5_	○
6	7	8	9	10	11	12	
_13_	14	15	16	17	18	19	◐
_20_	21	22	23	24	25	26	●
_27_	28						☽

FEB

M	T	W	T	F	S	S	
		1	2	3	4	5	
6	_7_	8	9	10	11	12	○
13	14	_15_	16	17	18	19	◐
20	_21_	22	23	24	25	26	●
27	28	_29_	30	31			☽

MAR

M	T	W	T	F	S	S	
31					1	2	
3	4	5	_6_	7	8	9	○
10	11	12	_13_	14	15	16	◐
17	18	19	_20_	21	22	23	●
24	25	26	_27_	28	29	30	☽

APR

MON 6 voc from 3:18 am to 3:38 am ingress into Virgo ♍ earth/ root/ salt

☽☍♄ ☽♂♍ ☽△♌ ☽☍☿ ☉⚹♅
• great evening for a full Moon ritual, read more about Moon in Virgo on page 37
• emphasis on health issues, work and daily routines
Labour Day (WA)

TUE 7 full Moon in Virgo ♍ 12:40 pm 16° 40′ earth/ root/ salt

☽△♅ ☽☍☉ ☽□♂ ♄♂♓
• today can be an intense day, try and transform your thoughts into insights
• try to avoid operations and vaccinations today

WED 8 voc from 2:07 pm to 2:43 pm ingress into Libra ♎ air/ flower/ fat

☽☍♆ ☽△♇ ☽♂♎
• cleansing and toning cosmetics are very effective
• good day for bookkeeping
International Women's Day

THU 9 waning Moon in Libra ♎ air/ flower/ fat

☽⚹⚸ ☽☍♃ ☽☍⚷
• favourable day for cleaning shoes and dusting
• excellent time to beautify your surroundings

☽Moon ☉Sun ☿Mercury ♀Venus ♂Mars ♃Jupiter ♄Saturn ♅Uranus ♆Neptune ♇Pluto ⚷Chiron
♌North Node ⚸Lilth ♂Conjunction, Ingress ⚹Sextile □Square ☍Opposition △Trine (page 46)

FRI 10 waning Moon in Libra ♎ voc from 11:36 pm   air/ flower/ fat

☾☌♀ ☾△♂ ☾□♆
• drink teas that support the kidneys, e.g. Stinging Nettle
• painting jobs turn out well

SAT 11 voc to 0:05 am ingress into Scorpio ♏   water/ leaf/ carbo

☾☌♏ ☾△♄ ☾☌♌ ☾□☽ ☿⚹♓ ♀⚹♂
• support your digestive system by taking 'Swedish Bitters'
• care for prickly plants today

SUN 12 waning Moon in Scorpio ♏   water/ leaf/ carbo

☾☌♓ ☾△☿ ☾△☉ ☾△♆ ♃☌♅
• good day to start treating warts and calluses (until next new Moon)
• appreciate yourself and indulge in a nurturing Lavender bath

*"Be careful with what seeds you allow
to take root in the garden of your heart.
Not all seeds bear good fruit."*

	M	T	W	T	F	S	S	
			1	2	3	4	5	○
F	6	7	8	9	10	11	12	
E	13	14	15	16	17	18	19	◐
B	20	21	22	23	24	25	26	●
	27	28						◗

	M	T	W	T	F	S	S	
			1	2	3	4	5	
M	6	7	8	9	10	11	12	○
A	13	14	15	16	17	18	19	◐
R	20	21	22	23	24	25	26	●
	27	28	29	30	31			◗

	M	T	W	T	F	S	S	
	31					1	2	
A	3	4	5	6	7	8	9	○
P	10	11	12	13	14	15	16	◐
R	17	18	19	20	21	22	23	●
	24	25	26	27	28	29	30	◗

MON 13   voc from 6:58 am to 7:20 am ingress into Sagittarius ♐   fire/ fruit/ protein

☽✶♆ ☽☌♐ ☽☐♄ ☽△☾
• a great day for dry brushing your skin to remove old skin cells
• good time to air bedding

TUE 14   waning Moon in Sagittarius ♐   fire/ fruit/ protein

☽△☾ ☽△♃ ☽☐☿ ♂☐♆
• great day for cleaning windows, mirrors and tiles
• excellent opportunity for a spontaneous outing

WED 15   voc from 8:49 am to 12:05 pm ingress into Capricorn ♑   earth/ root/ salt

☽☐☉ ☽☐♆ ☽☍♂ ☽△♀ ☽☌♑ ☽✶♄ ☽△☊ ☉☌♆
• don't overexert yourself, rather go for a relaxing walk
• avoid stress on bones and joints, particularly knees

THU 16   waning Moon in Capricorn ♑   earth/ root/ salt

☽☐☾ ☽☐♃ ☽△♅ ☉☐♂ ☿☌♆ ♀☐♆ ☽☌♅
• cleansing packs for hair, skin and nails show great results
• good day for earth works, paving and rendering

FRI 17 voc from 2:13 pm to 2:24 pm ingress into Aquarius ♒   air/ flower/ fat

☽✶♆ ☽✶☿ ☽✶☉ ☽♂♆ ☽♂♒ ☽□♀ ☽□♌ ☉♂☿ ☿□♂ ♀✶♄
- excellent for oiling, polishing wooden floors and furniture
- a gentle leg massage conditions the venous system

St. Patrick's Day

SAT 18 waning Moon in Aquarius ♒   air/ flower/ fat

☽♂♁ ☽✶♐ ☽✶♃ ☽□♅
- great for paint and glue jobs around the house
- favourable time for pest and weed control

SUN 19 voc from 10:32 am to 3:11 pm ingress into Pisces ♓   water/ leaf/ carbo

☽△♂ ☽♂♓ ☽♂♄ ☽✶♀ ☽✶♌ ☿✶♆ ☽♂♈
- good for sorting out and getting rid of things you don't need any more
- excellent time to connect with friends and meet new people

"I've always said I want a farmer, not a hunter.
Hunters go for the kill and they move on.
A farmer nurtures; he watches things grow."

       Eva Longoria, 15 March 1975

	M	T	W	T	F	S	S	
FEB			1	2	3	4	<u>5</u>	○
	6	7	8	9	10	11	12	
	<u>13</u>	14	15	16	17	18	19	◐
	<u>20</u>	21	22	23	24	25	26	●
	<u>27</u>	28						☽

	M	T	W	T	F	S	S	
MAR			1	2	3	4	5	
	6	<u>7</u>	8	9	10	11	12	○
	13	14	<u>15</u>	16	17	18	19	◐
	<u>20</u>	<u>21</u>	22	23	24	25	26	●
	27	28	<u>29</u>	30	31			☽

	M	T	W	T	F	S	S	
APR	31					1	2	
	3	4	5	<u>6</u>	7	8	9	○
	10	11	12	<u>13</u>	14	15	16	◐
	17	18	19	<u>20</u>	21	22	23	●
	24	25	26	<u>27</u>	28	29	30	☽

MON 20 waning Moon in Pisces ♓︎ water/ leaf/ carbo

☾⚹⛢ ☉⚹♆ ☉♂♈︎ ♀♂♌

• a relaxing foot massage or reflexology is very beneficial today
• excellent day for a lymphatic drainage massage
Spring Equinox, Ostara (see page 13)

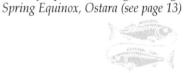

TUE 21 voc 3:57 pm to 4:01 pm ingress into Aries ♈︎ new Moon ♈︎ 5:22 pm 0° ♈︎ 49′

☾♂♆ ☾□♂ ☾⚹♆ ☾♂♈︎ ☾♂☉

• improve your digestive system by taking 'Swedish Bitters'
• for more info about Sun and Moon in Aries see page 27
International Day for the Elimination of Racial Discrimination
International Day of Forests

WED 22 waxing Moon in Aries ♈︎ fire/ fruit/ protein

☾♂☿ ☾△₵ ☾♂⚷ ☾♂♃

• excellent day for initiating changes and new beginnings
• avoid stimulants to prevent headaches and migraines
World Water Day

THU 23 voc from 5:12 pm to 6:41 pm ingress into Taurus ♉︎ earth/ root/ salt

☾⚹♂ ☾□♆ ☾♂♉︎ ☾⚹♄ ☿△₵ ♀□₵

• all things nourishing and regenerative for body and mind are beneficial
• moisturise skin to prevent dehydration

☾Moon ☉Sun ☿Mercury ♀Venus ♂Mars ♃Jupiter ♄Saturn ⛢Uranus ♆Neptune ♇Pluto ⚷Chiron
☊North Node ₵Lilth ♂Conjunction, Ingress ⚹Sextile □Square ☍Opposition △Trine (page 46)

FRI 24 waxing Moon in Taurus ♉ earth/ root/ salt

☽☌♌ ☽□⚷ ☽☌♀ ☽☌♅ ♆☌♒
• be aware of your and others' need for comfort and security
• work on projects which need endurance and vision

SAT 25 waxing Moon in Taurus ♉ voc from 4:18 pm earth/ root/ salt

☽⚹♆ ♂☌♋
• prepare and eat root vegetables, use less salt today
• great time to practise any desirable skills
Earth Hour Day

SUN 26 voc to 0:41 am ingress into Gemini ♊ air/ flower/ fat

☽☌♊ ☽△♆ ☽□♄ ☽⚹☉ ☽⚹⚷ ☿☌♃
• breathing and gentle singing exercises are beneficial for your lungs
• favourable day to visit a powerful place in nature and meditate

"Many of the qualities that come so effortlessly to dogs
- loyalty, devotion, selflessness, unflagging optimism,
unqualified love - can be elusive to humans."
John Grogan, 20 March 1957

M	T	W	T	F	S	S	
		1	2	3	4	<u>5</u>	○
F	6	7	8	9	10	11	12
E	<u>13</u>	14	15	16	17	18	19	◖
B	<u>20</u>	21	22	23	24	25	26	●
	<u>27</u>	28						◗

M	T	W	T	F	S	S	
		1	2	3	4	5	
M	6	<u>7</u>	8	9	10	11	12	○
A	13	14	<u>15</u>	16	17	18	19	◖
R	20	<u>21</u>	22	23	24	25	26	●
	27	28	<u>29</u>	30	31			◗

M	T	W	T	F	S	S	
	31					1	2
A	3	4	5	<u>6</u>	7	8	9	○
P	10	11	12	<u>13</u>	14	15	16	◖
R	17	18	19	<u>20</u>	21	22	23	●
	24	25	26	<u>27</u>	28	29	30	◗

MON 27   waxing Moon in Gemini ♊   air/ flower/ fat

☽﹡♄ ☽﹡☿ ☽﹡♃
• great for socialising, spend time with your siblings and friends
• good time to develop a product or advertising campaign

TUE 28   voc from 1:38 am to 10:21 am ingress into Cancer ♋   water/ leaf/ carbo

☽□♆ ☽♂♋ ☽♂♂ ☽△♄ ☽﹡☊ ☿♂♃
• favourable days for communication and business negotiations
• great time to potter around the home and kitchen

WED 29   waxing Moon in Cancer ♋   water/ leaf/ carbo

☽□☉ ☽﹡♀ ☽□♄ ☽﹡♅ ☽□♃ ☉△♵
• excellent opportunity to nurture yourself and your loved ones
• improve your digestive system by eating bitter herbs

THU 30   voc from 1:45 pm to 10:30 pm ingress into Leo ♌   fire/ fruit/ protein

☽□☿ ☽△♆ ☽♂♌ ☽♂♆ ♀♂♅ ♂△♄
• fresh leafy salads, herbs and sprouts are most nutritious now
• avoid cleaning windows, mirrors and tiles

FRI **31** waxing Moon in Leo ♌ fire/ fruit/ protein

☽□♌ ☽♂☾ ☽△☉
• anything nourishing and regenerative to the heart and back is beneficial now
• great day for hair cuts, colouring and streaks
Nowruz, Persian New Year

SAT **1** waxing Moon in Leo ♌ fire/ fruit/ protein

☽△♂ ☽□♅ ☽□♀ ☽△♃
• excellent day to make yourself and others feel special
• creative and fun endeavours are favoured now

SUN **2** voc from 6:02 am to 10:57 am ingress into Virgo ♍ earth/ root/ salt

☽△☿ ☽♂♍ ☽☍♄ ☽✶♂ ☽△♌ ♂✶♌
• eat fruit and fruiting vegetables for maximum nutritional benefit
• focus on health issues and your daily routine

"We should attempt to bring nature, houses,
and human beings together in a higher unity."

Mies van der Rohe 27 March 1886

M	T	W	T	F	S	S	
				1	2	3	4	<u>5</u>	○

	M	T	W	T	F	S	S	
F					1	2	3	4	<u>5</u>	○
E	6	7	8	9	10	11	12	
B	<u>13</u>	14	15	16	17	18	19	☾
	<u>20</u>	21	22	23	24	25	26	●
	<u>27</u>	28						☽

	M	T	W	T	F	S	S	
M			1	2	3	4	5	
A	6	<u>7</u>	8	9	10	11	12	○
R	13	14	<u>15</u>	16	17	18	19	☾
	20	<u>21</u>	22	23	24	25	26	●
	27	28	<u>29</u>	30	31			☽

	M	T	W	T	F	S	S	
	31					1	2	
A	3	4	5	<u>6</u>	7	8	9	○
P	10	11	12	<u>13</u>	14	15	16	☾
R	17	18	19	<u>20</u>	21	22	23	●
	24	25	26	<u>27</u>	28	29	30	☽

MON 3   waxing Moon in Virgo ♍   earth/ root/ salt

☽△♅ ☿♂♉ ☽□♇
- favourable day for projects requiring ingenuity and detailed work
- take care of private mail, email and messages

TUE 4   voc from 1:49 pm to 9:50 pm ingress into Libra ♎   air/ flower/ fat

☽△♀ ☽☍♆ ☽♂♎ ☽△♀
- eat high fibre root vegetables, avoid fatty and salty foods
- great for bookkeeping and administrative jobs

WED 5   waxing Moon in Libra ♎   air/ flower/ fat

☽□♂ ☽⚹⚸ ☉♂⚸ ☿⚹♄
- great evening for a full Moon ritual, read more about Moon in Libra on page 39
- good opportunity to beautify your surroundings

THU 6   full Moon in Libra ♎ 4:34 am 16° 07′ voc from 12:42 pm   air/ flower/ fat

☽☍⚸ ☽☍☉ ☽☍♃ ☿♂☊
- value and appreciate both your partner and yourself
- great evening to enjoy a hot Lavender bath

International Day of Sport for Development and Peace

FRI 7 voc to 6:29 am ingress into Scorpio ♏ water/ leaf/ carbo

☽☌♏ ☽□♇ ☽△♄ ☽☍☊ ☽☍☿ ☽△♂ ♀✶♆

- drink teas that support kidneys, e.g. Stinging Nettle
- enjoy a pleasant time with partners and friends

International Day of Reflection on the 1994 Genocide in Rwanda
World Health Day
Good Friday

SAT 8 waning Moon in Scorpio ♏ water/ leaf/ carbo

☽□⚸ ☽☍♅ ☿✶♂

- a coffee scrub helps tightens your skin and repair sun damage
- fresh leafy salads, herbs and sprouts are very nutritious

Holy Saturday

SUN 9 voc from 9:08 am to 12:56 pm ingress into Sagittarius ♐ fire/ fruit/ protein

☽△♆ ☽☍♀ ☽☌♐ ☽✶♇ ☽□♄

- don't overexert yourself; best to go for a relaxing walk
- dry brush your skin to remove old skin cells

Holy Sunday

"I think every young child can learn through any martial art. They would then learn to respect their life, respect their parents, respect their country, and respect the whole world."

Jackie Chan 7 April 1945

MAR	M	T	W	T	F	S	S	
			1	2	3	4	5	
	6	7	8	9	10	11	12	○
	13	14	15	16	17	18	19	◖
	20	21	22	23	24	25	26	●
	27	28	29	30	31			◗

APR	M	T	W	T	F	S	S	
	31					1	2	
	3	4	5	6	7	8	9	○
	10	11	12	13	14	15	16	◖
	17	18	19	20	21	22	23	●
	24	25	26	27	28	29	30	◗

MAY	M	T	W	T	F	S	S	
	1	2	3	4	5	6	7	○
	8	9	10	11	12	13	14	◖
	15	16	17	18	19	20	21	●
	22	23	24	25	26	27	28	◗
	29	30	31					

MON 10 waning Moon in Sagittarius ♐ fire/ fruit/ protein

☽△⛢ ☽△♄

- great time for meeting friends and new people
- excellent day for a spontaneous outing

Easter Monday

TUE 11 voc from 10:47 am to 5:32 pm ingress into Capricorn ♑ earth/ root/ salt

☽△☉ ☽△♃ ☽□♆ ☽♂♑ ☉♂♃ ☿□☾ ♀♂Ⅱ ☽△♅

- avoid weeding plants that spread via their root system, it encourages growth
- excellent day for cleaning windows, mirrors and tiles

Look for Mercury low in the western sky just after sunset

WED 12 waning Moon in Capricorn ♑ earth/ root/ salt

☽⚹♄ ☽△☊ ☽♂♂ ☽△☿ ☽□♄ ☽△♅

- good days for disciplined and hard work but avoid straining your knees
- favourable time for building and renovation work

THU 13 voc from 2:13 pm to 8:41 pm ingress into Aquarius ♒ air/ flower/ fat

☽□♃ ☽□☉ ☽⚹♆ ☽♂♒ ☽♂♆

- excellent day for oiling, polishing wooden floors and furniture
- focus on your dental hygiene today

FRI 14 waning Moon in Aquarius ♒ air/ flower/ fat

☽△♀ ☽□☊ ☽☍⚸ ☽□☿ ♀□♄ ♄✶☊

- good day for cleaning windows, mirrors and tiles
- favourable time for weed and pest management

SAT 15 voc from 3:15 pm to 10:56 pm ingress into Pisces ♓ water/ leaf/ carbo

☽✶⚷ ☽□♅ ☽✶♃ ☽✶☉ ☽☌♆

- great day for paint and glue jobs around the house
- good opportunity to go on a short trip

SUN 16 waning Moon in Pisces ♓ water/ leaf/ carbo

☽✶☊ ☽☌♄ ☽□♀ ☽△♂ ☽✶☿

- improve your digestive system by taking bitter herbs or 'Swedish Bitters'
- avoid haircuts and washing hair, encourages dandruff

*"If you don't like something, change it.
If you can't change it, change your attitude."*

Maya Angelou, 4 April 1928

MAR	M	T	W	T	F	S	S	
			1	2	3	4	5	
	6	7	8	9	10	11	12	○
	13	14	15	16	17	18	19	◖
	20	21	22	23	24	25	26	●
	27	28	29	30	31			◗

APR	M	T	W	T	F	S	S	
	31					1	2	
	3	4	5	6	7	8	9	○
	10	11	12	13	14	15	16	◖
	17	18	19	20	21	22	23	●
	24	25	26	27	28	29	30	◗

MAY	M	T	W	T	F	S	S	
	1	2	3	4	5	6	7	○
	8	9	10	11	12	13	14	◖
	15	16	17	18	19	20	21	●
	22	23	24	25	26	27	28	◗
	29	30	31					

MON 17   waning Moon in Pisces ♓ voc from 6:56 pm   water/ leaf/ carbo

☽✶♅ ☽♂♆
- a relaxing foot massage or reflexology is very beneficial today
- great evening for a relaxing movie

TUE 18   voc to 1:09 am ingress into Aries ♈   fire/ fruit/ protein

☽♂♈ ☽✶♆ ☽✶♀ ☽△⚸ ☽□♂
- walk barefoot in the morning dew, it is very grounding and
discharges electromagnetic pollution through the feet

WED 19   waning Moon in Aries ♈   fire/ fruit/ protein

☽♂⚸ ☽♂♃
- all things cleansing for body and mind are beneficial
- avoid stimulants to prevent headaches

THU 20   new Moon in Aries 4:12 am 29° ♈ 50′ voc 4:12 am to 4:29 am into Taurus ♉

☽♂☉ ☽♂♅ ☽□♆ ☽♂☊ ☽✶♄ ☉♂♅ ☽□♇
- cut back sick trees and hedges to encourage healthy regrowth
- for more info about Sun and Moon in Aries see page 27

Total Solar Eclipse

☽Moon ☉Sun ☿Mercury ♀Venus ♂Mars ♃Jupiter ♄Saturn ♅Uranus ♆Neptune ♇Pluto ⚷Chiron
☊North Node ⚸Lilth ♂Conjunction, Ingress ✶Sextile □Square ♂Opposition △Trine (page 46)

FRI 21 waxing Moon in Taurus ♉   earth/ root/ salt

☽□⚷ ☽⚹♂ ☽♂☿ ☽♂♅ ♀⚹⚷
- be aware of your and others' need for comfort and security
- excellent day to make new resolutions and plan ahead

SAT 22 voc from 3:40 am to 10:10 am ingress into Gemini ♊   air/ flower/ fat

☽⚹♆ ☽♂♊ ☽△♇ ☽□♄
- good day to attend to flowering plants, vines and herbs
- excellent time to fertilise the soil

Earth Day

Mercury ☿ retrograde until 15 May

Lyrids Meteor Shower

SUN 23 waxing Moon in Gemini ♊   air/ flower/ fat

☽⚹⚷ ☽♂♀ ☽⚹⚴
- breathing and gentle singing exercises are beneficial for your lungs
- great day for socialising, spend time with your family and friends

World Book and Copyright Day

"Science is organised knowledge.
Wisdom is organised life."
Immanuel Kant, 22 April 1724

	M	T	W	T	F	S	S	
						1	2	3	4	5	
M A R	6	7	8	9	10	11	12	○
	13	14	15	16	17	18	19	◐
	20	21	22	23	24	25	26	●
	27	28	29	30	31			◑

	M	T	W	T	F	S	S	
	31					1	2	
A P R	3	4	5	6	7	8	9	○
	10	11	12	13	14	15	16	◐
	17	18	19	20	21	22	23	●
	24	25	26	27	28	29	30	◑

	M	T	W	T	F	S	S	
	1	2	3	4	5	6	7	○
M A Y	8	9	10	11	12	13	14	◐
	15	16	17	18	19	20	21	●
	22	23	24	25	26	27	28	◑
	29	30	31					

MON 24 voc from 12:14 pm to 6:58 pm ingress into Cancer ♋ water/ leaf/ carbo

☽✶♃ ☽□♆ ☽☌♋ ☉☌♌ ☿✶♂
• stretches and exercise for shoulders have a strengthening effect
• great time for a spontaneous outing
International Day of Multilateralism and Diplomacy for Peace

TUE 25 waxing Moon in Cancer ♋ water/ leaf/ carbo

☽✶♌ ☽✶☉ ☽△♄ ☽✶☿ ☉✶♄ ♀✶⚷
• fresh leafy salads, herbs and sprouts are most nutritious now
• favourable day to focus on home, family and garden
Day of the Tree

WED 26 waxing Moon in Cancer ♋ voc from 11:40 pm water/ leaf/ carbo

☽☌♂ ☽□⚷ ☽✶♅ ☽□♃ ☽△♆
• avoid cutting and washing your hair today
• avoid cleaning windows, mirrors and tiles
Chernobyl Disaster Remembrance Day

THU 27 voc to 6:29 am ingress into Leo ♌ fire/ fruit/ protein

☽☌♌ ☽☍♆ ☽□♌ ☽□☉ ♂□⚷
• avoid removal of unwanted body hair, strong re-growth
• avoid anything troubling or irritating to the heart

APRIL 2023

FRI 28 waxing Moon in Leo ♌ — fire/ fruit/ protein

☽☌☿ ☽□☿ ☽△♃ ☽□♅ ☽⚹♀
• anything nourishing and regenerative to the heart and back is very effective
• good day for hair cuts (to strengthen re-growth), colouring and streaks

SAT 29 voc from 10:52 am to 6:58 pm ingress into Virgo ♍ — earth/ root/ salt

☽△♃ ☽☌♍ ♂⚹♅
• eat fruit and fruiting vegetables for maximum nutritional benefit
• all creative and fun endeavours are favoured now

SUN 30 waxing Moon in Virgo ♍ — earth/ root/ salt

☽△♌ ☽⚼♄ ☽△☉ ☽△☿ ☿□☽
• perfect day for working on home, building and renovating projects
• emphasis on health issues and daily routine matters
Beltaine (see page 13)

"It isn't where you came from.
It's where you're going that counts."
Ella Fitzgerald, 25 April 1917

M	T	W	T	F	S	S
		1	2	3	4	5
6	7	8	9	10	11	12	○
13	14	15	16	17	18	19	☾
20	21	22	23	24	25	26	●
27	28	29	30	31			☽

MAR

M	T	W	T	F	S	S
31					1	2
3	4	5	6	7	8	9	○
10	11	12	13	14	15	16	☾
17	18	19	20	21	22	23	●
24	25	26	27	28	29	30	☽

APR

M	T	W	T	F	S	S
1	2	3	4	5	6	7	○
8	9	10	11	12	13	14	☾
15	16	17	18	19	20	21	●
22	23	24	25	26	27	28	☽
29	30	31				

MAY

MAY 2023

MON 1   waxing Moon in Virgo ♍ voc from 11:52 pm   earth/ root/ salt

☽△♅ ☽⚹♂ ☽□♀ ☽☍♆ ☉♂☿
- favourable time for projects requiring ingenuity and detailed work
- opportune day to focus on practical business issues and tax

TUE 2   voc to 6:08 am ingress into Libra ♎   air/ flower/ fat

☽♂♎ ☽△♇
- accommodate your and others' need for beauty and harmony
- healing creams and ointments are very potent today

Pluto ♇ retrograde until 11 Oc

WED 3   waxing Moon in Libra ♎   air/ flower/ fat

☽⚹♐ ☽☍♅ ☽♂♂ ☉□♐
- take care of flowers, herbs and vines
- avoid diplomatic endeavours today

World Press Freedom Day

THU 4   voc from 9:16 am to 2:32 pm ingress into Scorpio ♏   water/ leaf/ carbo

☽△♀ ☽☍♃ ☽♂♏ ☽□♆ ☽☍☊ ♀□♃
- nurture and appreciate yourself, indulge in a nourishing Lavender bath
- careful, all medicines and drugs are very potent today and tomorrow

☽Moon ☉Sun ☿Mercury ♀Venus ♂Mars ♃Jupiter ♄Saturn ♅Uranus ♆Neptune ♇Pluto ⚷Chiron ☊North Node ⚸Lilth ♂Conjunction, Ingress ⚹Sextile □Square ☍Opposition △Trine (page 46)

FRI 5   full Moon in Scorpio ♏ 5:33 pm 14° 58′   water/ leaf/ carbo

☽△♄ ☽☌♀ ☽□☽ ☽☌☉ ♀✳♃

• great evening for a full Moon ritual, read more about Moon in Scorpio on page 41

• take it easy if you are pregnant

Lunar Eclipse
Wesak

SAT 6   voc from 2:37 pm to 8:03 pm ingress into Sagittarius ♐   fire/ fruit/ protein

☽☌♅ ☽△♂ ☽△♆ ☽☌♐ ☽✳♆

• a magical, magnetic time, careful what you ask for, accept gracefully what you receive

• great time to detoxify in the sauna

Eta Aquarids Meteor Shower

SUN 7   waning Moon in Sagittarius ♐   fire/ fruit/ protein

☽□♄ ☽△☽ ♀☌♋

• avoid weeding plants that spread via their root system, it encourages root growth

• don't over exert yourself, rather go for a relaxing walk

"A quality education has the power to transform societies in a single generation, provide children with the protection they need from the hazards of poverty, labour, exploitation and disease, and give them the knowledge and skills and confidence to reach their full potential."
Audrey Hepburn 4 May 1924

	M	T	W	T	F	S	S
	31					1	2
A	3	4	5	6	7	8	9	○
P	10	11	12	13	14	15	16	☽
R	17	18	19	20	21	22	23	●
	24	25	26	27	28	29	30	☽

	M	T	W	T	F	S	S
		1	2	3	4	5	6	7	○
M	8	9	10	11	12	13	14	☽
A	15	16	17	18	19	20	21	●
Y	22	23	24	25	26	27	28	☽
	29	30	31				

	M	T	W	T	F	S	S
				1	2	3	4	○
J	5	6	7	8	9	10	11	☽
U	12	13	14	15	16	17	18	●
N	19	20	21	22	23	24	25	
	26	27	28	29	30			☽

MAY 2023

MON 8   voc from 8:27 pm to 11:32 pm ingress into Capricorn ♑   earth/ root/ salt

☽△☿ ☽□♆ ☽△♃ ☽♂♅

• excellent day for cleaning windows, mirrors and tiles
• dry brush your skin to remove old skin cells

TUE 9   waning Moon in Capricorn ♑   earth/ root/ salt

☽♂♀ ☽△☊ ☽✳♄ ☽△☿ ☉♂♅

• great opportunity to patiently practise any desired skills
• explore business ideas and possibilities

WED 10   waning Moon in Capricorn ♑ voc from 11:52 pm   earth/ root/ salt

☽□☿ ☽△♅ ☽△☉ ☽♂♂ ☽✳♆ ☽□♃

• cleansing packs for hair, skin and nails show great results
• avoid stress on bones and joints, particularly knees

THU 11   voc to 2:05 am ingress into Aquarius ♒   air/ flower/ fat

☽♂♒ ☽♂♆ ☽□☊ ☽□☿ ♀✳☊

• great day for paint and glue jobs around the house
• excellent time for weed and pest management

☽Moon ☉Sun ☿Mercury ♀Venus ♂Mars ♃Jupiter ♄Saturn ♅Uranus ♆Neptune ♇Pluto ⚷Chiron
☊North Node ⚸Lilth ♂Conjunction, Ingress ✳Sextile □Square ♂Opposition △Trine (page 46)

FRI 12 waning Moon in Aquarius ♒ air/ flower/ fat

☽☍⚸ ☽⚹⚷ ☽□♅ ☽□☉ ☿⚹♄

• explore, express and network ideas and possibilities
• favourable days for stretches and light gymnastics

SAT 13 voc from 3:14 am to 4:38 am ingress into Pisces ♓ water/ leaf/ carbo

☽⚹♃ ☽☌♆ ☽⚹☊ ☽⚹☿ ☽☌♄ ☽△♀ ☿⚹♀ ♀△♄

• a relaxing foot massage or reflexology is very beneficial today
• avoid haircuts and washing hair, encourages dandruff

SUN 14 waning Moon in Pisces ♓ water/ leaf/ carbo

☽⚹♅ ☽⚹☉

• take your mother on a fun outing and let her know you care
• excellent day to watch an inspiring movie

Mother's Day

"It took me quite a long time to develop a voice, and now that I have it, I am not going to be silent."

Madeleine Albright, 15 May 1937

APR	M	T	W	T	F	S	S	
	31					1	2	
	3	4	5	6	7	8	9	○
	10	11	12	13	14	15	16	◐
	17	18	19	20	21	22	23	●
	24	25	26	27	28	29	30	◑

MAY	M	T	W	T	F	S	S	
	1	2	3	4	5	6	7	○
	8	9	10	11	12	13	14	◐
	15	16	17	18	19	20	21	●
	22	23	24	25	26	27	28	◑
	29	30	31					

JUN	M	T	W	T	F	S	S	
				1	2	3	4	○
	5	6	7	8	9	10	11	◐
	12	13	14	15	16	17	18	●
	19	20	21	22	23	24	25	
	26	27	28	29	30			◑

MON 15   voc from 2:56 am to 7:55 am ingress into Aries ♈   fire/ fruit/ protein

☽△♂ ☽♂♆ ☽♂♈ ☽⚹♇ ☽□♀ ♂△♆

• avoid straining your eyes and take short breaks when working at the computer
• all things cleansing for body and mind are beneficial
International Day of Families

TUE 16   waning Moon in Aries ♈   fire/ fruit/ protein

☽△⚸ ☽♂⚷ ⚷♂♅

• eyes benefit from relaxation under organic cucumber slices
• excellent for cleaning windows and mirrors
Mercury ☿ direct

WED 17   voc from 9:09 am to 12:27 pm ingress into Taurus ♉   earth/ root/ salt

☽□♂ ☽♂♉ ☽♂♃ ☽□♆ ☽♂☊ ☽♂☿ ☽⚹♄

• be easy on your throat and voice avoid drafts and noisy areas today
• avoid arguments and rash decisions

THU 18   waning Moon in Taurus ♉   earth/ root/ salt

☽⚹♀ ☽□⚸ ☽♂♅ ☉⚹♆ ♃□♆

• be aware of your and others' needs for comfort and security
• great gardening days, seed and plant root vegetables

FRI 19 new Moon 3:53 pm 28° ♉ 25′ voc 5:50 pm to 6:47 pm ingress into Gemini ♊

☽✶♆ ☽♂☉ ☽✶♂ ☽♂♊ ☽△♇ ☿✶♄
• excellent for building, laying wooden floors, setting timber fences and posts
• for more info about Sun and Moon in Taurus see page 29

SAT 20 waxing Moon in Gemini ♊   air/ flower/ fat

☽□♄ ☽✶⚸ ♂♂♌
• good time for musicians to practise finger and breathing techniques
• excellent day to set new intentions and start new healthy habits
World Bee Day

SUN 21 waxing Moon in Gemini ♊ voc from 10:11 pm   air/ flower/ fat

☽✶⚸ ☽□♆ ☉♂♊ ☽△♇ ♂♂♀
• good day to meet friends and new people
• cakes turn out well

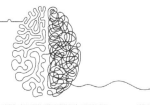

"The fundamental cause of the trouble is that in the modern world the stupid are cocksure while the intelligent are full of doubt."
Bertrand Russell, 18 May 1872

M	T	W	T	F	S	S	
31					1	2	
3	4	5	6	7	8	9	○
10	11	12	13	14	15	16	◐
17	18	19	20	21	22	23	●
24	25	26	27	28	29	30	◑

APR

M	T	W	T	F	S	S	
1	2	3	4	5	6	7	○
8	9	10	11	12	13	14	◐
15	16	17	18	19	20	21	●
22	23	24	25	26	27	28	◑
29	30	31					

MAY

M	T	W	T	F	S	S	
			1	2	3	4	○
5	6	7	8	9	10	11	◐
12	13	14	15	16	17	18	●
19	20	21	22	23	24	25	
26	27	28	29	30			◑

JUN

MON 22   voc to 3:28 am ingress into Cancer ♋   water/ leaf/ carbo

☽☌♋ ☽⚹♃ ☽⚹♌ ☽△♄ ☽⚹⚷ ☉⚹♂
- fresh leafy salads, herbs and sprouts are more nutritious now
- good day to focus on home and family

TUE 23   waxing Moon in Cancer ♋   water/ leaf/ carbo

☽☌♀ ☽□♀ ☽⚹♅ ♂□♃
- improve your digestive system by drinking bitter teas for liver, stomach and bile flow
- avoid washing hair, it becomes unruly

WED 24   voc from 9:11 am to 2:34 pm ingress into Leo ♌   fire/ fruit/ protein

☽△♆ ☽☌♌ ☽☍♇ ☽□♃ ☽☌♂ ☽⚹☉ ☽□♌ ♀□♀
- today can be an emotionally exhausting day
- mowing the lawn now encourages growth

THU 25   waxing Moon in Leo ♌   fire/ fruit/ protein

☽□☿ ☽☌⚸
- anything nourishing and regenerative to the heart and back is very effective
- make yourself and others feel special

FRI 26 waxing Moon in Leo ♌ voc from 6:38 am   fire/ fruit/ protein

☽△♂ ☽□⛢ ♀⚹♅ ♂□♌
- eat fruit and fruiting vegetables for maximum nutritional benefit
- sow and plant fruiting vegetables e.g. zucchinis

SAT 27 voc to 3:04 am ingress into Virgo ♍   earth/ root/ salt

☽☌♍ ☽△♃ ☽△♌ ☽□☉ ☽☍♄
- perfect day for working on home, building and renovating projects
- take care of private mail, email and messages

SUN 28 waxing Moon in Virgo ♍   earth/ root/ salt

☽△☿ ☽△♅ ☉□♄
- eat high fibre root vegetables, avoid fatty and salty foods
- emphasis on health issues and daily routine

"If we understood the power of our thoughts, we would guard them more closely. If we understood the power of our words, we would prefer silence to almost anything negative. In our thoughts and words, we create our own weaknesses and our own strengths. We can always replace negative with positive." *Betty Eadie*

	M	T	W	T	F	S	S
						1	2
A	3	4	5	6	7	8	9	○
P	10	11	12	13	14	15	16	◐
R	17	18	19	20	21	22	23	●
	24	25	26	27	28	29	30	☽

(APR 31 appears at top left of first block)

	M	T	W	T	F	S	S
	1	2	3	4	5	6	7	○
M	8	9	10	11	12	13	14	◐
A	15	16	17	18	19	20	21	●
Y	22	23	24	25	26	27	28	☽
	29	30	31				

	M	T	W	T	F	S	S
					1	2	3	○
J	5	6	7	8	9	10	11	◐
U	12	13	14	15	16	17	18	●
N	19	20	21	22	23	24	25	
	26	27	28	29	30			☽

MON 29   voc from 9:45 am to 2:50 pm ingress into Libra ♎︎   air/ flower/ fat

☽⚹♀ ☽☍♆ ☽☌♎︎ ☽△♅
- favourable time for projects requiring detailed work
- focus on practical business and tax issues

International Day of UN Peacekeepers

Look for Mercury low in the eastern sky just before sunrise

TUE 30   waxing Moon in Libra ♎︎   air/ flower/ fat

☽⚹♂ ☽△☉ ☽⚹⚸
- accommodate your and others' need for beauty and harmony
- great opportunity to practise diplomacy

WED 31   voc from 2:53 pm to 11:44 pm ingress into Scorpio ♏︎   water/ leaf/ carbo

☽☍⚷ ☽□♀ ☽☌♏︎
- excellent time to start growing sprouts for salads
- tend to flowers, herbs and vines in the garden

THU 1   waxing Moon in Scorpio ♏︎   water/ leaf/ carbo

☽□♆ ☽☍♃ ☽☍☊ ☽□♂ ☽△♄ ☿□⚸
- today can be an emotionally exhausting day
- mow lawns for strong regrowth

FRI 2   waxing Moon in Scorpio ♏︎   water/ leaf/ carbo

☽□♆ ☽☌♃ ☽☌♅ ♀△♆ ♃☌☊
- nurture yourself and indulge in a nourishing Lavender bath tonight
- all medicines and drugs are very powerful now

SAT 3   voc from 0:50 am to 5:03 am ingress into Sagittarius ♐︎   fire/ fruit/ protein

☽△♆ ☽△♀ ☽☌♐ ☽⚹♆ ☽□♄ ☽△♂
- great evening for a full Moon ritual, read more about Moon in Sagittarius on page 43
- excellent day for a spontaneous outing to meet friends and new people

World Bicycle Day

SUN 4   full Moon in Sagittarius ♐︎ 3:41 am 13° 18′   fire/ fruit/ protein

☽☍☉ ☽△♆ ☽△♃ ♀☌♅
- smudge yourself and your surroundings with Marjoram and Sage
- eat fruit and fruiting vegetables for maximum nutritional benefit

Look for Venus in the western sky after sunset

"There is no greater pillar of stability than a strong, free and educated woman."

Angelina Jolie 4 June 1975

	M	T	W	T	F	S	S	
		1	2	3	4	5	6	7	○
M	8	9	10	11	12	13	14	◗
A	15	16	17	18	19	20	21	●
Y	22	23	24	25	26	27	28	◖
	29	30	31					

	M	T	W	T	F	S	S	
				1	2	3	4	○
J	5	6	7	8	9	10	11	◗
U	12	13	14	15	16	17	18	●
N	19	20	21	22	23	24	25	
	26	27	28	29	30			◖

	M	T	W	T	F	S	S	
	31					1	2	
J	3	4	5	6	7	8	9	○
U	10	11	12	13	14	15	16	◗
L	17	18	19	20	21	22	23	●
	24	25	26	27	28	29	30	◖

JUNE 2023

MON 5 voc from 3:23 am to 7:30 am into Capricorn ♑ earth/ root/ salt

☽□♅ ☽♂♆ ☽△♇ ☽△♃ ☽⚹♄ ♀♂♌ ♀♂♆
• great opportunity to patiently practise any desired skills
• best days to remove unwanted body hair
World Environment Day

TUE 6 waning Moon in Capricorn ♑ earth/ root/ salt

☽□♀ ☽△♅ ☽△☿m
• favourable days for communication and business negotiations
• good day for disciplined work but avoid straining your knees

WED 7 voc from 4:39 am to 8:41 am ingress into Aquarius ♒ air/ flower/ fat

☽⚹♆ ☽♂♒ ☽♂♆ ☽♂♀ ☽□♌ ☽□♃ ☉⚹⚸
• great for cleaning wooden floors, windows and mirrors
• avoid strenuous exercise; better to elevate your legs

THU 8 waning Moon in Aquarius ♒ air/ flower/ fat

☽♂♂ ☽♂⚸ ☽△☉ ☽⚹♀ ☽□♅ ♀□♌
• great day for paint and glue jobs around the house
• excellent time for weed and pest management
World Oceans Day

FRI 9 voc from 4:23 am to 10:13 am ingress into Pisces ♓ water/ leaf/ carbo

☽□☿ ☽☌♓ ☽✶♌ ☽✶♃ ☽☌♄ ☿✶♆
• favourable day for stretches and light gymnastics
• ideal time for a lymphatic drainage massage

SAT 10 waning Moon in Pisces ♓ water/ leaf/ carbo

☽□☉ ☽✶♅ ☉✶♅ ♀☌♑
• a relaxing foot massage or reflexology is very beneficial
• avoid washing your hair today, encourages dandruff

SUN 11 voc from 1:19 pm to 1:20 pm ingress into Aries ♈ fire/ fruit/ protein

☽☌♆ ☽✶♇ ☽☌♈ ☽✶♀ ☽△♀ ♀△♇ ☽☌♊ ♀□♃
• improve your digestive system with bitter teas or 'Swedish Bitters'
• spend the day with your loved ones, excellent time for the movies

"Be careful with your words, once they are said,
they can only be forgiven, not forgotten."

Rob Hill 11 June 1967

	M	T	W	T	F	S	S	
		1	2	3	4	5	6	7	○
M A Y	8	9	10	11	12	13	14	◑
	15	16	17	18	19	20	21	●
	22	23	24	25	26	27	28	◗
	29	30	31					

	M	T	W	T	F	S	S	
				1	2	3	4	○
J U N	5	6	7	8	9	10	11	◑
	12	13	14	15	16	17	18	●
	19	20	21	22	23	24	25	
	26	27	28	29	30			◗

	M	T	W	T	F	S	S	
	31					1	2	
J U L	3	4	5	6	7	8	9	○
	10	11	12	13	14	15	16	◑
	17	18	19	20	21	22	23	●
	24	25	26	27	28	29	30	◗

MON 12   waning Moon in Aries ♈   fire/ fruit/ protein

☽△♂ ☽△☾ ☽♂⚷
• excellent for renovating, especially painting
• good day for a spontaneous outing
World Day against Child Labour

TUE 13   voc from 6:26 pm to 6:30 pm ingress into Taurus ♉   earth/ root/ salt

☽✶☉ ☽□♇ ☽♂♅
• avoid straining your eyes, take short breaks when working at the computer
• excellent time to clean windows, mirrors and tiles

WED 14   waning Moon in Taurus ♉   earth/ root/ salt

☽♂☊ ☽♂♃ ☽✶♄ ☽□♀ ☽□♂
• great time for building and renovating, particularly laying wooden floors
• be easy on your throat and voice avoid drafts and noisy areas today
World Blood Donor Day

THU 15   waning Moon in Taurus ♉   earth/ root/ salt

☽□☾ ☽♂♅ ☽✶♇ ☿□♄
• great day for paving, earth works and excavations
• a relaxing neck massage is very beneficent today

FRI 16   voc from 1:36 am to 1:45 am ingress into Gemini ♊   air/ flower/ fat

☽△♆ ☽♂♊ ☽□♄ ☽♂☿ ☽⚹♀

• wanting to give up smoking? Mentally prepare yourself and let go of it next Sunday
• treat your hands with a gentle hand scrub

SAT 17   waning Moon in Gemini ♊   air/ flower/ fat

☽⚹♂ ☽⚹⚞ ☽⚹♅ ☿⚹♀

• good time for musicians to practise finger and breathing techniques
• great day to have an outing with friends and/or family

SUN 18   new Moon 4:36 am 26° ♊43′ voc 6:23 am to 10:57 am ingress into Cancer ♋

☽♂☉ ☽□♆ ☽♂♋ ☽⚹♌

• for more info about Sun and Moon in Gemini see page 31
• excellent time to start new healthy habits

Saturn ♄ retrograde until 4 Novemberr

"If slaughterhouses had glass walls, everyone would be a vegetarian."

Paul McCartney 18 June 1942

	M	T	W	T	F	S	S	
	1	2	3	4	5	6	7	○
M	8	9	10	11	12	13	14	◑
A	15	16	17	18	19	20	21	●
Y	22	23	24	25	26	27	28	◐
	29	30	31					

	M	T	W	T	F	S	S	
				1	2	3	4	○
J	5	6	7	8	9	10	11	◑
U	12	13	14	15	16	17	18	●
N	19	20	21	22	23	24	25	
	26	27	28	29	30			◐

	M	T	W	T	F	S	S	
	31					1	2	
J	3	4	5	6	7	8	9	○
U	10	11	12	13	14	15	16	◑
L	17	18	19	20	21	22	23	●
	24	25	26	27	28	29	30	◐

MON 19   waxing Moon in Cancer ♋   water/ leaf/ carbo

☾⚹♃ ☾△♄ ☉□♆ ♃⚹♄
- favourable time for planning new family projects
- good day to potter around the home and kitchen
Father's Day

TUE 20   voc from 9:43 pm to 10:03 pm ingress into Leo ♌   fire/ fruit/ protein

☾□♀ ☾⚹♅ ☾△♆ ☾☍♇ ☾♂♌
- improve your digestive system by drinking bitter teas for liver, stomach and bile flow
- excellent evening for a nurturing family diner
World Refugee Day

WED 21   waxing Moon in Leo ♌   fire/ fruit/ protein

☾□♌ ☾□♃ ☉♂♋ ☿⚹☾ ☿⚹♂ ♂♂☾
- good day for hair colouring and streaks, shorter application time
- receive or give a strengthening back massage
Summer Solstice, Litha (see page 13)

THU 22   waxing Moon in Leo ♌ voc from 5:00 pm   fire/ fruit/ protein

☾♂♀ ☾♂☾ ☾♂♂ ☾△♃ ☾⚹☿ ☾□♅ ☿⚹♃
- excellent day to make yourself and others feel special
- creative and fun endeavours are favoured now

JUNE 2023

FRI **23** voc to 10:34 am ingress into Virgo ♍   earth/ root/ salt

☾♂♍ ☾⚹☉ ☾△♌ ☉⚹♌ ♂△☿
- anything nourishing and strengthening to the heart and back is very effective
- great day for bookkeeping and administrative jobs

International Widows Day

SAT **24** waxing Moon in Virgo ♍   earth/ root/ salt

☾☍♄ ☾△♃
- take care of business and private mail, email and messages
- favourable time to focus on your budget and savings

SUN **25** voc from 10:24 pm to 10:56 pm ingress into Libra ♎   air/ flower/ fat

☾△♅ ☾□☿ ☾☍♆ ☾△♇ ☾♂♎ ☿□♆
- eat root vegetables high in fibre, avoid fatty and salty foods
- emphasis on health issues and daily routine matters

	M	T	W	T	F	S	S	
M A Y	1	2	3	4	<u>5</u>	6	7	○
	8	9	10	11	<u>12</u>	13	14	◖
	15	16	17	18	<u>19</u>	20	21	●
	22	23	24	25	26	<u>27</u>	28	◗
	29	30	31					

	M	T	W	T	F	S	S	
J U N				1	2	3	<u>4</u>	○
	5	6	7	8	9	<u>10</u>	11	◖
	12	13	14	15	16	17	<u>18</u>	●
	19	20	21	22	23	24	25	
	<u>26</u>	27	28	29	30			◗

	M	T	W	T	F	S	S	
J U L	31					1	2	
	<u>3</u>	4	5	6	7	8	9	○
	<u>10</u>	11	12	13	14	15	16	◖
	<u>17</u>	18	19	20	21	22	23	●
	24	<u>25</u>	26	27	28	29	30	◗

MON 26   waxing Moon in Libra ♎   air/ flower/ fat

☽□☉ ♂□♅
- regenerative and nourishing cosmetics are very effective now
- drink teas that support the kidneys, e.g. Stinging Nettle

TUE 27   waxing Moon in Libra ♎   air/ flower/ fat

☽⚹♀ ☽⚹☾ ☽☍⚸ ☽⚹♂ ☿♂♋ ☿⚹♌
- accommodate your and others' needs for beauty and harmony
- take care of flowers, herbs and vines in the garden

WED 28   voc from 8:18 am to 8:55 am ingress into Scorpio ♏   water/ leaf/ carbo

☽□♆ ☽☌♏ ☽☍☊ ☽△☿ ☽△☉ ☽△♄ ♀☌☾
- favourable time for projects requiring communication and structure
- go for a nurturing walk with your partner, family or friends

THU 29   waxing Moon in Scorpio ♏   water/ leaf/ carbo

☽☍♃ ☽□☾ ☽□♀ ☉△♄ ♀△⚸
- excellent day for divining and drilling water bores
- great gardening days for almost everything

FRI   **30**   voc from 2:20 pm to 2:59 pm ingress into Sagittarius ♐   fire/ fruit/ protein

☽☌♊ ☽□♂ ☽△♆ ☽⚹♅ ☽♂♐ ☿△♄
• fresh herbs, sprouts and leafy vegetables are especially nutritious and tasty now
• enjoy a nourishing Lavender bath tonight

SAT   **1**   waxing Moon in Sagittarius ♐   fire/ fruit/ protein

☽□♄ ☉♂☿ ☉⚹♃ ☿⚹♃
• avoid too strenuous exercise, rather elevate your legs
• good days for planting and tending to fruit trees
Neptune ♆ retrograde until 6 December

SUN   **2**   voc from 1:33 pm to 5:19 pm ingress into Capricorn ♑   earth/ root/ salt

☽△☊ ☽△♂ ☽△♀ ☽△♂ ☽□♆ ☽♂♑ ☽△♌ ♀□♊
• great evening for a full Moon ritual, read more about Moon in Capricorn on page 21
• excellent day for a spontaneous outing

*"The best and most beautiful things in the world
cannot be seen or even touched.
They must be felt with the heart."*
Helen Keller 27 June 1880

M	T	W	T	F	S	S	
1	2	3	4	<u>5</u>	6	7	○
8	9	10	11	<u>12</u>	13	14	◐
15	16	17	18	<u>19</u>	20	21	●
22	23	24	25	26	<u>27</u>	28	◑
29	30	31					

M A Y

M	T	W	T	F	S	S	
				1	2	3	○
5	6	7	8	9	<u>10</u>	11	◐
12	13	14	15	16	17	<u>18</u>	●
19	20	21	22	23	24	25	
<u>26</u>	27	28	29	30			◑

J U N

M	T	W	T	F	S	S	
31					1	2	
<u>3</u>	4	5	6	7	8	9	○
<u>10</u>	11	12	13	14	15	16	◐
<u>17</u>	18	19	20	21	22	23	●
24	<u>25</u>	26	27	28	29	30	◑

J U L

MON 3   full Moon in Capricorn ♑ 11:38 am 11° ♑ 18′   earth/ root/ salt

☽⚹♄ ☽△♃ ☽☌☉ ☽☌☿
• potential tension between family, home and work interests
• smudge yourself and your surroundings with marjoram

TUE 4   voc from 4:45 pm to 5:29 pm ingress into Aquarius ♒   air/ flower/ fat

☽□♀ ☽△♅ ☽⚹♆ ☽☌♇ ☽☌♒ ☽□☊ ⚷△☽
• good time for deep cleansing skin and hair treatments
• great day for a cleansing manicure and pedicure

WED 5   waning Moon in Aquarius ♒   air/ flower/ fat

☽□♃
• great opportunity to patiently practise any desired skills
• favourable days for stretches and light gymnastics

THU 6   voc from 1:41 pm to 5:32 pm ingress into Pisces ♓   water/ leaf/ carbo

☽⚹♀ ☽☌☾ ☽□♅ ☽☌♀ ☽☌♂ ☽☌♓ ☽⚹☊ ☿□♀
• great for cleaning wooden floors, windows and mirrors
• favourable time for weed and pest management

FRI 7   waning Moon in Pisces ♓   water/ leaf/ carbo

☾☌♄ ☾⚹♃ ☾△☉ ☿⚹♅

• excellent time to walk barefoot in the morning dew, it is very grounding
and discharges electromagnetic pollution through the feet

SAT 8   voc from 6:21 pm to 7:18 pm ingress into Aries ♈   fire/ fruit/ protein

☾⚹♅ ☾△☿ ☾☌♆ ☾⚹♆ ☾☌♈

• improve your digestive system with bitter teas or 'Swedish Bitters'
• a relaxing foot massage or reflexology is very beneficial today

SUN 9   waning Moon in Aries ♈   fire/ fruit/ protein

☿△♆

• all things cleansing for body and mind are beneficial
• soothe your eyes with organic cucumber slices

"Happy people build their inner world.
Unhappy people blame their outer world."

Dalai Lama, 6 July 1935

	M	T	W	T	F	S	S	
					1	2	3	4	○
J	5	6	7	8	9	10	11	☽
U	12	13	14	15	16	17	18	●
N	19	20	21	22	23	24	25	
	26	27	28	29	30			☽

	M	T	W	T	F	S	S	
	31					1	2	
J	3	4	5	6	7	8	9	○
U	10	11	12	13	14	15	16	☽
L	17	18	19	20	21	22	23	●
	24	25	26	27	28	29	30	☽

	M	T	W	T	F	S	S	
	1	2	3	4	5	6	○
A	7	8	9	10	11	12	13	☽
U	14	15	16	17	18	19	20	●
G	21	22	23	24	25	26	27	☽
	28	29	30	31				○

MON 10   voc from 11:10 pm to 11:55 pm ingress into Taurus ♉   earth/ root/ salt

☽□☉ ☽♂☿ ☽△☾ ☽△♀ ☽□♇ ☽□☿ ☽♂♉ ☿⚹♇ ♂♂♍

- great day for renovating jobs, especially painting
- avoid stimulants to prevent headaches

TUE 11   waning Moon in Taurus ♉   earth/ root/ salt

☽△♂ ☽♂♌ ☽⚹♄ ☽♂♃ ☿♂♌ ☿□♌ ♂△♌

- be aware of your and others' needs for comfort and security
- a relaxing neck massage is very beneficent today

World Population Day

WED 12   waning Moon in Taurus ♉   earth/ root/ salt

☽⚹☉ ☽□☾ ☽♂♅ ☉□☿

- great day for earthworks, pavings and excavations
- prepare and eat root vegetables today

THU 13   voc from 6:10 am to 7:25 am ingress into Gemini ♊   air/ flower/ fat

☽□♀ ☽⚹♆ ☽△♇ ☽♂♊ ☽□♂ ☽⚹☿ ☽□♄

- good time for musicians to practise finger and breathing techniques
- attend to flowering plants, vines and herbs

☽Moon ☉Sun ☿Mercury ♀Venus ♂Mars ♃Jupiter ♄Saturn ♅Uranus ♆Neptune ♇Pluto ⚷Chiron
☊North Node ☾Lilth ♂Conjunction, Ingress ⚹Sextile □Square ♂Opposition △Trine (page 46)

FRI 14 waning Moon Gemini ♊   air/ flower/ fat

☽⚹♉ ☽⚹☿ ☉⚹♅
• best time to clean windows and mirrors
• good for pest and weed management

SAT 15 voc from 12:35 pm to 5:13 pm ingress into Cancer ♋   water/ leaf/ carbo

☽⚹♀ ☽□♆ ☽☌♋ ☽⚹♌ ☽⚹♂
• great day for socialising, spend time with your siblings and friends
• dusting and vacuuming is more effective now

SUN 16 waning Moon in Cancer ♋   water/ leaf/ carbo

☽△♄ ☽⚹♃
• excellent time to nurture and spend time with loved ones
• good day to potter around the home and garden

"Education is the great engine of personal development. It is through education that the daughter of a peasant can become a doctor. The son of a mine worker can become the head of the mine. The child of a farm worker can become the president of a great nation." — Nelson Mandela, July 18, 1918

	M	T	W	T	F	S	S	
					1	2	3	4	○
J U N	5	6	7	8	9	10	11	◐
	12	13	14	15	16	17	18	●
	19	20	21	22	23	24	25	
	26	27	28	29	30			◗

	M	T	W	T	F	S	S	
	31					1	2	
J U L	3	4	5	6	7	8	9	○
	10	11	12	13	14	15	16	◐
	17	18	19	20	21	22	23	●
	24	25	26	27	28	29	30	◗

	M	T	W	T	F	S	S	
		1	2	3	4	5	6	○
A U G	7	8	9	10	11	12	13	◐
	14	15	16	17	18	19	20	●
	21	22	23	24	25	26	27	◗
	28	29	30	31				○

MON 17 new Moon in Cancer ♋ 6:31 pm 24° 56′ water/ leaf/ carbo

☽□♄ ☽⚹♅ ☽☌☉ ☽△♆ ☿□♃ ☊☌♈
- excellent day to relax or meditate at a lake or the beach
- read more about Sun and Moon in Cancer on page 33

TUE 18 voc from 3:05 am to 4:39 am ingress into Leo ♌ fire/ fruit/ protein

☽☌♀ ☽□☊ ☽☌♌
- emotions might run high, tendency to overreact, overindulge or overeat
- enjoy a guided meditation in a relaxing bath tonight

WED 19 waxing Moon in Leo ♌ fire/ fruit/ protein

☽□♃ ☽☌☿ ☽△♄
- excellent day to set new goals and work out steps to be implemented
- good time for a healing and heart-to-heart communication

THU 20 voc from 2:08 pm to 5:12 pm ingress into Virgo ♍ earth/ root/ salt

☽☌⚸ ☽□♅ ☽☌♀ ☽△☊ ☽☌♍ ☉△♆ ♂☍♄
- great opportunity to make yourself and others feel special
- all creative and fun endeavours are favoured now

FRI **21** waxing Moon in Virgo ♍   earth/ root/ salt

☽☍♄ ☽♂♂ ☽△♃
- good time for projects requiring detailed work
- emphasis on health issues and daily routine

SAT **22** waxing Moon in Virgo ♍   earth/ root/ salt

☽△♅ ☉☍♆ ☉□♎ ☿△♄
- accommodate your and others' needs for hygiene and daily routines
- favourable days for de-cluttering and general garden maintenance

---

SUN **23** voc from 4:05 am to 5:53 am ingress into Libra ♎   air/ flower/ fat

☽☍♆ ☽△♆ ☽♂♎ ☽⚹☉ ☉♂♎ ♀♂☽ ♀□♅ ♆□♎
- regenerative and nourishing cosmetics are very effective now
- take care of flowers and vines in the garden

"People who master their emotions can manage and
change their feelings depending on the situation.
Being generally flexible and learning active listening
skills cultivates empathy, optimism and enthusiasm."

M	T	W	T	F	S	S	
				1	2	3	4 ○
J U N	5	6	7	8	9	10	11 ☽
	12	13	14	15	16	17	18 ●
	19	20	21	22	23	24	25
	26	27	28	29	30		☽

M	T	W	T	F	S	S	
	31					1	2
J U L	3	4	5	6	7	8	9 ○
	10	11	12	13	14	15	16 ☽
	17	18	19	20	21	22	23 ●
	24	25	26	27	28	29	30 ☽

M	T	W	T	F	S	S	
	1	2	3	4	5	6	○
A U G	7	8	9	10	11	12	13 ☽
	14	15	16	17	18	19	20 ●
	21	22	23	24	25	26	27 ☽
	28	29	30	31			○

MON 24   waxing Moon in Libra ♎   air/ flower/ fat

☽ ☌ ⚷

• drink teas that support the kidneys, e.g. Stinging Nettle
• start growing sprouts for salads

Chiron ⚷ retrograde until 27 December
Venus ♀ retrograde until 4 September

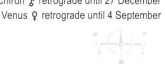

TUE 25   voc from 3:05 pm to 4:55 pm ingress into Scorpio ♏   water/ leaf/ carbo

☽⚹⚸ ☽⚹☿ ☽⚹♀ ☽□♆ ☽☌☊ ☽☌♏ ☽□☉ ♆□☊

• accommodate your and others' need for beauty and harmony
• a visit to the art gallery would be fun today

WED 26   waxing Moon in Scorpio ♏   water/ leaf/ carbo

☽△♄ ☽⚹♂ ☽☌♃

• fresh leafy salads, herbs and sprouts are more nutritious now
• good days to do small repairs around the house

THU 27   waxing Moon in Scorpio ♏ voc from 10:35 pm   water/ leaf/ carbo

☽□⚸ ☽☌⚸ ☽△♆ ☽□♀ ☽□☿ ☽⚹♆ ☿☌♀

• nurture and appreciate yourself, indulge in a nourishing Lavender bath tonight
• improve your digestive system by taking 'Swedish Bitters'

☽Moon ☉Sun ☿Mercury ♀Venus ♂Mars ♃Jupiter ♄Saturn ♅Uranus ♆Neptune ♇Pluto ⚷Chiron
☊North Node ⚸Lilth ♂Conjunction, Ingress ⚹Sextile □Square ⚼Opposition △Trine (page 46)

FRI 28   voc to 0:23 am ingress into Sagittarius ♐   fire/ fruit/ protein

☽ ☌ ♐   ☽ △ ☉   ☽ □ ♄   ☽ □ ♂   ☿ △ ♌   ☿ ☌ ♍   ♀ □ ♌

• avoid weeding plants which spread via their root system
• great days to plant and tend to fruit trees

Delta Aquarids Meteor Shower

SAT 29   waxing Moon in Sagittarius ♐ voc from 11:51 pm   fire/ fruit/ protein

☽ △ ♅   ☽ △ ☾   ☽ □ ♆   ☽ △ ♀

• eat fruit and fruiting vegetables for maximum nutritional benefit
• dry brushing your skin stimulates your overall circulation

SUN 30   voc to 3:43 am ingress into Capricorn ♑   earth/ root/ salt

☽ △ ♌   ☽ ☌ ♑   ☽ △ ☿   ☽ ✶ ♄   ♅ □ ☾

• excellent day for meeting friends and new people
• great opportunity for a spontaneous outing

"Life isn't about finding yourself,
It is about creating yourself."
George Brenhard Shaw, 26 July 1856

M	T	W	T	F	S	S	
				1	2	3	4	○
J 5	6	7	8	9	10	11	☽
U 12	13	14	15	16	17	18	●
N 19	20	21	22	23	24	25	
26	27	28	29	30			☽

M	T	W	T	F	S	S	
31					1	2	
J 3	4	5	6	7	8	9	○
U 10	11	12	13	14	15	16	☽
L 17	18	19	20	21	22	23	●
24	25	26	27	28	29	30	☽

M	T	W	T	F	S	S	
	1	2	3	4	5	6	○
A 7	8	9	10	11	12	13	☽
U 14	15	16	17	18	19	20	●
G 21	22	23	24	25	26	27	☽
28	29	30	31				○

MON 31   waxing Moon in Capricorn   earth/ root/ salt

○

☽△♂ ☽△♃ ☽□♅ ☽△♅ ☽⚹♆
• good day for researching and scrutinising new business trends
• allow yourself to be inspired and pursue knowledge

TUE 1   voc 2:12 am to 3:57 am ingress into Aquarius ♒ full Moon ♒ 6:31 pm 9° 15′

○

☽□♇ ☽♂♆ ☽♂♒ ☽♂☉ ♂△♃
• read more about Moon in Aquarius on page 23
• great evening for a full Moon ritual

Lammas (see page 13)
Super Moon

WED 2   waning Moon in Aquarius ♒ voc from 9:15 pm   air/ flower/ fat

○

☽□♃ ☽⚹♅ ☽□♅ ☽♂⚸ ☽♂♀ ☿♂♄
• favourable nights to put your crystals outside to bathe them in the full moonlight
• heightened sense of irritation, you might feel annoyed

THU 3   voc to 3:05 am ingress into Pisces ♓   water/ leaf/ carbo

○

☽⚹♌ ☽♂♓ ☽♂♄ ☽♂☿
• avoid haircuts and washing hair, encourages dandruff
• a positive attitude allows developments to take place

FRI 4 waning Moon in Pisces ♓   water/ leaf/ carbo

☽✶♃ ☽♂♂ ☽✶♅ ☽♂♆

• excellent time to walk barefoot in the morning dew, very grounding and discharges electromagnetic pollution through the feet

SAT 5 voc from 1:20 am to 3:19 am ingress into in Aries ♈   fire/ fruit/ protein

☽✶♆ ☽♂♈

• avoid stimulants to prevent headaches and migraines
• all things cleansing for body and mind are beneficial

SUN 6 waning Moon in Aries ♈   fire/ fruit/ protein

☽△☉ ☽♂♄ ☽△♀ ☽△♀

• eyes benefit from relaxation under cotton pads soaked in cold almond milk
• great day for a spontaneous outing

"The best Anti Poverty program
is a world class education."
Barack Obama 4 August 1961

	M	T	W	T	F	S	S
J U L	31					1	2
	3	4	5	6	7	8	9	○
	10	11	12	13	14	15	16	☽
	17	18	19	20	21	22	23	●
	24	25	26	27	28	29	30	☽

	M	T	W	T	F	S	S
A U G		1	2	3	4	5	6	○
	7	8	9	10	11	12	13	☽
	14	15	16	17	18	19	20	●
	21	22	23	24	25	26	27	☽
	28	29	30	31				○

	M	T	W	T	F	S	S
S E P					1	2	3
	4	5	6	7	8	9	10	☽
	11	12	13	14	15	16	17	●
	18	19	20	21	22	23	24	☽
	25	26	27	28	29	30	31	○

MON 7   voc from 4:12 am to 6:24 am ingress into Taurus ♉   earth/ root/ salt

☽ ♂ ♌ ☽ □ ♀ ☽ ♂ ♉ ☽ ✶ ♄ ☉ □ ♃
• excellent day for small maintenance jobs around the house and garden
• be easy on your throat and voice, avoid drafts and noisy areas today

TUE 8   waning Moon in Taurus ♉   earth/ root/ salt

☽ △ ☿ ☽ ♂ ♃ ☽ □ ☉ ☽ △ ♂ ☽ ♂ ♅ ♀ ♂ ☾
• favourable time for projects requiring ingenuity and detailed work
• good opportunity to practise patiently any desirable skill

WED 9   voc from 10:38 am to 1:04 pm ingress into Gemini ♊   air/ flower/ fat

☽ □ ♀ ☽ □ ☾ ☽ ✶ ♆ ☽ △ ♀ ☽ ♂ ♊ ☽ □ ♄ ♀ □ ♅
• relaxing exercises for shoulders and arms are very beneficial
• favourable time for focusing on dental hygiene
International Day of the World's Indigenous Peoples

THU 10   waning Moon in Gemini ♊   air/ flower/ fat

☽ □ ☿ ☽ ✶ ☉ ☿ △ ♃
• good time for cleaning windows, mirrors, tiles and floors
• dusting and vacuuming is most effective now
Look for Mercury low in the western sky just after sunset

☽ Moon ☉ Sun ☿ Mercury ♀ Venus ♂ Mars ♃ Jupiter ♄ Saturn ♅ Uranus ♆ Neptune ♇ Pluto ⚷ Chiron
☊ North Node ☾ Lilth ♂ Conjunction, Ingress ✶ Sextile □ Square ♂ Opposition △ Trine (page 46)

AUGUST 2023

FRI 11 voc from 5:27 pm to 10:51 pm ingress into Cancer ♋ water/ leaf/ carbo

☽□♂ ☽⚹♄ ☽⚹♀ ☽⚹♆ ☽□♅ ☽⚹♌ ☽♂♋
• good day for musicians to practise finger and breathing techniques
• great time to socialise and get fresh air

SAT 12 waning Moon in Cancer ♋ water/ leaf/ carbo

☽△♄ ☉△♄
• excellent day for a general cleanup and repairs around the house
• improve your digestive system by drinking bitter teas
Perseids Meteor Shower

SUN 13 waning Moon in Cancer ♋ water/ leaf/ carbo

☽⚹♃ ☽⚹☿ ☽□♄ ☽⚹♂ ☽⚹♅ ☉♂♀
• great day to nurture yourself and your loved ones
• opportune time to focus on home and family

*"A good rule for going through life
is to keep the heart a little softer
than the head."*
Anonymous

M	T	W	T	F	S	S
31					1	2
3	4	5	6	7	8	9
10	11	12	13	14	15	16
17	18	19	20	21	22	23
24	25	26	27	28	29	30

JUL

M	T	W	T	F	S	S
	1	2	3	4	5	6
7	8	9	10	11	12	13
14	15	16	17	18	19	20
21	22	23	24	25	26	27
28	29	30	31			

AUG

M	T	W	T	F	S	S
				1	2	3
4	5	6	7	8	9	10
11	12	13	14	15	16	17
18	19	20	21	22	23	24
25	26	27	28	29	30	31

SEP

AUGUST 2023

WEEK 33

MON 14 voc from 7:46 am to 10:35 am ingress into Leo ♌ fire/ fruit/ protein

☽△♆ ☽□☊ ☽☍♇ ☽☌♌ ♀△⚷

• nourishing and regenerative cosmetics are very effective today
• excellent for cleaning windows, mirrors and mopping floors

TUE 15 waning Moon in Leo ♌ fire/ fruit/ protein

☽□♃

• any creatively inspired endeavour or performance is favoured
• excellent day to make yourself and others feel special

WED 16 new Moon in Leo ♌ 9:37 am 23° 17′ voc 9:37 am to 11:13 pm into Virgo ♍

☽☌♀ ☽△⚷ ☽□♅ ☽☌☉ ☽☌⚸ ☽△☊ ☽☌♍ ☉□♅ ♂△♅

• all things relaxing for heart and back are very beneficial
• read more about Sun and Moon in Leo on page 35

THU 17 waxing Moon in Virgo ♍ earth/ root/ salt

☽☍♄ ☉☌⚸

• good day to recharge your batteries and start with a new and healthy attitude
• excellent day to set new goals and plan each step to be implemented

☽Moon ☉Sun ☿Mercury ♀Venus ♂Mars ♃Jupiter ♄Saturn ♅Uranus ♆Neptune ♇Pluto ⚷Chiron
☊North Node ⚸Lilith ☌Conjunction, Ingress ⚹Sextile □Square ☍Opposition △Trine (page 46)

FRI 18 waxing Moon in Virgo ♍   earth/ root/ salt

☽△♃ ☽☌☿ ☽△♅
- opportune day to focus on practical tax and business issues
- excellent time for bookkeeping

SAT 19 voc from 8:50 am to 11:53 am ingress into Libra ♎   air/ flower/ fat

☽☌♂ ☽☍♆ ☽△♀ ☽☌♎ ☉△☊
- perfect day for working on home, building and renovating projects
- favourable time for projects requiring ingenuity and detailed work

World Humanitarian Day

SUN 20 waxing Moon in Libra ♎   air/ flower/ fat

☽✶♀
- accommodate your own and others' needs for beauty and harmony
- support your kidneys by drinking Stinging Nettle tea

"Elegance is not the prerogative of those who
have just escaped from adolescence, but of those
who have already taken possession of their future."

Coco Chanel, 19 August 1883

	M	T	W	T	F	S	S	
JUL	31					1	2	
	3	4	5	6	7	8	9	○
	10	11	12	13	14	15	16	◐
	17	18	19	20	21	22	23	●
	24	25	26	27	28	29	30	◑

	M	T	W	T	F	S	S	
AUG		1	2	3	4	5	6	○
	7	8	9	10	11	12	13	◐
	14	15	16	17	18	19	20	●
	21	22	23	24	25	26	27	◑
	28	29	30	31				○

	M	T	W	T	F	S	S	
SEP					1	2	3	
	4	5	6	7	8	9	10	◐
	11	12	13	14	15	16	17	●
	18	19	20	21	22	23	24	◑
	25	26	27	28	29	30	31	○

MON 21   voc from 8:30 pm to 11:21 pm ingress into Scorpio ♏   water/ leaf/ carbo

☽☌♄ ☽⚹♆ ☽☌♌ ☽□♇ ☽⚹☉ ☽☌♏

- regenerative and nourishing cosmetics are very effective
- take care of flowers and vines in the garden

TUE 22   waxing Moon in Scorpio ♏   water/ leaf/ carbo

☽△♄ ♀□♃ ♂☌♆

- fresh leafy salads, herbs and sprouts are more nutritious now
- mow lawns for strong regrowth

WED 23   waxing Moon in Scorpio ♏   water/ leaf/ carbo

☽□♀ ☽☌♃ ☽⚹☿ ☽☌♅ ☽□♆ ☉☌♍

- today might be a tense day; maybe do something on your own
- improve your digestive system by taking 'Swedish Bitters'

THU 24   voc from 5:09 am to 8:07 am ingress into Sagittarius ♐   fire/ fruit/ protein

☽△♆ ☽⚹♂ ☽⚹♇ ☽☌♐ ☽□☉ ☽□♄

- dry brushing your skin stimulates your overall circulation
- nourish and soothe your soul today

Mercury ☿ retrograde until 15 Sep

☽Moon ☉Sun ☿Mercury ♀Venus ♂Mars ♃Jupiter ♄Saturn ♅Uranus ♆Neptune ♇Pluto ⚷Chiron
☊North Node ⚸Lilth ☌Conjunction, Ingress ⚹Sextile □Square ☍Opposition △Trine (page 46)

FRI 25   waxing Moon in Sagittarius ♐   fire/ fruit/ protein

☽△♀   ☽△♄   ☽□☿   ♂△♆
• great days for harvesting fruit trees and fruiting vegetables
• excellent day for a spontaneous outing

SAT 26   voc from 11:55 am to 1:05 pm ingress into Capricorn ♑   earth/ root/ salt

☽△☾   ☽△♌   ☽□♆   ☽□♂   ☽♂♑   ☽△☉   ☽⚹♄
• eat fruit and fruiting vegetables for maximum nutritional benefit
• avoid too strenuous exercise; instead, elevate your legs

SUN 27   waxing Moon in Capricorn ♑   earth/ root/ salt

☽△♃   ☽□♄   ☉⚼♄   ♂♂♎
• great opportunity to patiently practise any desired skills
• avoid stress on bones and joints, particularly knees
Best time to view and photograph Saturn and its moons

"I love being my age. I love getting older.
What you lose in good looks you gain in wisdom."
Delvene Delayney, 26 August 1951

	M	T	W	T	F	S	S
	31					1	2
J	3	4	5	6	7	8	9	○
U	10	11	12	13	14	15	16	◐
L	17	18	19	20	21	22	23	●
	24	25	26	27	28	29	30	◑

	M	T	W	T	F	S	S
		1	2	3	4	5	6	○
A	7	8	9	10	11	12	13	◐
U	14	15	16	17	18	19	20	●
G	21	22	23	24	25	26	27	◑
	28	29	30	31				○

	M	T	W	T	F	S	S
					1	2	3
S	4	5	6	7	8	9	10	◐
E	11	12	13	14	15	16	17	●
P	18	19	20	21	22	23	24	◑
	25	26	27	28	29	30	31	○

MON 28 voc from 11:48 am to 2:31 pm ingress into Aquarius ♒ air/flower/fat

☽△☿ ☽△♅ ☽□♆ ☽⚹♆ ☽♂♆ ☽♂♒ ☽△♂
• work on business projects, explore new trends and possibilities
• great day to structure tasks and workload

TUE 29 waxing Moon in Aquarius ♒ air/flower/fat

☽♂♀ ☽□♃ ☽⚹♄ ♌△☾
• be careful – herbs, medication and stimulants are very potent today!
• favourable time to put your crystals out in the full moonlight
International Day against Nuclear Tests

WED 30 voc from 3:04 am to 1:56 pm ingress into Pisces ♓ water/leaf/carbo

☽□♅ ☽⚹♌ ☽♂☾ ☽♂♓ ☽♂♄
• today and tomorrow are excellent days to buy shoes for people with sensitive feet
• great evening for a full Moon ritual, read more about Moon in Pisces on page 25
Uranus ♅ retrograde until 26 January 2024

THU 31 full Moon in Pisces ♓ 1:35 am 7° 25′ water/leaf/carbo

☽♂☉ ☽⚹♃ ☽♂☿
• avoid alcohol and stimulants to prevent headaches and migraines
• visit a magical nature spot near water and meditate
Blue Moon, Super Moon

FRI 1 voc 10:35 am to 1:24 pm ingress into Aries ♈ fire/ fruit/ protein

☽⚹♅ ☽☌♆ ☽⚹♇ ☽☌♈ ☽☍♂

- a relaxing foot massage or reflexology is very beneficial today
- excellent for renovating, especially painting

SAT 2 waning Moon in Aries ♈ fire/ fruit/ protein

☽△♀ ☽☌♅

- good day for cleaning windows and mirrors
- good time for pruning fruit trees

SUN 3 voc 11:56 am to 2:59 pm ingress into Taurus ♉ earth/ root/ salt

☽☌☊ ☽△☽ ☽□♇ ☽☌♉ ☽⚹♄

- relax your eyes under cotton pads soaked in cold almond milk
- all things cleansing for body and mind are beneficial

"There are only two lasting bequests we can hope to give our children. One of these is roots, the other one is wings." Goethe 28 August 1749

M	T	W	T	F	S	S	
	1	2	3	4	5	6	○
7	8	9	10	11	12	13	◗
14	15	16	17	18	19	20	●
21	22	23	24	25	26	27	◖
28	29	30	31				○

A
U
G

M	T	W	T	F	S	S	
				1	2	3	
4	5	6	7	8	9	10	◗
11	12	13	14	15	16	17	●
18	19	20	21	22	23	24	◖
25	26	27	28	29	30	31	○

S
E
P

M	T	W	T	F	S	S	
30	31					1	
2	3	4	5	6	7	8	◗
9	10	11	12	13	14	15	●
16	17	18	19	20	21	22	◖
23	24	25	26	27	28	29	○

O
C
T

SEPTEMBER 2023 WEEK 36

MON 4 waning Moon in Taurus ♉ earth/ root/ salt

☾△☉ ☾□♀ ☾△☿ ☾♂♃ ☿△♃
• good opportunity to think out of the box, to be inventive and resourceful
• ideal time to scrutinise contracts and agreements

TUE 5 voc from 4:45 pm to 8:06 pm ingress into Gemini ♊ air/ flower/ fat

☾♂♅ ☾⚹♆ ☾□♍ ☾△♇ ☾♂♊
• take it easy on your throat and voice; avoid drafts and noisy areas
• be aware of your and others' needs for comfort and security

Jupiter ♃ retrograde until 31 December
Venus ♀ direct

WED 6 waning Moon in Gemini ♊ air/ flower/ fat

☾□♄ ☾△♂ ☾⚹♀ ☾□☿ ☾□☉ ☉♂☿
• great day for a spontaneous outing with your friends or partner
• good time to work on a product or advertising campaign

THU 7 waning Moon in Gemini ♊ voc from 10:21 pm air/ flower/ fat

☾⚹⚷ ☾⚹☊ ☾□♆ ☾⚹♍
• excellent time for musicians to practise finger and breathing techniques
• dusting and vacuuming is most effective now

☾Moon ☉Sun ☿Mercury ♀Venus ♂Mars ♃Jupiter ♄Saturn ♅Uranus ♆Neptune ♇Pluto ⚷Chiron
☊North Node ⚸Lilth ♂Conjunction, Ingress ⚹Sextile □Square ☍Opposition △Trine (page 46)

FRI   8   voc to 4:59 am ingress into Cancer ♋   water/ leaf/ carbo

☽☌♋   ☽∆♄   ☽☐♂   ☉∆♃
• improve your digestive system by drinking bitter teas
• great day for handicrafts
International Literacy Day

SAT   9   waning Moon in Cancer ♋   water/ leaf/ carbo

☽✶☿   ☽✶♃   ☽✶☉   ☽☐♀
• excellent day for a general cleanup and repairs around the house
• favourable time to focus on home and family

SUN   10   voc from 12:47 pm to 4:35 pm ingress into Leo ♌   fire/ fruit/ protein

☽✶♅   ☽☐♌   ☽∆♆   ☽♂♇   ☽☌♌
• enjoy a relaxing meditation in a nurturing bath tonight
• avoid washing or cutting hair, it becomes unruly
World Suicide Prevention Day

"Someone will always be prettier. Someone will always
be smarter, someone will always be younger.
But they never will be you."
                              Freddie Mercury, 5 September 1946

	M	T	W	T	F	S	S	
	1	2	3	4	5	6		○
A U G	7	8	9	10	11	12	13	◐
	14	15	16	17	18	19	20	●
	21	22	23	24	25	26	27	☽
	28	29	30	31				○

	M	T	W	T	F	S	S	
					1	2	3	
S E P	4	5	6	7	8	9	10	◐
	11	12	13	14	15	16	17	●
	18	19	20	21	22	23	24	☽
	25	26	27	28	29	30	31	○

	M	T	W	T	F	S	S	
	30	31					1	
O C T	2	3	4	5	6	7	8	◐
	9	10	11	12	13	14	15	●
	16	17	18	19	20	21	22	☽
	23	24	25	26	27	28	29	○

MON 11　waning Moon in Leo ♌　　　fire/ fruit/ protein

☽⚹♂　☽☌♀　☽□♃
• eat fruit and fruiting vegetables for maximum nutritional benefit
• good day for hair cuts, colouring and streaks

TUE 12　waning Moon in Leo ♌ voc from 3:05 pm　　　fire/ fruit/ protein

☽△♀　☽□♅　☽△♌
• all creative and fun endeavours are favoured now
• avoid anything troubling or irritating to the heart

WED 13　voc to 5:17 am ingress into Virgo ♍　　　earth/ root/ salt

☽☌♌　☽☌♍　☽⚹♄　☽☌☿
• great days for bookkeeping and working on detailed projects
• take care of private mail, email and messages

THU 14　waning Moon in Virgo ♍　　　earth/ root/ salt

☽△♃
• favourable time for maintenance and sorting jobs around the house and garden
• excellent time to focus and analyse legal or tax issues

FRI 15 new Moon in Virgo 1:39 am 21° ♍ 58′ voc 1:49 pm to 5:44 pm into Libra ♎

☽☌☉ ☽△♅ ☽☍♆ ☽△♇ ☽☌♎
- great day to drop outdated habits, read more about Sun and Moon in Virgo on page 37
- perfect time to set new goals and steps to achieve them

International Day of Democracy

SAT 16 waxing Moon in Libra ♎   air/ flower/ fat

☽☌♂ ☽⚹♀ ☉△♅
- regenerative and nourishing cosmetics are very effective now
- accommodate your and others' need for harmony

Mercury ☿ direct

SUN 17 waxing Moon in Libra ♎   air/ flower/ fat

☽☍♄ ☽☍♌ ♀□♃
- excellent time to beautify your surroundings
- good day for diplomatic endeavours

"If you really want to do something,
You find a way.
If you don't, you find an excuse."

Jim Rohn 17 September 1930

	M	T	W	T	F	S	S	
A U G		1	2	3	4	5	6	○
	7	8	9	10	11	12	13	◐
	14	15	16	17	18	19	20	●
	21	22	23	24	25	26	27	◑
	28	29	30	31				○

	M	T	W	T	F	S	S	
S E P					1	2	3	
	4	5	6	7	8	9	10	◐
	11	12	13	14	15	16	17	●
	18	19	20	21	22	23	24	◑
	25	26	27	28	29	30	31	○

	M	T	W	T	F	S	S	
O C T	30	31					1	
	2	3	4	5	6	7	8	◐
	9	10	11	12	13	14	15	●
	16	17	18	19	20	21	22	◑
	23	24	25	26	27	28	29	○

SEPTEMBER 2023

MON 18   voc from 1:06 am to 4:57 am ingress Scorpio ♏   water/ leaf/ carbo

☽□♇ ☽⚹⚸ ☽☌♏ ☽△♄ ☽⚹☿
- drinking Stinging Nettle tea is beneficial to your kidneys and bladder
- fresh leafy salads, herbs and sprouts are more nutritious now

TUE 19   waxing Moon in Scorpio ♏   water/ leaf/ carbo

☽☍♃ ☽□♀ ☉☍♆
- nurture and indulge yourself in a Lavender bath
- nourish and soothe your soul today

best time to view and photograph Neptune ♆

WED 20   voc from 10:21 am to 2:05 pm ingress into Sagittarius ♐   fire/ fruit/ protein

☽☍♅ ☽△♆ ☽⚹☉ ☽⚹♇ ☽□⚸ ☽☌♐ ☽□♄
- improve your digestive system by drinking bitter teas
- mow lawns to strengthen regrowth

THU 21   waxing Moon in Sagittarius ♐   fire/ fruit/ protein

☽□☿ ☽⚹♂ ☽△♀ ☽△⚵ ☉△♆
- avoid weeding plants that spread via their root system, it encourages root growth
- tend to fruit trees

International Day of Peace

FRI 22   voc from 7:31 pm to 8:20 pm ingress into Capricorn ♑   earth/root/salt

☽△♌ ☽□♇ ☽△♀ ☽□☉ ☽♂♃ ☽✳♄
- don't overexert yourself; instead go for a relaxing walk
- good time to meet friends and new people

Look for Mercury low in the eastern sky just before sunrise

SAT 23   waxing Moon in Capricorn ♑   earth/root/salt

☽△☿ ☽△♃ ☉♂︎︎♎ ♀△♂
- good day for disciplined work and structuring your workload
- a positive attitude allows developments to take place

Autumn Equinox, Mabon (see page 13)

SUN 24   voc from 8:05 pm to 11:29 pm ingress into Aquarius ♒   air/flower/fat

☽□♂ ☽□♂ ☽△♅ ☽□♌ ☽✳♇ ☽♂♇ ☽♂♒ ♂♂♂
- opportune time to work on projects, explore new trends and possibilities
- avoid stress on bones and joints, particularly knees

"Let your love be stronger than your hate or anger. Learn the wisdom of compromise, for it is better to bend a little than to break."

H.G.Wells, 21 September 1866

	M	T	W	T	F	S	S	
A U G		1	2	3	4	5	6	○
	7	8	9	10	11	12	13	◐
	14	15	16	17	18	19	20	●
	21	22	23	24	25	26	27	☽
	28	29	30	31				○

	M	T	W	T	F	S	S	
S E P					1	2	3	
	4	5	6	7	8	9	10	◐
	11	12	13	14	15	16	17	●
	18	19	20	21	22	23	24	☽
	25	26	27	28	29	30	31	○

	M	T	W	T	F	S	S	
O C T	30	31					1	
	2	3	4	5	6	7	8	◐
	9	10	11	12	13	14	15	●
	16	17	18	19	20	21	22	☽
	23	24	25	26	27	28	29	○

MON 25   waxing Moon in Aquarius ♒   air/ flower/ fat

)

☽△☉ ☽□♃ ☿△♃
• good night to put your crystals out in the full moonlight
• business trips and networking is rewarding today

TUE 26   waxing Moon in Aquarius ♒ voc from 12:38 pm   air/ flower/ fat

☽✶♄ ☽△♂ ☽♂♀ ☽□♅ ☽✶☊ ☽♂⚸
• great day for communication, networking and working on projects
• opportune time to connect with friends and meet new people

WED 27   voc to 0:17 am ingress into Pisces ♓   water/ leaf/ carbo

☽♂♓ ☽♂♄ ☽✶♃
• excellent days to buy new shoes, especially if you have sensitive feet
• avoid alcohol and stimulants to prevent headaches and migraines

THU 28   waxing Moon in Pisces ♓ voc from 8:57 pm   water/ leaf/ carbo

☽♂☿ ☽✶♅ ☽♂♆ ☽✶♇
• great evening for a full Moon ritual, read more about Moon in Aries on page 27
• careful: herbs, stimulants and medication are very potent now

FRI 29

voc to 0:17 am into Aries ♈ full Moon 9:57 am 6° ♈ 00′   fire/ fruit/ protein

☽♂♈ ☽☍☉ ♀☐♅

- improve your digestive system with bitter tasting teas or 'Swedish Bitters'
- avoid alcohol and stimulants to prevent headaches and migraines

SAT 30

waning Moon in Aries ♈ voc from 9:49 pm   fire/ fruit/ protein

☽♂♅ ☽☍♂ ☽△♀ ☽♂♌ ☽☐♆ ☿△♅

- eyes benefit from relaxation under warm Chamomile tea bags
- watch out for impulsiveness to avoid accidents

SUN 1

voc to 1:17 am ingress into Taurus ♉   earth/ root/ salt

☽△☽ ☽♂♉ ☽✶♄

- relaxing exercises for your neck and shoulders are very beneficial now
- be aware of your and others' need for comfort and security

"I will not be lectured about sexism and misogyny by this man. I will not. I am sick of crawling towards a world of gender equality. It is time to run."

Julia Gillard Libra 29 September 1961

	M	T	W	T	F	S	S	
A		1	2	3	4	5	6	○
U	7	8	9	10	11	12	13	☽
G	14	15	16	17	18	19	20	●
	21	22	23	24	25	26	27	☽
	28	29	30	31				○

	M	T	W	T	F	S	S	
S					1	2	3	
E	4	5	6	7	8	9	10	☽
P	11	12	13	14	15	16	17	●
	18	19	20	21	22	23	24	☽
	25	26	27	28	29	30	31	○

	M	T	W	T	F	S	S	
O	30	31					1	
C	2	3	4	5	6	7	8	☽
T	9	10	11	12	13	14	15	●
	16	17	18	19	20	21	22	☽
	23	24	25	26	27	28	29	○

OCTOBER 2023

WEEK 40

MON 2 waning Moon in Taurus ♉ — earth/ root/ salt

☽☌♃ ☽☌♅ ☽□♀ ☽✶♆ ☽△☿ ☿☍♆ ♀△☊

• excellent day for small maintenance jobs around the house and garden
• favourable time for projects requiring ingenuity and detailed work

International Day of Non-Violence

TUE 3 voc from 1:19 am to 5:02 am ingress into Gemini ♊ — air/ flower/ fat

☽△♇ ☽□⚸ ☽☌♊ ☽□♄ ☿△♇ ⚸☌♍

• good time for musicians to practise finger and breathing techniques
• spend time with your partner, siblings or friends

WED 4 waning Moon in Gemini ♊ — air/ flower/ fat

☽△☉ ☽✶⚷ ♂☍☊

• best time to clean windows and mirrors
• good time to focus on dental hygiene

THU 5 voc from 6:34 am to 12:31 pm ingress into Cancer ♋ — water/ leaf/ carbo

☽✶☊ ☽△♂ ☽□♆ ☽✶♀ ☽☌♋ ☽✶⚸ ☽□☿ ☽△♄ ☿☌♎

• opportune time to socialise, communicate and network
• good day for dusting and vacuuming

World Teachers' Day

☽Moon ☉Sun ☿Mercury ♀Venus ♂Mars ♃Jupiter ♄Saturn ♅Uranus ♆Neptune ♇Pluto ⚷Chiron
☊North Node ⚸Lilth ☌Conjunction, Ingress ✶Sextile □Square ☍Opposition △Trine (page 46)

FRI 6 · waning Moon in Cancer ♋ · water/ leaf/ carbo

☽□☉ ☽⚹♃ ☽□♅

• fresh leafy salads, herbs and sprouts are more nutritious now
• favourable time to focus on your family

SAT 7 · voc from 7:11 pm to 11:24 pm ingress into Leo ♌ · fire/ fruit/ protein

☽⚹♅ ☽□♎ ☽△♆ ☽□♂ ☽☍♀ ☽♂♌

• improve your digestive system eating bitter herbs
• good day to potter around the home and kitchen

Draconids Meteor Shower

SUN 8 · waning Moon in Leo ♌ · fire/ fruit/ protein

☽⚹☿

• eat fruit and fruiting vegetables for maximum nutritional benefit
• good day for any creatively inspired endeavour or performance

"If we are going to see real development in the world, then our best investment is women!"

Desmond Tutu 7 October 1931

M	T	W	T	F	S	S
				1	2	3
4	5	6	7	8	9	10
11	12	13	14	15	16	17
18	19	20	21	22	23	24
25	26	27	28	29	30	31

SEP ◖ ● ☽ ○

M	T	W	T	F	S	S
30	31					1
2	3	4	5	6	7	8
9	10	11	12	13	14	15
16	17	18	19	20	21	22
23	24	25	26	27	28	29

OCT ◖ ● ☽ ○

M	T	W	T	F	S	S
		1	2	3	4	5
6	7	8	9	10	11	12
13	14	15	16	17	18	19
20	21	22	23	24	25	26
27	28	29	30			

NOV ◖ ● ☽ ○

MON 9 waning Moon in Leo ♌ fire/ fruit/ protein

☽□♃ ☽✶☉ ☽△⚷ ☽□♅ ♀☌♍ ♀☌⚸ ♂□♇

- avoid anything troubling or irritating to the heart
- opportune day to make a good impression

TUE 10 voc from 9:36 am to 12:01 pm ingress into Virgo ♍ earth/ root/ salt

☽△☊ ☽✶♂ ☽☌♍ ☽☌⚸ ☽☍♄ ☽☌♀ ♀☍♄

- take care of business and private mail, email and messages
- a back massage helps you relax today

World Mental Health Day

WED 11 waning Moon in Virgo ♍ earth/ root/ salt

☽△♃ ☉☍⚷

- eat high fibre vegetables, e.g. roots, and avoid fatty and salty foods
- great time for bookkeeping and administrative jobs

THU 12 waning Moon in Virgo ♍ voc from 8:10 pm earth/ root/ salt

☽△♅ ☽☍♆ ☽△♇ ♂☌♏ ♄☍⚸

- opportune day to work on detailed projects
- good day for maintenance and sorting jobs

Pluto ♇ direct

☽Moon ☉Sun ☿Mercury ♀Venus ♂Mars ♃Jupiter ♄Saturn ♅Uranus ♆Neptune ♇Pluto ⚷Chiron
☊North Node ⚸Lilth ☌Conjunction, Ingress ✶Sextile □Square ☍Opposition △Trine (page 46)

FRI 13 voc to 0:21 am ingress into Libra ♎ — air/ flower/ fat

☽☌♎ ♂△♄ ☽✶⚸

• cleansing and toning cosmetics are very effective
• good day to beautify your surroundings

SAT 14 new Moon in Libra ♎ 5:54 pm 21° ♎ 07′ — air/ flower/ fat

☽☌☿ ☽☍⚷ ☽☌☉ ☿☍⚷

• perfect time to reflect and let go of outdated habits, set positive intentions tomorrow
• more info about Sun and Moon in Libra see page 39

Solar Eclipse

SUN 15 voc from 7:00 am to 11:03 am into Scorpio ♏ — water/ leaf/ carbo

☽☍☊ ☽□♇ ☽☌♏ ☽△♄ ☽✶⚸ ☽☌♂ ☽✶♀

• opportune day to set new goals and implement steps to reach them
• nurture and indulge yourself in a Lavender bath

International Pregnancy and Infant Loss Remembrance Day

"Great minds discuss ideas;
Average minds discuss events;
Small minds discuss people."

Eleanor Roosevelt, 11 October 1884

SEP	M	T	W	T	F	S	S	
					1	2	3	
	4	5	6	7	8	9	10	◖
	11	12	13	14	15	16	17	●
	18	19	20	21	22	23	24	◗
	25	26	27	28	29	30	31	○

OCT	M	T	W	T	F	S	S	
	30	31					1	
	2	3	4	5	6	7	8	◖
	9	10	11	12	13	14	15	●
	16	17	18	19	20	21	22	◗
	23	24	25	26	27	28	29	○

NOV	M	T	W	T	F	S	S	
			1	2	3	4	5	◖
	6	7	8	9	10	11	12	
	13	14	15	16	17	18	19	●
	20	21	22	23	24	25	26	◗
	27	28	29	30				○

OCTOBER 2023

MON 16 waxing Moon in Scorpio ♏︎ water/ leaf/ carbo

☽☌♃

• fresh leafy salads, herbs and sprouts are most nutritious now
• improve your digestive system by taking 'Swedish Bitters'
World Food Day

TUE 17 voc from 3:43 pm to 7:36 pm ingress into Sagittarius ♐︎ fire/ fruit/ protein

☽☌♅ ☽△♆ ☽✶♇ ☽☌♐︎ ☽□♄ ☽□☽

• drinking Stinging Nettle tea is beneficial to your kidneys and bladder
• fresh leafy salads, herbs and sprouts are more nutritious now

WED 18 waxing Moon in Sagittarius ♐︎ fire/ fruit/ protein

☽□♀ ☉☌☊

• eat fruit and fruiting vegetables for maximum nutritional benefit
• dry brushing your skin stimulates your overall circulation

THU 19 waxing Moon in Sagittarius ♐︎ voc from 7:01 pm fire/ fruit/ protein

☽△☿ ☽△☊ ☽□♆ ☽✶♅ ☽✶☉ ☿☌☊

• a gentle leg massage conditions the venous system today
• excellent day for a spontaneous outing

FRI 20   voc to 1:54 am ingress into Capricorn ♑   earth/ root/ salt

☽☌♑ ☽⚹♄ ☽△♆ ☽⚹♂ ☽△♀ ☽△♃ ☉☌☿
- eat root vegetables today for maximum nutritional benefit
- avoid too strenuous exercise; instead, elevate your legs

SAT 21   waxing Moon in Capricorn ♑   earth/ root/ salt

☽□♄ ☽△♅ ☽□♌ ☽⚹♆ ☉□♀ ☿□♆
- great opportunity to re-structure and be inspired
- favourable day for stretches and light gymnastics

Orionids Meteor Shower

SUN 22   voc from 6:00 am to 6:05 am ingress into Aquarius ♒   air/ flower/ fat

☽☌♆ ☽□☉ ☽□☿ ☽☌♒ ☽□♂ ☿☌♏ ☿△♄ ♀△♃
- avoid emotional outbursts and arguments, rather practise self control
- healing creams and facial packs are very beneficial today

I think if I'd quit years ago, I'd never have known what I was capable of doing.

Tom Petty 20 October 1950

	M	T	W	T	F	S	S			M	T	W	T	F	S	S			M	T	W	T	F	S	S	
					1	2	3			30	31					1					1	2	3	4	5	◗
S	4	5	6	7	8	9	10	◗	O	2	3	4	5	6	7	8	◗	N	6	7	8	9	10	11	12	
E	11	12	13	14	15	16	17	●	C	9	10	11	12	13	14	15	●	O	13	14	15	16	17	18	19	●
P	18	19	20	21	22	23	24	◖	T	16	17	18	19	20	21	22	◖	V	20	21	22	23	24	25	26	◖
	25	26	27	28	29	30	31	○		23	24	25	26	27	28	29	○		27	28	29	30				○

OCTOBER 2023

MON 23   waxing Moon in Aquarius ♒ voc from 7:04 pm   air/ flower/ fat

◐

☽□♃ ☽✳♅ ☽□♅ ☉♂♏ ☿✳(

• excellent day to start weaning babies (until next full Moon)
• opportune time to work with crystals

Look for Venus in the eastern sky before sunrise

TUE 24   voc to 8:32 am ingress into Pisces ♓   water/ leaf/ carbo

◐

☽✳♌ ☽♂♓ ☽♂♄ ☽△☉ ☽☍(☽△☿ ☽△♂ ☉△♄

• great day to buy new shoes, especially if you have sensitive feet
• excellent day for nourishing and regenerative treatments

United Nations Day

WED 25   waxing Moon in Pisces ♓   water/ leaf/ carbo

◑

☽✳♃ ☽☍♀ ☽✳♅

• a gentle foot reflexology massage has an invigorating effect on your organs
• opportune time to refine and restock your shop display today

THU 26   voc from 6:38 am to 10:01 am ingress into Aries ♈   fire/ fruit/ protein

◑

☽♂♆ ☽✳♅ ☽♂♈ ☉✳(

• all things nourishing and regenerative for body and mind are beneficial
• avoid washing and cutting hair to prevent dandruff

FRI **27**   waxing Moon in Aries ♈   fire/ fruit/ protein

○   ☽☌☿
• if possible, avoid dental treatments and operations on face, ears, jaw and neck
• avoid alcohol and stimulants to prevent headaches and migraines

SAT **28**   voc 8:19 am to 11:43 am ingress into Taurus ♉ full Moon 8:23 pm 5° ♉ 09′

○   ☽☌♌ ☽□♆ ☽☌♅ ☽⚹♄ ☽△♇ ☽☍☉ ♂☍♃
• great evening for a full Moon ritual, read more about Moon in Taurus on page 29
• overindulgence and drama can turn this into an emotionally challenging day
Lunar Eclipse

SUN **29**   waning Moon in Taurus ♉   earth/ root/ salt

○   ☽☌♃ ☽☍☿ ☽☍♂ ☽△♀ ☿☍♃ ☿☌♂
• be aware of your own and others' needs for comfort and security
• favourable day visit a powerful place in nature and meditate

"Women are the largest untapped
reservoir of talent in the world."

Hillary Clinton, 26 October 1947

	M	T	W	T	F	S	S	
						1	2	3
S	4	5	6	7	8	9	10	◐
E	11	12	13	14	15	16	17	●
P	18	19	20	21	22	23	24	◑
	25	26	27	28	29	30	31	○

	M	T	W	T	F	S	S	
	30	31					1	
O	2	3	4	5	6	7	8	◐
C	9	10	11	12	13	14	15	●
T	16	17	18	19	20	21	22	◑
	23	24	25	26	27	28	29	○

	M	T	W	T	F	S	S	
			1	2	3	4	5	◐
N	6	7	8	9	10	11	12	
O	13	14	15	16	17	18	19	●
V	20	21	22	23	24	25	26	◑
	27	28	29	30				○

MON 30   voc from 11:35 am to 3:07 pm ingress into Gemini ♊   air/ flower/ fat

☽♂♅ ☽✶♇ ☽△♀ ☽♂♊ ☽□♄ ☽□☾

• favourable time to tend to indoor flowering plants, vines and herbs
• a relaxing neck and shoulder massage is very beneficial today

TUE 31   waning Moon in Gemini ♊   air/ flower/ fat

☽✶♃ ♀△♅

• dusting and vacuuming is more effective now
• good day to clean windows, mirrors and tiles
Halloween

WED 1   voc from 12:36 pm to 9:30 pm ingress into Cancer ♋   water/ leaf/ carbo

☽□♀ ☽✶♋ ☽□♇ ☽♂♋ ☽△♄

• relaxing exercises for shoulders and arms are very beneficial now
• good time to focus on dental hygiene
Samhain (see page 13)

THU 2   waning Moon in Cancer ♋   water/ leaf/ carbo

☽✶☾ ☽△☉ ☽✶♃

• great day to centre your attention on home, family and garden
• improve your digestive system by drinking bitter teas

FRI 3   waning Moon in Cancer ♋   water/ leaf/ carbo

☽△♂ ☽□♂ ☽△♀ ☽✶♅ ☽□♋ ☽✶♀ ☽△♆ ☉⚹♃ ♀⚹♆

- great time to write those Christmas cards to family and friends overseas
- excellent opportunity to nurture yourself and loved ones

best time to view and photograph Jupiter and its moons

SAT 4   voc from 3:27 am to 7:20 am ingress into Leo ♌   fire/ fruit/ protein

☽⚹♆ ☽♂♌ ☿⚹♅

- enjoy giving or receiving a relaxing back massage today
- good day for hair cuts colouring and streaks

Taurids Meteor Shower

SUN 5   waning Moon in Leo ♌   fire/ fruit/ protein

☽□♃ ☽□☉ ☽△♂ ☽□♂

- avoid anything troubling or irritating to the heart
- fresh fruit is especially nutritious now

Saturn ♄ direct

"Nothing in life is to be feared, it is only to be understood. Now is the time to understand more, so that we may fear less."

Marie Curie 7 November 1867

M	T	W	T	F	S	S
30	31					1
2	3	4	5	6	7	8
9	10	11	12	13	14	15
16	17	18	19	20	21	22
23	24	25	26	27	28	29

OCT

M	T	W	T	F	S	S
		1	2	3	4	5
6	7	8	9	10	11	12
13	14	15	16	17	18	19
20	21	22	23	24	25	26
27	28	29	30			

NOV

M	T	W	T	F	S	S
				1	2	3
4	5	6	7	8	9	10
11	12	13	14	15	16	17
18	19	20	21	22	23	24
25	26	27	28	29	30	31

DEC

NOVEMBER 2023

MON 6   voc from 7:25 am to 7:38 pm ingress into Virgo ♍   earth/ root/ salt

☽□♅ ☽□☿ ☽△☊ ☽☌♍ ☽⚍♄ ♀△♇
- deep cleansing skin and hair treatments are very effective today
- Moon voc all day, great opportunity for a clean up

TUE 7   waning Moon in Virgo ♍   earth/ root/ salt

☽☌⚸ ☽△♃ ☿△♇
- focus on health and daily routine
- good day for bookkeeping

WED 8   waning Moon in Virgo ♍   earth/ root/ salt

☽⚹☉ ☽⚹♂ ☽△♅ ☽⚍♇ ♀☌♎
- opportune time for laying pavers, excavations and earth moving
- favourable day for maintenance and sorting jobs

THU 9   voc from 4:54 am to 8:07 am ingress into Libra ♎   air/ flower/ fat

☽△♇ ☽⚹☿ ☽☌♎ ☽☌♀ ☿⚹♇
- express yourself clearly, take care of e-mails and messages
- excellent opportunity to beautify your surroundings

☽Moon ☉Sun ☿Mercury ♀Venus ♂Mars ♃Jupiter ♄Saturn ♅Uranus ♆Neptune ♇Pluto ⚷Chiron
☊North Node ⚸Lilth ☌Conjunction, Ingress ⚹Sextile □Square ⚍Opposition △Trine (page 46)

FRI 10 waning Moon in Libra ♎   air/ flower/ fat

☽☍☿ ♀♂♐ ☿□♄
• good day to attend to indoor flowering plants, vines and herbs
• great time to detoxify in the sauna or have a hot Lavender bath
World Science Day for Peace and Development

SAT 11 voc from 3:05 pm to 6:38 pm ingress into Scorpio ♏   water/ leaf/ carbo

☽☍♌ ☽□♇ ☽♂♏ ☽△♄ ♂☍♅
• drink teas that support the kidneys, e.g. Stinging Nettle
• painting jobs turn out well

SUN 12 waning Moon in Scorpio ♏   water/ leaf/ carbo

☽⚹⚷ ☽☍♃
• nourish and soothe your soul today, take it easy if you are pregnant
• a coffee body scrub helps to firm and tighten your skin

"Obstacles, of course, are developmentally necessary:
they teach kids strategy, patience, critical thinking,
resilience and resourcefulness."

Naomi Wolf 12 November 1962

M	T	W	T	F	S	S
30	31					1
2	3	4	5	6	7	8
9	10	11	12	13	14	15
16	17	18	19	20	21	22
23	24	25	26	27	28	29

OCT

M	T	W	T	F	S	S
		1	2	3	4	5
6	7	8	9	10	11	12
13	14	15	16	17	18	19
20	21	22	23	24	25	26
27	28	29	30			

NOV

M	T	W	T	F	S	S
				1	2	3
4	5	6	7	8	9	10
11	12	13	14	15	16	17
18	19	20	21	22	23	24
25	26	27	28	29	30	31

DEC

MON 13 new Moon in Scorpio ♏ 9:27 am 20° ♏ 43′ voc from 11:03 pm

☽☌☉ ☽☍♅ ☽☌♂ ☽△♆ ☽⚹♇ ☉☍♅ ☿□☾
- opportune day to set goals and work out steps to achieve them
- for more info about Sun and Moon in Scorpio see page 41

TUE 14 voc to 2:22 am ingress into Sagittarius ♐   fire/ fruit/ protein

☽☌♐ ☽□♄ ☽□☾ ☽☌☿ ☽⚹♀
- eat fruit and fruiting vegetables for maximum nutritional benefit
- avoid too strenuous exercise, rather elevate your legs

WED 15 waxing Moon in Sagittarius ♐ voc from 10:56 pm   fire/ fruit/ protein

☽△♀ ☽△☊ ☽□♆ ☿⚹♀
- dry brushing your skin stimulates your overall circulation
- excellent day for a spontaneous outing

THU 16 voc to 7:41 am ingress into Capricorn ♑   earth/ root/ salt

☽☌♑ ☽⚹♄ ☽△☾ ☽△♃
- great time for a conditioning manicure and pedicure
- avoid stress on bones and joints, particularly knees

FRI 17 waxing Moon in Capricorn ♑ earth/ root/ salt

☽□♀ ☽□♄ ☽△♅ ☉△♆ ♂△♆
• nourishing skin treatments, wraps and facials are beneficial now
• eat root vegetables today for maximum nutritional benefit

Leonids Meteor Shower

SAT 18 voc from 8:27 am to 11:27 am ingress into Aquarius ♒ air/ flower/ fat

☽□♌ ☽⚹♆ ☽⚹☉ ☽⚹♂ ☽☌♆ ☽☌♒ ☉☌♂
• stretches and light gymnastics are very beneficial today
• great opportunity to re-structure and be inspired

SUN 19 waxing Moon in Aquarius ♒ air/ flower/ fat

☽□♃ ☽△♀ ☽⚹☿ ☽⚹♄ ☽□♅
• favourable day to explore, research and network new trends
• good day to start weaning babies until the next full Moon

"Don't let them get you down.
Be cheeky and wild and wonderful.

Pippi Longstocking by Astrid Lindgren, 14 Nov 1907

M	T	W	T	F	S	S	
30	31					1	
2	3	4	5	6	7	8	◐
9	10	11	12	13	14	15	●
16	17	18	19	20	21	22	◑
23	24	25	26	27	28	29	○

OCT

M	T	W	T	F	S	S	
		1	2	3	4	5	◐
6	7	8	9	10	11	12	
13	14	15	16	17	18	19	●
20	21	22	23	24	25	26	◑
27	28	29	30				○

NOV

M	T	W	T	F	S	S	
				1	2	3	
4	5	6	7	8	9	10	◐
11	12	13	14	15	16	17	●
18	19	20	21	22	23	24	◑
25	26	27	28	29	30	31	○

DEC

MON 20   voc from 10:49 am to 2:28 pm ingress into Pisces ♓   water/ leaf/ carbo

☽✶☊ ☽□♂ ☽□☉ ☽♂♅ ☽♂♄ ☽☍♆ ☉✶♆
- healing creams and facial packs are very beneficial today
- a gentle leg massage conditions the venous system

TUE 21   waxing Moon in Pisces ♓   water/ leaf/ carbo

☽✶♃ ☽□☿ ☿△♆
- excellent time to refine and restock your shop display
- avoid washing and cutting hair to prevent dandruff

WED 22   voc from 3:09 pm to 5:19 pm ingress into Aries ♈   fire/ fruit/ protein

☽✶♅ ☽♂♆ ☽✶♇ ☽△♂ ☽♂♈ ☽△☉ ☉♂♐ ♀☍♅ ♂✶♆
- great day to buy new shoes, especially if you have sensitive feet
- foot reflexology massage is very effective now

THU 23   waxing Moon in Aries ♈   fire/ fruit/ protein

☽♂♅ ☽☍♀ ☉□♄
- all things nourishing and regenerative for body and mind are beneficial
- good day for hair colouring and streaks, shorter application time

FRI 24 voc from 5:40 pm to 8:28 pm ingress into Taurus ♉ earth/ root/ salt

☽△☿ ☽♂☊ ☽□♆ ☽♂♅ ☽⚹♄ ♂♂♐
- avoid alcohol and stimulants to prevent headaches and migraines
- nurture your eyes with cotton pads soaked in almond milk

SAT 25 waxing Moon in Taurus ♉ earth/ root/ salt

☽△♆ ☽♂♃ ♂□♄
- be aware of your and others' need for comfort and security
- good day to shop for Christmas presents

SUN 26 waxing Moon in Taurus ♉ voc from 9:51 pm earth/ root/ salt

☽♂♅ ☽⚹♆ ☽△♆
- gentle with your voice and throat; for sore throats gargle with Sage or Chamomile tea
- great evening for a full Moon ritual, read more about Moon in Gemini on page 31

"When the power of love
overcomes the love of power,
the world will know peace."
Jimi Hendrix 27 November 1942

M	T	W	T	F	S	S
30	31					1
2	3	4	5	6	7	8
9	10	11	12	13	14	15
16	17	18	19	20	21	22
23	24	25	26	27	28	29

OCT

M	T	W	T	F	S	S
		1	2	3	4	5
6	7	8	9	10	11	12
13	14	15	16	17	18	19
20	21	22	23	24	25	26
27	28	29	30			

NOV

M	T	W	T	F	S	S
				1	2	3
4	5	6	7	8	9	10
11	12	13	14	15	16	17
18	19	20	21	22	23	24
25	26	27	28	29	30	31

DEC

NOVEMBER 2023

MON 27 voc to 0:39 am into Gemini ♊ full Moon 9:16 am 4° ♊ 51'   air/ flower/ fat

☽☌♊ ☽□♄ ☽☍♂ ☽☍☉ ☽□◐ ☿△♌ ☿□♆
• relaxing exercises for shoulders and arms are very beneficial today
• avoid paint, solvents and paint stripping jobs

TUE 28 waning Moon in Gemini ♊   air/ flower/ fat

☽✶♀ ☽△♀ ☽✶♌ ☽□♆ ☉◐
• breathing and gentle singing exercises are beneficial for your lungs
• good day to attend to your indoor flowering plants

WED 29 voc from 1:02 am to 6:53 am ingress into Cancer ♋   water/ leaf/ carbo

☽☍☿ ☽☌♋ ☽△♄ ☽✶◐ ☽✶♃ ♀☍♌
• improve your digestive system by drinking bitter teas
• spend time with your siblings and friends

THU 30 waning Moon in Cancer ♋   water/ leaf/ carbo

☽□♀ ☽✶♅
• favourable day to focus on your home and garden
• avoid washing or cutting hair, it becomes unruly

FRI 1   voc from 1:06 pm to 4:00 pm ingress into Leo ♌   fire/ fruit/ protein

☽□♎ ☽△♇ ☽□♀ ☽☍♅ ☽♂♌ ☿♂♑

• a moody day; meditations and relaxing massages are very beneficial
• enjoy a nourishing Lavender bath tonight

SAT 2   waning Moon in Leo ♌   fire/ fruit/ protein

☽△♂ ☽□♃ ☽△☉ ☽△♀ ☿⚹♄

• excellent day for cleaning windows, mirrors and mopping floors
• all creative and fun endeavours are favoured now

SUN 3   waning Moon in Leo ♌   fire/ fruit/ protein

☽□♅ ☽△♌ ♀□♇ ♃△☽

• everything relaxing for heart and back is very beneficial today
• receive or give a relaxing back massage

*"The pessimist sees difficulty in every opportunity.
The optimist sees opportunity in every difficulty."*

W. Churchill 30 November 1874

M	T	W	T	F	S	S
30	31					1
2	3	4	5	<u>6</u>	7	8
9	10	11	12	13	<u>14</u>	15
16	17	18	19	20	21	<u>22</u>
23	24	25	26	27	<u>28</u>	29

OCT

M	T	W	T	F	S	S
		1	2	3	4	<u>5</u>
6	7	8	9	10	11	12
<u>13</u>	14	15	16	17	18	19
<u>20</u>	21	22	23	24	25	26
<u>27</u>	28	29	30			

NOV

M	T	W	T	F	S	S
				1	2	3
4	<u>5</u>	6	7	8	9	10
11	<u>12</u>	13	14	15	16	17
18	<u>19</u>	20	21	22	23	24
25	26	<u>27</u>	28	29	30	31

DEC

DECEMBER 2023

MON 4   voc from 2:11 am to 3:50 am ingress into Virgo ♍   earth/ root/ salt

☽✳♀ ☽♂♍ ☽☍♄ ☽△☿ ☽△♃ ☽♂☾ ☽☐♂ ♀♂♏ ♂☐☾
- express yourself clearly, take care of emails and messages
- the emphasis is on health and daily routine

Look for Mercury low in the western sky just after sunset

TUE 5   waning Moon in Virgo ♍   earth/ root/ salt

☽☐☉ ☽△♅ ♀△♄
- great time for bookkeeping and administrative jobs
- excellent day to work on detailed project

World Soil Day

WED 6   voc from 1:49 pm to 4:34 pm ingress into Libra ♎   air/ flower/ fat

☽☍♆ ☽△♇ ☽♂♎
- favourable time to de-clutter and for general garden maintenance
- haircuts and perms are very accurate and last longer

THU 7   waning Moon in Libra ♎   air/ flower/ fat

☽☐☿ ☽✳♂ ☽✳☉ ☽☍♃
- good day to attend to indoor flowering plants
- painting jobs turn out well

Neptune ♆ direct

FRI 8   waning Moon in Libra ♎   air/ flower/ fat

☽☍♌   ☉△♅   ☿△♃

• good time to start beautifying your home for Christmas
• cleansing and toning cosmetics are very effective

SAT 9   voc from 1:05 am to 3:34 am ingress into Scorpio ♏   water/ leaf/ carbo

☽□♆   ☽♂♏   ☽△♄   ☽♂♀   ☽☍♃   ☽⚹☿   ☽⚹⚸   ☿△⚸

• support your digestive system by taking 'Swedish Bitters'
• excellent day to wrap Christmas presents

SUN 10   waning Moon in Scorpio ♏   water/ leaf/ carbo

☽☍♅   ♀☍♃

• a coffee body scrub helps to firm and tighten your skin
• great time to detoxify in the sauna
Human Rights Day

"It always takes the truth a little bit
longer to cross the finishing line."

Kim Basinger 8 December 1953

	M	T	W	T	F	S	S	
N O V			1	2	3	4	5	◗
	6	7	8	9	10	11	12	
	13	14	15	16	17	18	19	●
	20	21	22	23	24	25	26	◑
	27	28	29	30				○

	M	T	W	T	F	S	S	
D E C					1	2	3	
	4	5	6	7	8	9	10	◗
	11	12	13	14	15	16	17	●
	18	19	20	21	22	23	24	◑
	25	26	27	28	29	30	31	○

	M	T	W	T	F	S	S	
J A N	1	2	3	4	5	6	7	◗
	8	9	10	11	12	13	14	●
	15	16	17	18	19	20	21	◑
	22	23	24	25	26	27	28	○
	29	30	31					

MON 11   voc from 8:57 am to 11:10 am ingress into Sagittarius ♐   fire/ fruit/ protein

☽△♅ ☽⚹♆ ☽♂♐ ☽□♄ ☿⚹♀ ♀⚹☾
- lymphatic drainage massages are more beneficial today
- tie up loose ends before the holiday season begins

TUE 12   new Moon in Sagittarius ♐ 11:31 pm 20° ♐ 40′   fire/ fruit/ protein

☽□☾ ☽♂♂ ☽△☥ ☽♂☉
- spend a moment and reflect on the last year; consolidate and let go of excess
- for more info about Sun and Moon in Sagittarius see page 43

WED 13   voc from 6:48 am to 3:31 pm ingress into Capricorn ♑   earth/ root/ salt

☽△♎ ☽□♆ ☽♂♑ ☽⚹♄
- excellent time to set goals and work on strategies to reach them
- dry brushing your skin invigorates your circulation

Geminids Meteor Shower

THU 14   waxing Moon in Capricorn ♑   earth/ root/ salt

☽△♃ ☽△☾ ☽♂☿ ☽⚹♀ ☽□♅
- opportune day to think about and plan the upcoming business year
- brainstorm with others, take note of good ideas today

Mercury ☿ retrograde until 1 January 2024

☽Moon ☉Sun ☿Mercury ♀Venus ♂Mars ♃Jupiter ♄Saturn ♅Uranus ♆Neptune ♇Pluto ⚷Chiron
☊North Node ☾Lilith ♂Conjunction Ingress ⚹Sextile □Square ⚼Opposition △Trine (page 46)

168

FRI 15 voc from 4:03 pm to 5:55 pm ingress into Aquarius ♒ air/ flower/ fat

☽△♅ ☽□♎ ☽✶♄ ☽☌♆ ☽☌♒ ☉△♎ ☿△♆ ♂△♊
- good day for researching and scrutinising business trends
  - great day for business projects and networking

SAT 16 waxing Moon in Aquarius ♒ air/ flower/ fat

☽□♃ ☽□♀ ☽✶♊ ☽✶♂
- excellent time to start weening a baby and feed more solids
  - good day to attend to indoor flowering plants

SUN 17 voc from 12:03 pm to 7:58 pm ingress into Pisces ♓ water/ leaf/ carbo

☽□♅ ☽✶♓ ☽✶☉ ☽☌♓ ☽☌♄ ☉□♆
- a warm Epsom Salts foot soak helps you sleep
  - great day for baking

You say I'm great, thank you very much.
But I know what I am. I could be better, man, you know?

Keith Richards 18 December 1943

	M	T	W	T	F	S	S	
N			1	2	3	4	5	◐
O	6	7	8	9	10	11	12	
V	13	14	15	16	17	18	19	●
	20	21	22	23	24	25	26	◗
	27	28	29	30				○

	M	T	W	T	F	S	S	
D					1	2	3	
E	4	5	6	7	8	9	10	◗
C	11	12	13	14	15	16	17	●
	18	19	20	21	22	23	24	◗
	25	26	27	28	29	30	31	○

	M	T	W	T	F	S	S	
J	1	2	3	4	5	6	7	◐
A	8	9	10	11	12	13	14	●
N	15	16	17	18	19	20	21	◗
	22	23	24	25	26	27	28	○
	29	30	31					

MON 18   waxing Moon in Pisces ♓ water/ leaf/ carbo

☽✳♃   ☽✳☿   ☽☌☾   ☿△♃
- good time for a nurturing foot-soak and foot reflexology massage
- great day to refine and restock your shop display

International Migrants Day

TUE 19   voc from 9:03 pm to 10:46 pm ingress into Aries ♈ fire/ fruit/ protein

☽△♀   ☽□♂   ☽✳♅   ☽☌♆   ☽□☉   ☽✳♇   ☽☌♈
- excellent day for nourishing and regenerative treatments
- avoid washing and cutting hair to prevent dandruff

WED 20   waxing Moon in Aries ♈ fire/ fruit/ protein

☽□☿
- good days for hair colouring and streaks, shorter application time
- good time for a pre-Christmas get-together

International Human Solidarity Day

THU 21   waxing Moon in Aries ♈ fire/ fruit/ protein

☽☌♄   ☽△♂   ☽☌☊   ☿✳♄   ♀☍♅
- avoid stimulants to prevent headaches and migraines
- great day for a spontaneous outing

Ursids Meteor Shower

FRI 22   voc from 2:46 am to 2:49 am ingress into Taurus ♉   earth/ root/ salt

☽□♀ ☽△☉ ☽♂♉ ☽△☿ ☽⚹♄ ☽♂♃ ☽△☾ ☉♂♑ ☉♂☿
- eat root vegetables today for maximum nutritional benefit
- excellent time to prepare for Christmas

Winter Solstice, Yule (see page 13)

SAT 23   waxing Moon in Taurus ♉   earth/ root/ salt

☽♂♅ ☽⚬♀ ☽⚹♆ ☿♂♐
- great opportunity to prepare nourishing food for family and friends
- be aware of your and others' need for comfort and security

SUN 24   voc from 6:39 am to 8:14 am ingress into Gemini ♊   air/ flower/ fat

☽△♀ ☽♂♊ ☽□♄ ☉⚹♄
- we at Moontime Diary wish you a wholesome Christmas in best health and company

Christmas Eve

"It's never too late - never too late to start over, never too late to be happy."

June Fonda 21 December 1937

	M	T	W	T	F	S	S	
N			1	2	3	4	5	◗
O	6	7	8	9	10	11	12	
V	13	14	15	16	17	18	19	●
	20	21	22	23	24	25	26	◑
	27	28	29	30				○

	M	T	W	T	F	S	S	
D					1	2	3	
E	4	5	6	7	8	9	10	◗
C	11	12	13	14	15	16	17	●
	18	19	20	21	22	23	24	◑
	25	26	27	28	29	30	31	○

	M	T	W	T	F	S	S	
	1	2	3	4	5	6	7	◗
J	8	9	10	11	12	13	14	●
A	15	16	17	18	19	20	21	◑
N	22	23	24	25	26	27	28	○
	29	30	31					

DECEMBER 2023

MON 25   waxing Moon in Gemini ♊   air/ flower/ fat

☽□⚷   ☽⚹♅   ♀△♆   ♂△☊
- be aware of your communication style to avoid possible misunderstanding
- emotions run high, tendency to overreact, overindulge and overeat

Christmas Day

TUE 26   voc from 7:55 am to 3:14 pm ingress into Cancer ♋   water/ leaf/ carbo

☽⚹☊   ☽☍♂   ☽□♆   ☽☍☿   ☽♂♋   ☽△♄
- great evening for a full Moon ritual, read more about moon in Cancer on page 33
- favourable time to spend time with friends and family

Boxing Day

WED 27   full Moon in Cancer ♋ 0:32 am 4° ♋ 58′   water/ leaf/ carbo

☽☍☉   ☽⚹♃   ☽⚹⚷   ☽□⚸   ☉△♃   ☿□♅
- excellent day to relax or meditate at a lake or the beach
- good time for a family movie tonight

THU 28   waning Moon in Cancer ♋ voc from 10:57 pm   water/ leaf/ carbo

☽⚹♅   ☽□☊   ☽△♆   ☽△♀   ☽☍♇   ☿♂♂   ♂□♅
- favourable day to focus on home and family
- nurture yourself and your loved ones today

Chiron ⚷ direct

FRI 29   voc to 0:22 am ingress into Leo ♌   **fire/ fruit/ protein**

☽☌♌   ☽□♃   ♀⚹♆   ♀☌♐

• all creative and fun endeavours are favoured now
• a back massage is wonderfully relaxing today

SAT 30   waning Moon in Leo ♌   **fire/ fruit/ protein**

☽△♅   ☽□♅   ☽△♎   ☽△☿

• excellent day to make yourself and others feel special
• great evening to perform, entertain and dine out

SUN 31   voc from 5:18 am to 11:53 am ingress into Virgo ♍   **earth/ root/ salt**

☽△♂   ☽☌♍   ☽□♀   ☽☍♄   ☽△♃   ☉△☽

• Moontime Diary wishes you good health, prosperity and wisdom for 2024
• excellent time for a party or gathering with friends and family
New Year's Eve

"Nature is pleased with simplicity.
And nature is no dummy."

Sir Isaac Newton, 25 December 1642

	M	T	W	T	F	S	S	
					1	2	3	4	5	◗
N	6	7	8	9	10	11	12	
O	13	14	15	16	17	18	19	●
V	20	21	22	23	24	25	26	◐
	27	28	29	30				○

	M	T	W	T	F	S	S	
						1	2	3	
D	4	5	6	7	8	9	10	◗
E	11	12	13	14	15	16	17	●
C	18	19	20	21	22	23	24	◐
	25	26	27	28	29	30	31	○

	M	T	W	T	F	S	S	
	1	2	3	4	5	6	7	◗
J	8	9	10	11	12	13	14	●
A	15	16	17	18	19	20	21	◐
N	22	23	24	25	26	27	28	○
	29	30	31					

NOTES & NUMBERS

NOTES & NUMBERS

NOTES & NUMBERS

Notes & Numbers

Notes & Numbers

NOTES & NUMBERS

Moontime Menstruation Chart 2023

	1	2	3	4	5	6	7	8	9	10	11	12	13	14	15
Jan	○	○	○	○	○	○	○	○	○	○	○	○	○	○	○
Feb	○	○	○	○	○	○	○	○	○	○	○	○	○	○	○
Mar	○	○	○	○	○	○	○	○	○	○	○	○	○	○	○
Apr	○	○	○	○	○	○	○	○	○	○	○	○	○	○	○
May	○	○	○	○	○	○	○	○	○	○	○	○	○	○	○
Jun	○	○	○	○	○	○	○	○	○	○	○	○	○	○	○
Jul	○	○	○	○	○	○	○	○	○	○	○	○	○	○	○
Aug	○	○	○	○	○	○	○	○	○	○	○	○	○	○	○
Sep	○	○	○	○	○	○	○	○	○	○	○	○	○	○	○
Oct	○	○	○	○	○	○	○	○	○	○	○	○	○	○	○
Nov	○	○	○	○	○	○	○	○	○	○	○	○	○	○	○
Dec	○	○	○	○	○	○	○	○	○	○	○	○	○	○	○

| | 1 | 2 | 3 | 4 | 5 | 6 | 7 | 8 | 9 | 10 | 11 | 12 | 13 | 14 | 15 |

Mark your period in this menstruation flow chart to discover your period pattern and how your body relates to the lunar cycle.

Moontime Menstruation Chart 2023

16	17	18	19	20	21	22	23	24	25	26	27	28	29	30	31
O	O	O	O	O	O	O	O	O	O	O	O	O	O	O	O
O	O	O	O	O	O	O	O	O	O	O	O	O			
O	O	O	O	O	O	O	O	O	O	O	O	O	O	O	O
O	O	O	O	O	O	O	O	O	O	O	O	O	O		
O	O	O	O	O	O	O	O	O	O	O	O	O	O	O	O
O	O	O	O	O	O	O	O	O	O	O	O	O	O		
O	O	O	O	O	O	O	O	O	O	O	O	O	O	O	O
O	O	O	O	O	O	O	O	O	O	O	O	O	O	O	O
O	O	O	O	O	O	O	O	O	O	O	O	O	O	O	
O	O	O	O	O	O	O	O	O	O	O	O	O	O	O	O
O	O	O	O	O	O	O	O	O	O	O	O	O	O	O	
O	O	O	O	O	O	O	O	O	O	O	O	O	O	O	O

16	17	18	19	20	21	22	23	24	25	26	27	28	29	30	31

This method keeps you on track with your ovulation cycle and helps predict future periods..

Yearly Planner

	January	February	March	April	May	June
1						
2						
3						
4						
5						
6						
7						
8						
9						
10						
11						
12						
13						
14						
15						
16						
17						
18						
19						
20						
21						
22						
23						
24						
25						
26						
27						
28						
29						
30						
31						

YEARLY PLANNER

July	August	September	October	November	December	
						1
						2
						3
						4
						5
						6
						7
						8
						9
						10
						11
						12
						13
						14
						15
						16
						17
						18
						19
						20
						21
						22
						23
						24
						25
						26
						27
						28
						29
						30
						31

MOON CHART 2023

	January		February		March		April		May		June	
1	SUN	♉	WED	♊	WED	♋	SAT	♌	MON	♍	THU	♏
2	MON	♉	THU	♋	THU	♋	SUN	♍	TUE	♎	FRI	♏
3	TUE	♊	FRI	♋	FRI	♋	MON	♍	WED	♎	SAT	♐
4	WED	♊	SAT	♌	SAT	♌	TUE	♍	THU	♎	SUN ○	♐
5	THU	♊	SUN ○	♌	SUN	♌	WED	♎	FRI ○	♏	MON	♑
6	FRI ○	♋	MON	♌	MON	♍	THU ○	♎	SAT	♏	TUE	♑
7	SAT	♋	TUE	♍	TUE ○	♍	FRI	♏	SUN	♐	WED	♒
8	SUN	♋	WED	♍	WED	♍	SAT	♏	MON	♐	THU	♒
9	MON	♌	THU	♎	THU	♎	SUN	♏	TUE	♑	FRI	♓
10	TUE	♌	FRI	♎	FRI	♎	MON	♐	WED	♑	SAT ☾	♓
11	WED	♍	SAT	♎	SAT	♏	TUE	♐	THU	♒	SUN	♓
12	THU	♍	SUN	♏	SUN	♏	WED	♑	FRI ☾	♒	MON	♈
13	FRI	♎	MON ☾	♏	MON	♐	THU ☾	♑	SAT	♓	TUE	♈
14	SAT	♎	TUE	♐	TUE	♐	FRI	♒	SUN	♓	WED	♉
15	SUN ☾	♎	WED	♐	WED ☾	♐	SAT	♒	MON	♈	THU	♉
16	MON	♏	THU	♑	THU	♑	SUN	♓	TUE	♈	FRI	♊
17	TUE	♏	FRI	♑	FRI	♑	MON	♓	WED	♈	SAT	♊
18	WED	♐	SAT	♒	SAT	♒	TUE	♈	THU	♉	SUN ●	♊
19	THU	♐	SUN	♒	SUN	♒	WED	♈	FRI ●	♉	MON	♋
20	FRI	♑	MON ●	♓	MON	♓	THU ●	♈	SAT	♊	TUE	♋
21	SAT ●	♒	TUE	♓	TUE ●	♈	FRI	♉	SUN	♊	WED	♌
22	SUN	♒	WED	♈	WED	♈	SAT	♊	MON	♋	THU	♌
23	MON	♒	THU	♈	THU	♈	SUN	♊	TUE	♋	FRI	♍
24	TUE	♓	FRI	♉	FRI	♉	MON	♊	WED	♋	SAT	♍
25	WED	♓	SAT	♉	SAT	♉	TUE	♋	THU	♌	SUN	♍
26	THU	♈	SUN	♉	SUN	♊	WED	♋	FRI	♌	MON ☽	♎
27	FRI	♈	MON ☽	♊	MON	♊	THU ☽	♌	SAT ☽	♍	TUE	♎
28	SAT	♉	TUE	♊	TUE	♋	FRI	♌	SUN	♍	WED	♏
29	SUN ☽	♉			WED ☽	♋	SAT	♌	MON	♍	THU	♏
30	MON	♊			THU	♋	SUN	♍	TUE	♎	FRI	♏
31	TUE	♊			FRI	♌			WED	♎		

● New Moon; ☽ 1st Quarter; ○ Full Moon; ☾ 3rd Quarter; Moon listed at 12 noon (except some ○ & ●)

184

Moon Chart 2023

July	August	September	October	November	December	
SAT ♐	TUE ○ ♒	FRI ♓	SUN ♉	WED ♊	FRI ♋	1
SUN ♐	WED ♒	SAT ♈	MON ♉	THU ♋	SAT ♌	2
MON ○ ♑	THU ♓	SUN ♈	TUE ♊	FRI ♋	SUN ♌	3
TUE ♑	FRI ♓	MON ♉	WED ♊	SAT ♌	MON ♍	4
WED ♒	SAT ♈	TUE ♉	THU ♊	SUN ◐ ♌	TUE ◐ ♍	5
THU ♒	SUN ♈	WED ◐ ♊	FRI ◐ ♋	MON ♌	WED ♍	6
FRI ♓	MON ♉	THU ♊	SAT ♋	TUE ♍	THU ♎	7
SAT ♓	TUE ◐ ♉	FRI ♋	SUN ♌	WED ♍	FRI ♎	8
SUN ♈	WED ♉	SAT ♋	MON ♌	THU ♎	SAT ♏	9
MON ◐ ♈	THU ♊	SUN ♋	TUE ♌	FRI ♎	SUN ♏	10
TUE ♉	FRI ♊	MON ♌	WED ♍	SAT ♎	MON ♐	11
WED ♉	SAT ♋	TUE ♌	THU ♍	SUN ♏	TUE ● ♐	12
THU ♊	SUN ♋	WED ♍	FRI ♎	MON ● ♏	WED ♐	13
FRI ♊	MON ♌	THU ♍	SAT ● ♎	TUE ♐	THU ♑	14
SAT ♊	TUE ♌	FRI ● ♍	SUN ♏	WED ♐	FRI ♑	15
SUN ♋	WED ● ♌	SAT ♎	MON ♏	THU ♑	SAT ♒	16
MON ● ♋	THU ♍	SUN ♎	TUE ♏	FRI ♑	SUN ♒	17
TUE ♌	FRI ♍	MON ♏	WED ♐	SAT ♒	MON ♓	18
WED ♌	SAT ♎	TUE ♏	THU ♐	SUN ♒	TUE ◑ ♓	19
THU ♌	SUN ♎	WED ♏	FRI ♑	MON ◑ ♒	WED ♈	20
FRI ♍	MON ♎	THU ♐	SAT ♑	TUE ♓	THU ♈	21
SAT ♍	TUE ♏	FRI ◑ ♐	SUN ◑ ♒	WED ♓	FRI ♉	22
SUN ♎	WED ♏	SAT ♑	MON ♒	THU ♈	SAT ♉	23
MON ♎	THU ◑ ♐	SUN ♑	TUE ♓	FRI ♈	SUN ♊	24
TUE ◑ ♎	FRI ♐	MON ♒	WED ♓	SAT ♉	MON ♊	25
WED ♏	SAT ♐	TUE ♒	THU ♈	SUN ♉	TUE ♊	26
THU ♏	SUN ♑	WED ♓	FRI ♈	MON ○ ♊	WED ○ ♋	27
FRI ♐	MON ♑	THU ♓	SAT ○ ♉	TUE ♊	THU ♋	28
SAT ♐	TUE ♒	FRI ○ ♈	SUN ♉	WED ♊	FRI ♌	29
SUN ♑	WED ♒	SAT ♈	MON ♉	THU ♋	SAT ♌	30
MON ♑	THU ○ ♓		TUE ♊		SUN ♍	31

For Eclipses, Blue and Super Moons please refer to page 189

2023

JAN
M	T	W	T	F	S	S	
30	31					1	
2	3	4	5	6	7	8	○
9	10	11	12	13	14	15	◖
16	17	18	19	20	21	22	●
23	24	25	26	27	28	29	◗

FEB
M	T	W	T	F	S	S	
		1	2	3	4	5	○
6	7	8	9	10	11	12	
13	14	15	16	17	18	19	◖
20	21	22	23	24	25	26	●
27	28						◗

MAR
M	T	W	T	F	S	S	
		1	2	3	4	5	
6	7	8	9	10	11	12	○
13	14	15	16	17	18	19	◖
20	21	22	23	24	25	26	●
27	28	29	30	31			◗

APR
M	T	W	T	F	S	S	
31					1	2	
3	4	5	6	7	8	9	○
10	11	12	13	14	15	16	◖
17	18	19	20	21	22	23	●
24	25	26	27	28	29	30	◗

MAY
M	T	W	T	F	S	S	
1	2	3	4	5	6	7	○
8	9	10	11	12	13	14	◖
15	16	17	18	19	20	21	●
22	23	24	25	26	27	28	◗
29	30	31					

JUN
M	T	W	T	F	S	S	
			1	2	3	4	○
5	6	7	8	9	10	11	◖
12	13	14	15	16	17	18	●
19	20	21	22	23	24	25	
26	27	28	29	30			◗

JUL
M	T	W	T	F	S	S	
31					1	2	
3	4	5	6	7	8	9	○
10	11	12	13	14	15	16	◖
17	18	19	20	21	22	23	●
24	25	26	27	28	29	30	◗

AUG
M	T	W	T	F	S	S	
	1	2	3	4	5	6	○
7	8	9	10	11	12	13	◖
14	15	16	17	18	19	20	●
21	22	23	24	25	26	27	◗
28	29	30	31				○

SEP
M	T	W	T	F	S	S	
				1	2	3	
4	5	6	7	8	9	10	◖
11	12	13	14	15	16	17	●
18	19	20	21	22	23	24	◗
25	26	27	28	29	30	31	○

OCT
M	T	W	T	F	S	S	
30	31					1	
2	3	4	5	6	7	8	◖
9	10	11	12	13	14	15	●
16	17	18	19	20	21	22	◗
23	24	25	26	27	28	29	○

NOV
M	T	W	T	F	S	S	
		1	2	3	4	5	◖
6	7	8	9	10	11	12	
13	14	15	16	17	18	19	●
20	21	22	23	24	25	26	◗
27	28	29	30				○

DEC
M	T	W	T	F	S	S	
				1	2	3	
4	5	6	7	8	9	10	◖
11	12	13	14	15	16	17	●
18	19	20	21	22	23	24	◗
25	26	27	28	29	30	31	○

2024

● New Moon   ◗ 1st Quarter   ○ Full Moon   ◖ 3rd Quarter

JAN
M	T	W	T	F	S	S	
1	2	3	4	5	6	7	◖
8	9	10	11	12	13	14	●
15	16	17	18	19	20	21	◗
22	23	24	25	26	27	28	○
29	30	31					

FEB
M	T	W	T	F	S	S	
			1	2	3	4	◖
5	6	7	8	9	10	11	●
12	13	14	15	16	17	18	◗
19	20	21	22	23	24	25	○
26	27	28	29				

MAR
M	T	W	T	F	S	S	
				1	2	3	◖
4	5	6	7	8	9	10	●
11	12	13	14	15	16	17	◗
18	19	20	21	22	23	24	
25	26	27	28	29	30	31	○

APR
M	T	W	T	F	S	S	
1	2	3	4	5	6	7	◖
8	9	10	11	12	13	14	●
15	16	17	18	19	20	21	◗
22	23	24	25	26	27	28	○
29	30						

MAY
M	T	W	T	F	S	S	
		1	2	3	4	5	◖
6	7	8	9	10	11	12	●
13	14	15	16	17	18	19	◗
20	21	22	23	24	25	26	○
27	28	29	30	31			◖

JUN
M	T	W	T	F	S	S	
31					1	2	
3	4	5	6	7	8	9	●
10	11	12	13	14	15	16	◗
17	18	19	20	21	22	23	○
24	25	26	27	28	29	30	◖

JUL
M	T	W	T	F	S	S	
1	2	3	4	5	6	7	●
8	9	10	11	12	13	14	◗
15	16	17	18	19	20	21	○
22	23	24	25	26	27	28	◖
29	30	31					

AUG
M	T	W	T	F	S	S	
			1	2	3	4	●
5	6	7	8	9	10	11	
12	13	14	15	16	17	18	◗
19	20	21	22	23	24	25	○
26	27	28	29	30	31		◖

SEP
M	T	W	T	F	S	S	
30						1	
2	3	4	5	6	7	8	●
9	10	11	12	13	14	15	◗
16	17	18	19	20	21	22	○
23	24	25	26	27	28	29	◖

OCT
M	T	W	T	F	S	S	
	1	2	3	4	5	6	●
7	8	9	10	11	12	13	◗
14	15	16	17	18	19	20	○
21	22	23	24	25	26	27	◖
28	29	30	31				

NOV
M	T	W	T	F	S	S	
				1	2	3	●
4	5	6	7	8	9	10	◗
11	12	13	14	15	16	17	○
18	19	20	21	22	23	24	◖
25	26	27	28	29	30		

DEC
M	T	W	T	F	S	S	
30	31					1	●●
2	3	4	5	6	7	8	◗
9	10	11	12	13	14	15	○
16	17	18	19	20	21	22	◖
23	24	25	26	27	28	29	

INTERNATIONAL DAYS

Jan	01	New Year's Day
Jan	22	Chinese New Year
Jan	24	International Day of Education
Feb	11	Day of Women & Girls in Science
Feb	13	World Radio Day
Feb	14	Valentine's Day
Feb	20	World Day of Social Justice
Mar	01	Zero Discrimination Day
Mar	03	World Wildlife Day
Mar	08	International Women's Day
Mar	17	St. Patrick's Day
Mar	21	Elimination of Racial Discrimination
Mar	21	International Day of Forests
Mar	22	World Water Day
Mar	25	Earth Hour Day
Mar	31	Nowruz, Persian New Year
Apr	06	International Day of Sport for Development and Peace
Apr	07	World Health Day
Apr	07	International Day of Reflection on the 1994 Genocide in Rwanda
Apr	07	Good Friday
Apr	09	Easter Sunday
Apr	10	Easter Monday
Apr	22	Earth Day
Apr	23	World Book and Copyright Day
Apr	24	International Day of Multilateralism & Diplomacy for Peace
Apr	25	Day of the Tree
Apr	26	Chernobyl Disaster Remembrance Day
May	03	World Press Freedom Day
May	14	Mother's Day
May	15	International Day of Families
May	20	World Bee Day
May	29	International Day of UN Peacekeepers

Jun	03	World Bicycle Day
Jun	05	World Environment Day
Jun	08	World Oceans Day
Jun	12	World Day Against Child Labour
Jun	14	World Blood Donor Day
Jun	19	Father's Day
Jun	20	World Refugee Day
Jun	23	International Widows' Day
Jul	11	World Population Day
Aug	09	International Day of the World's Indigenous Peoples
Aug	19	World Humanitarian Day
Aug	29	International Day against Nuclear Tests
Sep	08	International Literacy Day
Sep	10	World Suicide Prevention Day
Sep	15	International Day of Democracy
Sep	21	International Day of Peace
Oct	02	International Day of Non-Violence
Oct	05	World Teachers' Day
Oct	10	World Mental Health Day
Oct	15	Pregnancy & Infant Loss Remembrance Day
Oct	16	World Food Day
Oct	24	United Nations Day
Nov	10	World Science Day for Peace and Development
Dec	05	World Soil Day
Dec	10	Human Rights Day
Dec	18	International Migrants Day
Dec	20	Internat. Human Solidarity Day
Dec	24	Christmas Eve
Dec	25	Christmas Day
Dec	26	Boxing Day
Dec	31	New Year's Eve

ECLIPSES, BLUE & SUPER MOONS

Apr	20	Solar Eclipse
May	05	Lunar Eclipse
Aug	01	Super Moon
Aug	31	Super Moon, Blue Moon
Oct	14	Solar Eclipse
Oct	28	Lunar Eclipse

For more info visit:

www.timeanddate.com

www.seasky.org

ASTROLOGICAL AFFINITIES

Sign Ruled by Planet	Element Quality	Plant Part	Nutrient	Temperament	Body Part/Organ System	Metal	Fertility	Polarity Quality
Aries ♈ Mars ♂	fire cardinal	fruit	protein	choleric	head, eyes, nose, brain, outer layer of the skin	iron	barren	+ hot
Taurus ♉ Venus ♀	earth fixed	root	salt	melancholic	ears, throat, voice box, jaw, teeth, neck, tonsils	copper	fertile	- cold
Gemini ♊ Mercury ☿	air mutable	flower	fat	sanguine	shoulders, arms, hands, lungs, bronchi, nervous system	mercury	barren	+ dry
Cancer ♋ Moon ☽	water cardinal	leaf	carbo- hydrate	phlegmatic	breast, stomach, liver, bile, kidneys, lymphatic fluids	silver	fertile	- moist
Leo ♌ Sun ☉	fire fixed	fruit	protein	choleric	heart, back, diaphragm, blood and circulatory system	gold	barren	+ hot
Virgo ♍ Mercury ☿	earth mutable	root	salt	melancholic	lips, hands, digestive system, spleen, nerves, pancreas	mercury	semi fertile	- cold
Libra ♎ Venus ♀	air cardinal	flower	fat	sanguine	hips, kidneys, bladder, lower back	copper	semi fertile	+ dry
Scorpio ♏ Mars ♂ Pluto ♇	water fixed	leaf	carbo- hydrate	phlegmatic	sexual organs, liver, urethra, bone marrow, lymphatic fluids	iron, steel	fertile	- moist
Sagittarius ♐ Jupiter ♃	fire mutable	fruit	protein	choleric	hips, thighs, venous system, liver	tin	semi barren	+ hot
Capricorn ♑ Saturn ♄	earth cardinal	root	salt	melancholic	knees, bones, joints, skin, nails, teeth, gall bladder, spleen	lead	semi barren	- cold
Aquarius ♒ Saturn ♄ Uranus ♅	air fixed	flower	fat	sanguine	venous system, shins, ankles, nervous system	lead, uranium	barren	+ dry
Pisces ♓ Jupiter ♃ Neptune ♆	water mutable	leaf	carbo- hydrate	phlegmatic	feet, toes, red blood cells, lymphatic fluids	tin, platinum	fertile	- moist

YOUR PERSONAL NATAL CHART

Tuning to the Moon phases is a great way to become more aware of the cyclic nature of life, growth and death. Once we realise how we are affected by the Moon and the Sun, we start getting the idea that other planets too have an effect on us.

Astrology is a wonderful tool for self discovery and awareness. Astrology can guide us to heal and find our true potential. It facilitates growth on many levels and helps us take action at the right time.

For your quick reference, transcribe your personal Natal Chart into the wheel below. You then can follow the planetary movements with reference to the monthly Planetary Tables, pages 56–67, and relate aspects to your personal chart. For aspect interpretations see pages 46–55.

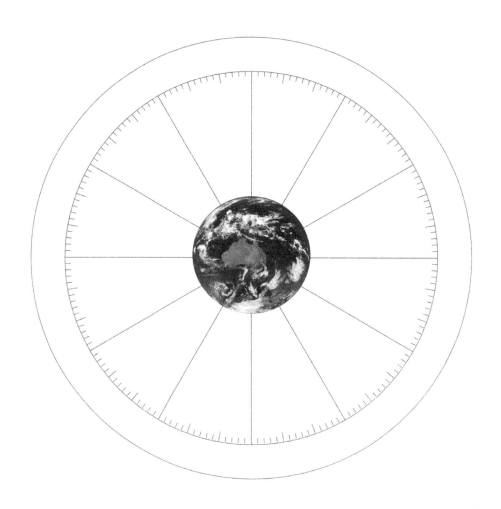

<u>Important Phone Numbers</u>

Ambulance - Police - Fire	
Emergency	Have exact address ready
24 Hours support for people impacted by sexual assault, domestic or family violence and abuse call	
Lifeline Crisis Support	
Local Hospital	
Next of Kin	
School	
Work	
Doctor	
Vet	
Dentist	
Herbal Apothecary	
Naturopath	
Homoeopath	
Acupuncturist	
Massage Clinic	
Practitioner	
Hairdresser	
Beautician	
Car Mechanic	
Computer Support	
Electrician	
Plumber	
Library	
Takeaway Restaurant	
Pizza	

MOONTIME DIARY 2024

This diary combines traditional Moon lore with new age knowledge and is filled with practical tips for your health and wellbeing, home and garden.

The Moontime Diary is the only diary with a detailed Astrological section providing planetary data for students of Astrology and professionals alike.

MOONTIME CALENDAR 2024

The Moontime Calendar 2024 Moon Chart shows you the whole year in one glance. It tells you the Moon phases, positions, eclipses, Super and Blue Moons in 2024.

The downloadable version is useful as desktop background on your computer and can also be colour printed on A3 paper.

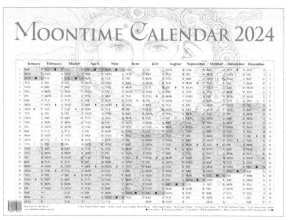

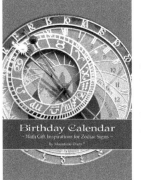

BIRTHDAY CALENDAR

This Birthday Calendar with a difference, provides birthday gift inspirations and party suggestions which resonate with the birthday person's Sun or Moon sign.

This handy Birthday Calendar will remind and inspire you to find the perfect gift for many years to come.

A FUTURE WITH NATURAL WOOD by Dr. Erwin Thoma

A passionate plea for one of our most significant natural resources — our trees and forests. This book is for people who want their children to grow up in a healthy environment, free from harmful substances, and for timber and building professionals interested in traditional methods for a sustainable future.

Austrian author Dr. Erwin Thoma brings forth a wealth of traditional and scientific knowledge. For more information visit www.thoma.at.

Lightning Source UK Ltd.
Milton Keynes UK
UKHW050340150223
416696UK00010B/119